Ba_____

MW01120614

# A Social and Economic Theory of Consumption

# A Social and Economic Theory of Consumption

Kaj Ilmonen

Edited by

**Pekka Sulkunen**
*University of Helsinki, Finland*

**Jukka Gronow**
*Uppsala University, Sweden*

**Arto Noro**
*University of Helsinki, Finland*

**Keijo Rahkonen**
*University of Helsinki, Finland*

**Alan Warde**
*University of Manchester, UK*

Translated by

David Kivinen

palgrave
macmillan

First published 2011 by
PALGRAVE MACMILLAN

Palgrave Macmillan in the UK is an imprint of Macmillan Publishers Limited,
registered in England, company number 785998, of Houndmills, Basingstoke,
Hampshire RG21 6XS.

Palgrave Macmillan in the US is a division of St Martin's Press LLC,
175 Fifth Avenue, New York, NY 10010.

Palgrave Macmillan is the global academic imprint of the above companies
and has companies and representatives throughout the world.

Palgrave® and Macmillan® are registered trademarks in the United States,
the United Kingdom, Europe and other countries.

ISBN: 978–0–230–24410–8 hardback

This book is printed on paper suitable for recycling and made from fully
managed and sustained forest sources. Logging, pulping and manufacturing
processes are expected to conform to the environmental regulations of the
country of origin.

A catalogue record for this book is available from the British Library.

A catalog record for this book is available from the Library of Congress.

10  9  8  7  6  5  4  3  2  1
20  19  18  17  16  15  14  13  12  11

Printed and bound in Great Britain by
CPI Antony Rowe, Chippenham and Eastbourne

# Contents

# Figures

# Foreword

Professor Kaj Ilmonen died prematurely at the height of his creative career in 2007. Sadly, he was unable to finish his *chef-d'oeuvre* in English – but he did see the publication of its Finnish version a couple of months before he passed away. This book, now translated and published in English, is a summary of his studies on consumption but spiced with his fresh theoretical viewpoints. It is not only a very comprehensive and systematic presentation of the sociology of consumption but also an original treatise of the new consumer society in which we live. He develops his views on classical issues in the sociological theory of modernity, including the social bond in general, the market, theory of money, the capitalist state and the relationship between the materiality of consumption and its economic and social constitution.

Professor Ilmonen had been a pioneer since the 1970s in what he called the *third wave of the sociology of consumption*, but most of all he was an original and erudite scholar and sociological theorist. This book gives a balanced overview of the main themes and topics in the sociology of consumption, reaching out towards its current and future development. The author's main argument is that the early enthusiasm of the 'third wave' exaggerated the role of the symbolic and imaginary, not only in consumption but in social life in general, at the expense of the materiality of human societies. At the same time he joins the sociological critiques of the neo-liberalist utopia of the autonomous market, which are based on the persistent but long-since invalidated imageries of *Homo economicus*. Going back to Marx he reminds us that consumption should be seen as part of the metabolism between nature and human societies in general, with specific characteristics in modern capitalism. In a curious way, affluent societies present and highlight features of the fundamental mechanisms of the social bond, such as gift exchange. Even money, the institution that we instinctively associate with calculative rationality, obeys laws that violate the rules of equivalent exchange and quantitative measurement.

The book, as it came out in Finnish, grew from years of research and lecturing and covered more than 400 pages. The current English version was shortened by the editors in two ways. First, sections on gift exchange and the politics of consumption were deleted from the translation because the points on these themes relevant to the author's argument are already covered in other chapters. Secondly, rich and detailed references to empirical research available only in Finnish were left out. Otherwise, only minor editorial changes were made in consultation with the translator. The English version will serve as an important source of reference to researchers of consumption, marketing and the contemporary social order anywhere in the world.

We wish to thank the Finnish Ministry of Education and the Kone Foundation for financial support for the translation.

The editors
PEKKA SULKUNEN, JUKKA GRONOW,
ARTO NORO, KEIJO RAHKONEN
AND ALAN WARDE

# 1
# The Sociology of Consumption: a Brief History

The sociological study of consumption goes as far back as sociology itself. Its empirical roots can be traced to the early development of statistical methods.[1] The first household budgets were collected across Europe in the mid-nineteenth century to determine minimum income needs, and therefore the main focus was on the consumption of food. This work led to the now famous *Engel's Law*, named after its inventor Ernst Engel, which stated that the proportion of income spent on food falls with rising income (Stigler 1954). This law still seems to apply today (Ilmonen & Pantzar 1986).

Despite this theoretically interesting result, household-budget research was still essentially pre-theoretical and driven by a political agenda. The sociological study of consumption achieved greater theoretical rigour with Karl Marx's distinction between the *use value* and *exchange value* of commodities. Marx suggested that in a market economy, the latter began to dominate the former because goods were no longer produced for personal consumption, but for exchange in the marketplace. At the same time, relations of production between people were blurred as they transformed into relations between commodities. Marx called this phenomenon *the fetishism of commodities* (Marx 1976). Both of these views had a major influence on twentieth-century sociology of consumption.

Marx did not, however, consider consumption in society in any way problematic, other than that there were large numbers of workers who were not earning enough even to reproduce their labour power. This, in turn, he maintained, was solely attributable to the relations of production. In general, Marx took the view that consumption was subordinate to production – a view that was widely shared at the time. Man was conceived primarily as a producer, *Homo faber*. The concept of consumer hadn't even been invented yet. This concept is commonly attributed to Étienne de Condillac, although his *consommateur* is ambivalent in that it can refer either to a consumer or to a person eating a meal. Perhaps Condillac shared with Engel the view that this, the ingestion of food, was the most basic form of consumption. More significant than that, however, was that he understood the consumer in the same way as in modern Gallup polls as an abstract statistical unit that seeks need satisfaction in the market (Préteceille & Terrail 1986).

## 1.1 Classical stage of sociology: the first wave of the sociology of consumption

It was not until the classical stage of sociology that consumption began to receive attention as a distinct sphere of human activity. This surge in interest is easy to understand in view of the unprecedented flood of consumer goods into the marketplace with industrialization in the late nineteenth century. These goods were eagerly embraced by consumers, especially in major towns and cities where they were on prominent display. It is hardly surprising, therefore, that sociologists took an interest. This stage marks the first wave of the sociology of consumption. It opened up perspectives on consumption that remain current to the present day.

However, this first wave of the sociology of consumption was not a unified and coherent movement. Some sociologists, among them Émile Durkheim (1995), denounced commercialism and considered it the ultimate cause of the new social condition of *anomie*. Other prominent sociologists, for their part, decided to leave the moral issue aside and deal with consumption as an integral part of the growth and development of capitalism. Here, much weight was placed on the consumption of luxury goods (Werner Sombart). Furthermore, consumption was seen as part of the modern way of life (Max Weber 1978), of which fashion was considered an important aspect. For Gabriel Tarde, a leading critic of Durkheim's sociology, fashion was an indication of people's endless desire to imitate others.

However, the single most important name in the sociology of consumption was Georg Simmel, whose major work on *The Philosophy of Money* explored the mediating role of money in consumption and various qualitative relationships (Simmel 1978). Simmel also drew attention to the prominence of consumption as a manifestation of the metropolitan high life and, furthermore, to the mechanisms of fashion in the modern world (Simmel 2005).

Simmel (1997 [1900]; 2005) took the view that all fashions were class-based. The upper echelons, he said, discarded the prevailing fashion as soon as it began to trickle down in the social hierarchy. However, it was not in fact Simmel but Torstein Veblen who created this trickle-down theory. Veblen described the tendencies of the upper classes to set themselves apart from other social classes as 'conspicuous consumption'. Most typically, this involved buying expensive consumer goods for the express purpose of raising one's social status. Since the consumption of these status goods usually caught on in the middle classes first and only then spread to the working class, it was a constant struggle for the upper classes to demonstrate their status through consumption (Veblen 1994). This was the force that ultimately drove consumption, as C. Wright Mills (1976) later stressed in his comments about middle-class 'status panic'.

The trickle-down mechanism continues to attract interest even today. The class structure of Western society may have changed significantly since Veblen's days, but conspicuous consumption is still very much in our midst. Most recently, it received attention in connection with the yuppie phenomenon (from the Gallup poll abbreviation YUP: young, urban, professional).

## 1.2   The second wave of the sociology of consumption

The second wave in the sociology of consumption initially gathered momentum during the interwar period, and picked up again after the Second World War. It was during these years that Marcel Mauss (1990), better known as an anthropologist, developed his theory of *gift exchange*. Mauss argues that gift giving is not as altruistically motivated as it might seem at first glance. In practice, everyone who gives a gift expects to receive one in exchange – even if they deny this. Mauss's observation was to have far-reaching implications for the sociology of consumption.

Another line of sociological inquiry that delves into consumption is associated with the critical theory of the Frankfurt School. On the one hand, Walter Benjamin (2003 [1939]) followed up on the work started by Simmel to describe life in the large metropoles. His main focus was on their grand shopping passages; on popular culture as a manifestation of modern life; on the *flâneurs* who strolled the streets of major cities; and on fashion as a manifestation of time rather than class. In the United States, Herbert Blumer (1969) continued to develop this same theme.

Theodor W. Adorno and Max Horkheimer (1979), on the other hand, launched a critical attack against the growth of commodity fetishism through popular culture. However, their critique was aimed not just at consumption: ultimately what they wanted to show was that through its subordination of use values to exchange value, capitalist society was destined to a dead end. This theme was pursued further both in the German sociological tradition, among others in the critique of commodity aesthetics by Wolfgang F. Haug (1986), and in the line of American sociology of consumption that drew attention to the artificial ageing of products and to consumer manipulation (e.g. Packard 1966; 1970). The roots of this research tradition can be tracked all the way back to Adam Smith's (1904) critique of 'unnecessary' consumption, and they continue to grow and expand in present-day critiques of marketing and consumerism.

Another American line of research takes a more nuanced view of consumption. Here, consumers are seen not just as victims of the manipulation of 'captains of consciousness' (Ewen 1976) but as active subjects who consciously follow and pursue their own values and objectives. Paul Lazarsfeld (1982), for example, observed that the consumer's mind is not a blank canvas for marketing communication to paint on but the commercial message is always relayed to the general public via opinion leaders; and even then its reception depends on existing tastes and preferences. As the focus then turned to tastes, it was realized that consumption provides excellent source material for an analysis of social change. David Riesman (1969), among others, used consumption data sets to describe the moral sea change that had taken place in American society. In the 1950s, he argued, a new modern type of 'outer-directed' personality had developed, for whom consumption had become a central aspect of everyday life. Riesman was very much ahead of his time, at least from a European point of view. Today, however, he seems to enjoy greater currency than ever.

## 1.3   The discipline takes shape: the third stage of the sociology of consumption

The third stage of sociological research on consumption, which at once marks the birth of the sociology of consumption proper, began in the late 1970s. While most previous sociological analyses of consumption involved a strong moralizing element, consumption was now approached, in the same vein as Riesman, as a meaningful social activity that provides a unique view into various facets of society.

This new stage was instigated by Pierre Bourdieu, who is also known for his work in the field of anthropology. Bourdieu combined and mixed the classics of sociology (Marx, Weber) and via consumption offered a description of the maintenance of the class structure in French society that is reminiscent of Simmel's and Veblen's idea of the trickling down of status goods in the social hierarchy. But Bourdieu's view is nevertheless different from his predecessors'. While Veblen suggests that consumption has taken over from other differences as an important means of social distinction, Bourdieu (1984) argues that distinctions are *embodied* in 'habitus' and *internalized* in dispositions.

Bourdieu is not alone in suggesting that consumption is used to maintain lines of demarcation between social classes and to make social distinctions. Research in the English-speaking world has also shown that consumption preferences reflect key social distinctions and social time (Sahlins 1976; Douglas & Isherwood 1980). Social distinctions, this tradition has it, are repeated in consumption, which is used to demonstrate the time (evening dress, nightgown), place (opera, rock concert) and nature (wedding, funeral) of events.

In the 1980s and early 1990s, there were at least four strands in the sociology of consumption. First of all, closely associated with the postmodern turn, there was the line of sociological theorizing that, inspired by Simmel and Benjamin, focused on the meanings of consumption. Like Jean Baudrillard (1988), it stressed, in a post-structuralist vein, that consumption was not a language. Clothes or food do not constitute a language-like system of signs that can be read and decoded in the same way by all members of the same culture. From this vantage point, the focus is turned to the role of consumption in the formation of and struggle over *social identities* and to the corporeality of consumption. The view that consumption rather than production plays a major constitutive role in identity formation has been used to defend the view of a historical turn in the modernization process.

Secondly, there was the empirically oriented line of sociology that was concerned with food. Its focus was on the continuity and change of consumer habits, a theme that has gained increasing currency with globalization. Concretely, these studies were interested in the symbolism of different foods, the national and cultural dimensions of meals, the class-, gender- and age-related characteristics of meals, eating habits, the 'problem' of omnivorousness and eating disorders, eating out and preparing meals at home and the breakdown of the family meal (Mennell, Murcott & van Otterloo 1992; Warde 1997). Food sociologists have discovered that people's food choices are surprisingly constant despite the huge variety of foods that has become available. At the same time, they have shown that the direction of change is not necessarily from centres to peripheries ('McDonaldization'), and that the flow of prestigious products in the social hierarchy does not only run from the top downwards, but history knows of many examples where simple peasant foods have achieved great popularity among the upper classes (pizza, traditional Chinese dishes etc.) (McCracken 1988).

The third trend in the sociology of consumption tied in with the sociological tradition initiated by Durkheim and Mauss, which was concerned with the circulation of goods. This line of work has elaborated on the characteristics of the institution of gift exchange and has drawn attention to how, in the process of gift giving, the aim is to *detach the good from its commodity status*. Gifts are wrapped and price tags removed because in Western countries they are not appreciated for their exchange value. A gift should in some way be special; it should reflect the personal characteristics of its giver so that the recipient could appreciate its value (Kopytoff 1988).

Another area of interest in this tradition concerns leisure activities and exceptional consumption habits, and collecting in particular. Researchers here have discovered that people can collect anything and everything, and that when they become collectibles, items lose their commodity status and take on a new meaning in relation to the existing collection. There are no fast rules, but when a collection is considered 'full and complete', it can be returned to the market for sale.

The fourth trend in the sociology of consumption was concerned with the aesthetics of commodities, with what it is in goods that appeals to us as consumers. These deliberations lead to the rejection of various theories of basic needs and set need hierarchies. Needs are seen instead as being mediated by a cultural filter and as historically variable forces that not only drive our actions, but also result from our actions. Another area of concern was the role of unsatisfied needs and unsatisfied desires emanating from those needs in instigating the growth of consumer society (Baudrillard 1988; Falk 1995). In this connection Colin Campbell (1987) has made the point that with the process of modernization, gluttony, the deadly sin for the Protestant Ethic, became refined into hedonism, which was concerned with the quality of pleasures. In contrast to Weber's assertions, the romantic 'spirit' that is sympathetic to consumption and self-realization has also played a significant role in this process of refinement.

## 1.4   Current trends in the sociology of consumption

The sociology of consumption focused on meanings has begun to attract criticism since the late 1990s. The sociology of meaning paradigm is committed to the idea of agency and reflexivity, ignoring the fact that only part of consumption is reducible to agency. Secondly, the sphere of consumption is reduced exclusively to meanings. The main interest is focused on meanings imposed on goods from the outside, usually by the researcher. Inverse inferences are then drawn from the consumers' intentions as to what they have wanted to communicate to others (Campbell 1996). The subjective side of meanings (meaning to oneself) has not been ignored altogether, but where it has been considered the emphasis is firmly placed on the cognitive element, disregarding the experiential side of consumption. Thirdly, only the publicly visible aspect of consumption has attracted the interest of sociology that is concerned with meanings.

For the reasons stated above, the sociology of consumption is now broadening its perspective. Work is continuing to unravel the meanings associated with consumption and to investigate how those meanings tie in with society's temporal, spatial and social structures and with identity formation – after all, it is impossible to imagine consumption without meanings. Indeed, there is every reason to expect that the key mechanisms of consumption and their associations with social order will continue to receive attention in future research (e.g. Gronow 1997). But otherwise, there are clear indications that the sociology of consumption, which became institutionalized in a relatively short space of time, is now breaking up into several different strands.

Firstly, it seems that, as in the field of market research, there is growing interest in the experiential side of consumption and at the same time in the *emotional link* between person and object. This is opening up new perspectives on how individual and collective identities are historically constructed through consumption.

Another new direction of research is focused on non-reflexive consumption, on *consumption routines*. This is drawing attention to questions of everyday consumption and the temporal and spatial arrangements embedded in that consumption: the way in which consumption routines are gendered (cleaning, cooking etc.) and how these routines change with age, ethnic background and religion (Gronow & Warde 2001; Shove 2003). However, routines are in constant flux under the pressure of accelerating social change, increasing health awareness and the consumption risks from gene technology and counterfeit goods, which are forcing consumers to reconsider and possibly to change their routines. This has thrown up a new challenge for reflexive sociology, forcing it to look into the ways that people deal with *consumption risks*. This latter theme has brought the concept of trust and confidence to the centre of the sociology of consumption and inspired studies into trust and confidence as one way of routinizing consumer behaviour. This line of research is creating a theoretically interesting tension between reflexive and non-reflexive action more generally.

The third area of growing research interest is the impact that everyday IT products, today's new supergoods, are having on the way that time and place are experienced. These changing perceptions of time and place are not only eroding old forms of social interaction and related practices (e.g. shopping), but also creating an entirely new kind of *virtual interaction* that is independent of time and place. This raises interesting new questions for sociological research: how does this interaction evolve and take shape – how is it reflected back into information technology?

The fourth rising trend in the sociology of consumption is concerned with the end-products of consumption, i.e. waste, the processing of waste and the recycling of semi-used goods. Waste management and recycling have already grown into multi-million industries, and research into the rubbish society is fast emerging as a new counterpart to research into the consumer society. This is expected to offer interesting insights into waste-processing routines but also into the opportunity for consumers to commodify their waste and sell it on the waste market.

There is plenty, then, for sociologists of consumption to research. Consumption not only reflects social practices but it also has a dynamic all of its own. This dynamic seems to imply that consumption is a self-sustaining process that feeds itself. The concept of a petrol-driven car implies the presence of petrol stations, which in turn implies the idea of filling up. This self-motion of consumption, an aspect first highlighted by Simmel, is emerging as an independent area of sociological research that ties in with the idea of path dependence as emphasized by institutional economics: future decisions on production, according to this idea, are influenced by existing technological solutions.

The sociology of consumption is thus splintering into a number of different strands, and it is no longer easy to identify any single coherent core – if indeed there ever was one. For this reason, I have searched out one general frame of reference for my treatment of the sociology of consumption. Despite Marx's claims, the commodity cannot provide such a unifying frame, for it is a much more complex entity than he assumed.

Since the 1980s, both economics and the social sciences have given increasing prominence to the markets, which, strangely enough, have remained rather peripheral in the sociology of consumption. It is now time to rectify this omission, to turn our attention not only to goods but to the markets as well, for the markets have become a superinstitution at the same time as the role of the state has been de-emphasized.

# 2
# Markets and the Neo-liberal Utopia of Omnipotent Markets

Towards the end of the twentieth century the world witnessed a sea change in economic policy thinking. The Reagan Administration in the United States and Margaret Thatcher's Cabinets in the United Kingdom began to champion a new kind of thinking that effectively put an end to some of the key principles of Keynesian economic policy (Julkunen 2001, 22). 'Private enterprise' was the magic word used to justify clampdowns on trade unions, to dismantle welfare-state mechanisms and to unload responsibilities onto private citizens in cases where the markets were not working as intended and where initially cyclical unemployment and then structural unemployment threatened to marginalize large portions of the wage-earning population. It was not the state that was supposed to solve these problems, but the markets. In fact many state-owned companies were to be privatized in the name of global competition. On the promise of increased efficiency, the grand scheme was to introduce market principles into public administration and to privatize public services. These views and measures formed an integral part of neo-liberal economic policy.

Public administrations around the world have taken up these ideas with great gusto (Julkunen 2001, 22–23, 27). And if and where they have failed to do so voluntarily, the World Bank and the World Trade Organization have ensured compliance by waving their batons and threatening to withdraw international loans. No country (with the possible exception of the United States) has been allowed to stand in the way of the expansion of the global markets. The prevailing thinking is that

1. The world has changed completely already. We are now living in a global marketplace. No one and nothing is responsible for this. It's just happened and there is very little that anyone can do.[1]

2. For this reason it is impossible to undo or reverse past developments by recourse to collective political action. Since the collapse of the Soviet Union, any dreams of a revolution have vanished into thin air. Keeping such dreams alive can only lead to green or heaven knows what other colour of totalitarian nightmare. It is even condemnable to try and alter the course of politics by means of election, for that, it is said, will only undermine competitiveness – whatever that means. Having said that, there seems to be no fear that any such efforts will materialize, because neo-liberal political thinking has transformed political governance into technologies (Scott 1996, 105; Graeber 2001, x–xi, Dean 1999, 149–175). And herein lies the strength of the neo-liberal economic doctrine. It turns decisions that have already been made into necessities (Bourdieu 1998, 29).

3. Although it may seem that only very little room is left for democracy, one should not despair. The markets will ensure that social order is maintained. They are just about all that democracy needs in the global world (cf. Graeber 2001, x–xi).

These three steps are typical of the neo-liberal train of thinking, which always represents the unfolding of events as a deterministic historical process that has no alternatives. Any attempt to discover such an alternative will only lead to more serious problems. Indeed, those problems can hardly be avoided, at least so long as the world's leading economic power, the United States (together with the World Bank and the WTO that have furthered its interests) continues to push for the liberalization of world markets when that is in its best interests, but then imposes protective duties (e.g. in the steel industry, clothing industry, agriculture) when its interests are threatened by the free operation of markets. And even when the United States does agree to open up the markets, it hands out huge subsidies to American businesses that are struggling to compete in the American internal market. However, my focus here is not on these questions, but rather on the third aspect of the globalization thesis, i.e. the sociological question of the role of markets in maintaining and guaranteeing social order and on its underlying premise, the question of the economic agent and its freedom in market society.

## 2.1  Adam Smith, the state and markets

It is interesting to observe that the third globalization thesis can be traced back to the thinking of Adam Smith. In fact many of Smith's views have shown remarkable staying power over the years, both in the field of economics and economic policy.

Adam Smith outlined the basic principles of the capitalist market in his magnum opus *The Wealth of the Nations* (1904, originally 1776). His description rests largely on Hobbesian premises, highlighting people's contrasting interests, although it is also influenced by David Hume. Smith's thinking was grounded, firstly, in the notion of what Norbert Elias (1978a) termed *Homo clausus*, the idea that competition in the market takes place between individuals who are independent of one another and who lack other social ties. They enter the market not out of benevolence but to seek their own interest. As Smith (1904, 8) famously wrote,

> It is not from the benevolence of the butcher, the brewer, or the baker, that we expect our dinner, but from their regard to their own self-interest. We address ourselves, not to their humanity but to their self-love, and never talk to them of our own necessities but of their advantages.

In other words, the people who participate in the markets are *individual entrepreneurs* whose interest in our needs as consumers extends no further than is necessary for the advancement of their own interests. In pursuing those interests in the markets, they put themselves into a competitive situation with one another, if not engaging in outright war (cf. modern business terminology that has companies organized into divisions and [profit] units and pursuing strategies that are applied 'in the field'). The markets, then, constitute a distinct sphere in society, i.e. the economy, which is governed by its own set of rules and laws. Despite disturbances at the micro level, these rules and laws produce, in the best case, a state of equilibrium at the macro level, which ultimately benefits all members of society. The benefits are not only economic but also social. The market, Smith says, is the mechanism that ultimately is responsible for social order. For that reason intervention by the state or some other body in the economy will not only disrupt the accumulation of national wealth but in the long term also threaten social order.[2]

Nonetheless, the state does have a role to play in Smith's thinking. The state was to defend its citizens from outside enemies, to build roads and other infrastructure and to provide education. By education, Smith did not mean vocational training; that was to be undertaken by trades-men and masters. Instead, the state was to educate moral and respon-sible citizens (Gronow 1996, 49, 54). This was necessary because in the market all that people really learned was how to protect their own interests. Even that, however, was constrained by the division of labour, which made people increasingly dependent on the work done by others and therefore promoted the civilization of their behaviour.

The social division of labour combined with the markets to create the famous 'invisible hand', which promoted 'an end which was no part of his [the entrepreneur's, KI] intention'. The metaphor of the invisible hand was intended to draw attention to the importance of unintended consequences to our actions. Where Smith went wrong was to suggest that these consequences were always beneficial. But since this is what he thought, it is understandable that in his view the 'invisible hand' posed on entrepreneurs no obligations to moral rectitude (Smith 1982, 184–185, originally 1759). They did have to take account of what other people were doing within the existing division of labour but this did still not provide a sufficient counterbalance to entrepreneurial selfishness. Smith insisted that in addition, it was necessary to have moral sentiments to guarantee a true sense of caring about other people (Gronow 1996, 54). Associations and organizations formed within civil society played a major role in evoking such sentiments, Smith argued, thus pointing the way for the current debate on what is now called social capital. This debate shares the same point of view that associations promote not only human virtue but also sound administration. This view that social order is reinforced through association is analogous to Smith's idea of the role of the market in guaranteeing order (Kangas 2001, 227).

All in all, Smith was convinced that despite its 'fomenting' of human selfishness, market society was far superior to earlier mercantilist systems. The reasons for this, he said, were that it raised people's standard of living; that it advanced the freedom of citizens; it did away with arbitrary relations of subordination and replaced them with contractual (wage labour) relations; and finally that a market-based society generally was conducive to the advancement of individual rights. Smith was by no means alone in his views. Quite the contrary, they were widely held in the eighteenth century (Kangas 2001, 210–211).

Towards the end of his life Smith became rather more pessimistic in his outlook. He was disappointed to see that economic growth did not appear to have the kind of moral effects he had assumed and that the development of the division of labour and trade did not have the kind of civilizing effects he had thought it would. If anything, 'commercial society' seemed to destroy the feelings of sympathy Smith had talked about in *The Theory of Moral Sentiments* (Smith 1982; see Kangas

2001, 239–241). It was becoming increasingly clear that the state had to intervene in market society[3] and to elevate social morality. However, these deliberations have been completely ignored in twentieth-century liberal economic understanding of market economy.

What did later gain increasing currency and support was Smith's definition of the relationship between the economy and the state and more generally the new ground rules for capitalism, the state and civil society. Firstly, he resolved the contradiction that continued to persist in the eighteenth century between the organized (state) economy and trade by declaring that this is what the economy was, trade. Secondly, thus redefined, the economy is a tool with which to tame both trade and the state.[4] Indeed, it has been suggested that the rhetorical force of political economy derived precisely from these new definitions (Meuret 1988, 228, 232, 241). This is no doubt true, but it is important to note that the breakthrough of political economy was also aided by the new terminology it used ('investment', 'capital') in describing economic functions.

## 2.2   Markets and twentieth-century neo-liberal economics

Many of the key concepts and fundamental assumptions adopted first by political economy and later by liberal (formal) economics can be traced back to the foundations laid by Adam Smith. They have been used to develop various definitions of the market. One element shared by all these definitions is that the market is understood as a tool for coordinating grassroots economic activities. Its main distinctive features are as follows: a) market agents are *ahistorical and mutually anonymous individuals or units*; b) they are in *competition* with one another, they further *their own interests* in competition and to this end make *calculations* or *rational assessments* of what course of action benefits them the most; c) market agents have *diverging interests* which force them into economic *exchange* in the market; d) the market resolves the *conflicts of interest among market agents by determining market prices* (cf. Callon 1999, 183); and e) *consumer choices provide information* about whether products are acceptable in the first place and whether they sell at market prices. This list must be further expanded by observing that f) market agents are *autonomous* and *market prices are fixed independently of personal feelings or individuals* (Smart 2003, 86). When market agents act independently of one another, g) their actions produce an *outcome that is optimal to the national economy* in that *resources are allocated according to demand*.

For this reason h) *there must be no outside intervention in this process,* for that would distort both the information created through consumer choices and, consequently, resource allocation (Carrier 1997, 6). This list also covers most of the basic concepts of neo-liberal economic theory. Provided that these concepts are followed the markets will become self-regulatory. That, in turn, means increased freedom for everyone in society.

My choice here for the two most prominent names of twentieth-century neo-liberal economic theory are Friedrich Hayek and Milton Friedman, who serve as representative examples of neo-liberal thinking more generally. First, however, it is necessary to point out that there are marked differences in their thinking – which in itself goes to illustrate the broad range of neo-liberal economic thinking. Hayek was not at all comfortable with the *laissez faire* concept associated with economic liberalism. The liberal argument, he said, is in favour of 'making the best possible use of the forces of competition as a means of coordinating human efforts, not an argument for leaving things just as they are' (Hayek 1994, 41). Hayek also took a sceptical view of econometric models and their powers of prediction, for he did not believe in social laws or regularities of any kind. Our knowledge of society, he maintained, is based on an understanding of our beliefs and intentions. That, however, is hardly very useful if neo-liberalism is seen as a doctrine of benefit maximization. For Hayek, it is impossible to measure the benefits of a given act either to the individual or to society at large, since we can never know what kinds of effects our actions will have. This ignorance explains why we have to rely on existing rules rather than conscious reflection (Lagerspetz 2004, 97–98, 103). (Hayek here approximates John Maynard Keynes's views on the underlying motivations for investment decisions.)

Friedman, one of the most prominent economists of the Chicago School, did, on the other hand, believe in economic laws and econometric models, even though he must have been aware of their flaws and inability to produce reliable forecasts. Unlike Hayek, he subscribed to the principle of benefit maximization at both individual and aggregate level, without troubling himself with the outcomes that would inevitably follow from this kind of universal rush to maximize one's own interests.[5] Every market agent would have to be wary of other people wanting to take advantage and cheat at every possible opportunity. So why have anything to do with these people in the first place?

These differences notwithstanding, both Hayek and Friedman start from the premise that the markets must remain free from state (and all other outside) intervention. Only markets that are independent of the state can guarantee free decision-making in the marketplace.[6] Insofar as the market is free in this respect, it consists of a wide range of individual decision-making and actions. It would be impossible to make sense of this complex web unless the market were a mechanism that aggregated information and responded to that information and to a countless range of activities to which individual market agents adapted their own actions (Hayek 1949, 87). *It is this ability of the market to aggregate and respond to information that both Hayek and Friedman say makes it more effective than any other economic system.* The reason for this, as Smith and Adam Ferguson argued, lies in the very complexity of the economy, which prevents the state from gaining detailed information about the market and from responding quickly and rationally at the aggregate level of society (see also Dean 1999, 49). All information about the economy is always incomplete, and neither the state nor any other entity can react quickly enough to mount a planned response to individual economic initiatives. This is no doubt true.

Both Hayek and Friedman are thus opposed to state intervention into the markets on *epistemological grounds.* Hayek (1949) makes two further points, which certainly make sense. First, he says that part of knowledge is 'practical' (today we would say *tacit* or *silent* knowledge) and cannot be expressed in abstract concepts and communicated onwards. Other than those people who are involved in maintaining this knowledge, everyone is fundamentally unaware of its existence. Hayek himself fails to realize this – but marketization is no solution.[7] The market is no more knowledgeable than the state about how to convey tacit knowledge. Second, another reason for the ignorance at the aggregate economic level is that there is no way to find out about consumers' current, let alone their future needs (see Smart 2003, 90) – although in the twentieth century socialism did of course try, and notoriously failed. According to Agnes Heller (1980), such attempts have only led to *political dictatorship over needs.*

According to Hayek this problem is resolved by the *price mechanism,* which *tells economic agents how to adapt to each situation.* This will ensure the efficient operation of the markets. This, however, only holds if there is a large number of competing agents in the markets. The situation is more problematic when the global marketplace is dominated by major corporations that can price their products as they please. Their *economic dictatorship over needs,* i.e. their intervention into the market mechanism to bolster their own interests, is no solution to the information problem raised by Hayek. Nor does it help to further the escape from the despotism of others, as Hayek wants to understand freedom (Lagerspetz 2004, 109). The spread of tacit knowledge to other market agents, then, is prevented by patenting – the registration of innovations for economic purposes.

If Hayek's views once made sense as he sought to oppose centralized socialist control, they are no longer entirely compatible with present-day economic realities. What about the much talked about association between freedom and the capitalist market that neo-liberalism is so keen to propagate? Hayek takes the unambiguous position that capitalism is a necessary condition for freedom because it is beyond anyone's control (Lagerspetz 2004, 112). Friedman's conclusion from his treatment of the relationship between the state and the market, on the other hand, is that 'capitalism is a necessary condition for political freedom' (Friedman 1982, 10). The state can certainly contribute to promoting that freedom, but only to a limited extent, because it is such a large power concentration.

At the same time, the state presents a serious threat to freedom. Even though the state has achieved significant success in the housing market, in nutrition, education and health care, these trends will not necessarily continue. The state is quite simply not in the position to guarantee welfare, as has become increasingly clear with the continued withering of the welfare state under neo-liberal economic policy. For this reason the power concentration that is the state must be curtailed. This is achieved via two routes: a) by developing free business cooperation and b) by decentralizing state power. This fits in well with Friedman's assertion that centralized government power is unable to respond to and promote 'the variety and diversity of individual action' (Friedman 1982, 4). Neo-liberal thinking has it that only the markets can do this, and by the same token that it is only the markets that can advance economic and political welfare. But this has proved untrue.

Besides, a new emerging problem is the question of how the markets can *effectively* coordinate the variety and diversity of individual initiatives and actions. It can no doubt do that when the future can be predicted with reasonable accuracy, as Keynes (1964) observes in his discussion of business investment decisions. However, the problem is exacerbated in times of *increasing world uncertainty*. Economics likes to portray itself as a predictive discipline but in fact its powers of prediction have proved quite limited even in reasonably stable and predictable conditions. As soon as uncertainty begins to grow in the economy and in consumer behaviour, its limited predictive powers cave in. Alan Greenspan, Former Chairman of the US Federal Reserve whose staff included a whole army of economists, has defended his actions ahead of the bursting of the stock bubble by admitting that *it is hard to know in advance* whether and when rising stock prices are an indication of a bubble and how to react, i.e. whether to keep interest rates unchanged or to put them up (Isotalus 2004).

So the more complex the economy and the greater the uncertainty, the harder it becomes to predict and calculate. Calculation is replaced simply by *ignorance*, as the Greenspan example goes to show. This does not increase the efficiency of the markets, but on the contrary produces economic failures at huge costs (cf. the launch of 3G mobile phones). However, every effort is made to conceal the significance of those failures. According to Keynes (1964, 114–117, 152; Callon 1999, 184), ignorance is hidden by resorting to old cultural solutions and related rhetoric, to simple rules of thumb learned in the national economy and to (business management) fashions in order to save the faces of business managers – or to what nowadays is appropriately described as garbage-can or muddling-through decision-making (Beckert 1996, 830). This approach may easily lead market agents onto the wrong track, often with catastrophic consequences for themselves and possibly for entire national economies.

In order to lower the risks of taking the wrong course, businesses may resort to *contingent agreements*, which will allow them to renegotiate if the economic situation changes dramatically (Beckert 1996, 830). However the greater the uncertainty, the more difficult it is to implement this procedure in practice. The growth of uncertainty means that *market agents do not know how to act rationally, to optimize their interests* (Beckert 1996, 823; Carrier 1997, 12).

Besides, the more the parties have to talk and negotiate about their contracts, the more expensive they become. Recurring meetings and contacts mean increased business costs. What is more, this interaction will transform anonymous market relations into personal relationships (Callon 1999, 184). People working for different companies learn to know one another, which is naturally reflected both in pricing and in future collaboration (cf. the US tobacco industry). In either case, part of the initial assumptions of neo-liberal economic theory will collapse.

Friedman has no solution to the coordination problem caused by this uncertainty, but he *believes* with absolute certainty (i.e. axiomatically) that the market has the capacity for self-adjustment and self-regulation. This conviction is quite understandable because if he were to critically explore the nature of economic decisions taken under conditions of uncertainty, he would *have to admit that many of them are fundamentally normative* (e.g. should the government increase national debt to keep unemployment rates in check or should it try to maintain balance in public finances and let unemployment balloon), in other words they are based on a mixture of what is, what could be and what should be. This in turn raises an uneasy question for economic theory: if and when economic decisions are normative by nature, *how does one define a rational choice* (Beckert 1996, 819, 823)?

The difficulty of defining rational choice spells big problems for neo-liberal economic theory. It is unable to show on what conditions it is possible to achieve relatively constant (*Pareto-optimal*) balance in the macroeconomy.[8] If those conditions cannot be specified, the *outcome* is always *political*, not economic. In this situation some businesses suffer more losses than others. The Hobbesian problem of social order consequently moves centre stage in the economy but apparently *not* in economic theory.

In general the market cannot, in itself, maintain social order. In the end the pursuit of private interests always has unintended consequences – most notably the growth of economic uncertainty. This undermines the social system outside the market, as for instance the growth rate of private business output exceeds that of consumption and as the macroeconomy is consequently thrown into disequilibrium. 'When the market operates freely, it does not out of itself generate social order' (Beckert 1996, 827), let alone harmony. That's when suddenly the state is called upon to intervene. However, the state has only limited opportunity to turn things around, for policies grounded in neo-liberal economic doctrines have effectively curtailed its freedom of movement. Rather than the optimal universally beneficial situation that Smith's 'invisible hand' would have painted, the outcome is arational or even irrational.

It is of course possible to circumvent these theoretical problems by extending the concept of rationality and referring instead to *intentional rationality*. This implies that economic agents are rational when they are pursuing a goal that optimizes their benefits. However, they do not know how best to achieve that desired goal (Beckert 1996, 819). This leads, in practice, to some curious forms of economic line-dancing. For example, banks may at sometimes feel they have every right and justification to enter the accident insurance business; at others it may be felt that this is wholly inappropriate. For the outsider, however, it is hard to see any clear reason for this about-turn.

The uncertainty fuelled by the market economy's operation presents a serious problem for economic theory,[9] but Friedman skates around that problem. Instead, he arbitrarily creates a juxtaposition between state

coercion and voluntary market coordination, as if there were no alternatives (Boyer 2005, 533–536). Reluctant even to consider the possibility
of such alternatives, he sets out to draw generalizations about a simple
exchange economy. According to those generalizations, independent
households used to produce goods and services that they exchanged for
various other goods and services by negotiating with other households.
Exchange only took place if both parties benefited. Cooperation, therefore, was achieved without coercion (Friedman 1982, 13).

Friedman's idea is that this simple and individual exchange can be
generalized to the complex system that is market economy, but only
providing that business enterprises are privately owned and that
individuals are free to enter or not to enter into exchange (Friedman
1982, 14). Hayek (1960, 11) shared this same view. For him, too, the
most important point was free exchange without external coercion.
Other than general references to 'law and order', neither gentlemen
say anything about the conditions under which such exchange could
take place.

Friedman also sees no problem in shifting up from exchange between
individual households at micro level to a market economy driven by
large business (see Smart 2003, 92). In that context competition is
waged not between private households but between profit-seeking business companies. Another inaccurate assumption on Friedman's part
is the idea that the people who sell their labour power to companies
are anonymous to them. In actual fact, employees are hired based on
information gained through rumour or observation and based on family, friendship and other social network factors (e.g. through employee
agencies) rather than on the free market (Carrier 1997, 9; Pahl 2000,
150; Halpern 2005, 45). These people, in turn, do not make their product choices in the marketplace based on individual preferences only;
they also follow mechanisms of collective choice, fashion, style and
taste (see Chapter 8).

Freedom of exchange nevertheless remains at the core of Friedman's
neo-liberal thinking. Freedom, he maintains, is guaranteed by the
existence of other producers. Producers, for their part, are protected
by the existence of consumers who always use their products. There
is no real threat of purchase boycotts. The freedom and independence
of employees from employers, then, is guaranteed by the existence of
other companies in the marketplace who are always willing to purchase
their labour power. The market, in other words, 'gives people what they
want' (Friedman 1982, 15). This is a crude idealization of how the economy works.

It is easy to give examples of how major market leaders aim to design their production with a view to building a strong monopoly position. There is no alternative but to buy Microsoft products because the organization's electronic network is based on Microsoft systems. Similarly, electricity generation and many other industries, especially in small national economies, seem to have a strong temptation to engage in oligopolistic pricing. It is equally simple to observe that both the current situation of mass unemployment and underemployment (low-pay 'garbage jobs', part-time and temporary jobs) in first-world economies as well as in the global economy at large are at variance with Friedman's third assumption, for people are actually being forced to work by political and sometimes even armed means (see e.g. Klein 2000). Rather than upholding freedom of exchange, these economies are imposing a necessity of exchange: in order to live people have no option but to sell their labour power.

The workings of the modern global economy, its 'China (or India or Brazil) phenomenon', structural unemployment and monopolistic tendencies all go to show just how far removed Friedman's thinking is from economic reality, and was so even in the 1980s. Even then, he was unable to justify the linkage between markets and freedom, on the one hand, and the state and coercion, on the other. He completely ignores the fact that even in the United States, large swathes of the private sector depend on direct or indirect state support, and that a large proportion of private companies have grown under the protective wing of the state. On the other hand, he also fails to pay attention to the constant demands imposed by business on the state, both with respect to monetary and customs' policy and taxation. In other words, Friedman fails to give any thought to the limiting conditions imposed by business companies, interest organizations and other market agents on democracy and freedom.

For a more analytical treatment than Hayek and Friedman themselves can offer of their notion of freedom, we need to look at the concept of freedom in somewhat more detail. Isaiah Berlin (2001, 47) famously made the distinction between negative and positive freedom. Hayek and Friedman are interested only in the former, which refers to the absence of sanctioned rules in some area of society, particularly in the economy, and which therefore could also be called *economic freedom*. In the hands of Hayek and Friedman, this is transformed into the *idea that anyone can further their economic interests without any limitation*. This is not a novel idea, but it comes more or less directly from British utilitarians and their predecessors, Nicolaus Cusanus, Giovanni Pico della

Mirandola, Niccolo Machiavelli, Giambattista Vico, Claude Adrien Helvetius and Thomas Hobbes (see Sahlins 2000, 535–537). However, this notion fits uneasily with the modern democratic idea of equality, for its connection to 'positive' freedom is problematic to say the least.[10]

'Positive' or *personal freedom* means more or less the same as what nowadays is called *empowerment*. It is the ability to lead one's life according to one's own views and values, to be the captain of one's life, to be an agent who can always choose to do otherwise. However, this notion of freedom must not be favoured because neo-liberalism says it may give rise to opposition against the current type of market economy and to a critical attack on society. 'Proper' neo-liberal personal freedom is only achieved when it is voluntarily restricted or when it can be used to further administrative goals.

Hayek does not favour individual empowerment and emancipation, but 'educated' and 'responsible' citizenship that lends itself to supporting various neo-liberal political projects. This is a constant problem for neo-liberal thinking. Indeed, Mitchell Dean, for one, stresses the duality of the neo-liberal concept of freedom. In order for individuals to have freedom of action, they must first of all be subjected to social and political indoctrination and taught to assume personal responsibility for their freedom. Adaptation and individual freedom go hand in hand (Dean 1999, 155, 165). One integral aspect of this is that employees are forced to comply with new business strategies and human resource policies at the same time as management in major companies seek relative freedom in their decision-making with a view to maximizing the interests of company owners or directors. Hayek and Friedman do not consider this lack of freedom a problem, since they maintain that employees can always change jobs if they want to.

Thirdly, there is the *freedom to promote common interests within a community, or the 'republican' right* to apply the collective political resources at one's disposal to pursue and promote what one believes is right (Ilmonen & Jokinen 2002, 138). Again, neo-liberalism wants to impose restrictions in the name of world market expansion and competitiveness, at least in the sense that all social movements seeking emancipation should be replaced by responsible individuality – i.e. individuality that supports neo-liberal policy (Dean 1999, 155).

If Hayek's and Friedman's understanding of freedom is one-sided, given that they ignore all other freedoms except economic freedom, or, more precisely, given that they confuse 'freedom from external coercions' with 'the ability to be one's own captain', there are also serious shortcomings in their analysis of the conditions of freedom (Smart

2003, 97). It is hardly an exaggeration to say that the concept of freedom advocated by neo-liberal economic doctrine, at least Hayek's and Friedman's version, is deeply one-sided. This is evidenced, among other things, by Friedman's failure to provide any serious analysis of the institutional conditions for the operation of the markets.

## 2.3   Institutional conditions for markets

When Friedman extrapolates from a pure barter exchange economy to modern capitalist markets, he fails to discuss the historical validity of his examples. That would have been important, however, to give credence to his idea of markets and how they have evolved into what they are today. Besides, his sporadic historical observations are fraught with mistakes. The first of these is the ironic comment by Oliver Williamson (1975, 20), creator of the concept of transaction costs, on neo-liberal thinking. According to Williamson, neo-liberal thinking is grounded in the maxim, 'In the beginning was the market'. In Friedman's world, then, in the beginning was not the word, but the merchant, *Homo economicus*. This, of course, is not true.

When the famous anthropologist Bronislaw Malinowski studied the Trobriand Islanders of Polynesia and their system of exchange known as the *kula* ring, he came to the conclusion that this did not amount to trade in other than a very general sense. This exchange was carried out not by Friedman's households but by clans. It was also not a trading of goods that the clans needed but an exchange of seashell necklaces, armbands and other 'valuables' in the *kula* ring. Their exchange involved various ceremonies and magical rites that had nothing at all to do with the promotion of self-interest. The same can be said of all other 'economic' activities among the islanders, including the growing of their staple agricultural produce, yam. Most of the harvest, Malinowski says, did not go to the farmer, but to the members of the farmer's extended family. Indeed he concludes (1992, 60–61, 84–86) that textbook notions of 'Primitive Economic Man (...) must be exploded, once and forever'. The Trobrianders were engaging not in an exercise in economy but in the maintenance of social relations (see Graeber 2001).

Malinowski's observations from the Trobriand Islands are not unique nor of course can they be generalized to Europe. To be sure, some mechanisms of exchange have evolved even among the Islanders with the growing division of labour – but we must not make the same mistake as Ludwig von Mises, Herbert Spencer and Walter Lippman and confuse the existence of a division of labour with exchange and exchange trade.

von Mises, Spencer and Lippman all uncritically follow Smith's notion of commodity exchange in archaic communities and assume that this exchange is driven by the pursuit of economic benefit. However, in Europe neither production nor the distribution of products has ever been *directly linked* with *private* economic interests associated with commodity ownership. Yes, these interests have existed, but exchange economy has fundamentally been driven by *social* interests. Those interests have been mainly related to kinship and family systems, to the gender division of labour and to some measure of reciprocity of services. Indeed, Karl Polanyi (1957, 44–47, 49), scholar of the roots of market economy, observes that in pre-capitalist society 'the economic system is, in effect, a mere function of social organization'. In the words of anthropological historian Henri Pirenne (1967, 419), it was 'an economy without markets'. It has also been characterized by a redistribution of products. Historian Edward P. Thompson (1983) describes this economic principle as a 'moral economy'.

In Europe, the moral economy only began to break down around the turn of the fifteenth and sixteenth century, when members of the great families began to compete for prestige and favour in European courts (Ilmonen 1993, 26). This coincided with the growth of world trade and with the consequent expansion of markets for luxury goods such as spices, silk, sugar, salt, tea and coffee. There had of course been markets in Europe even before this, mainly in the form of local weekend markets. Although some food was exchanged, these markets were mainly about amusement and entertainment, excuses for people to get together and have fun: to dance, to drink and to eat. Even the great families and their lords did not engage in trading with the intention of earning a profit. Profit-seeking quite simply did not fit with the thinking of lords of the manors, for they too were still living in a 'subsistence economy' (Pirenne 1967, 421, 429).

The first ever 'supranational' markets were held in the thirteenth century in Burgundy and Champagne, in an area that is now part of France, attracting traders and merchants from across Europe. They were quite different in nature from local markets. In Champagne, most of the trading was done with money, and predominantly on credit. Payment for goods purchased was made at next year's market, plus interest. Not for nothing were these markets known as the 'the money market of Europe' (Pirenne 1967, 436). They were instrumental in paving the way for the *credit institution* in Europe.

Trade was practised very early on in European cities, too. In fact according to Max Weber (1978, 1214), this was the meaning of 'city': it was a place for conducting trade and commerce, a market settlement, often with money changing hands. However, the local markets in cities did not develop from barter between individual households (Polanyi 1957, 61); they developed on the basis of the strict class hierarchy that prevailed in cities and a gild system – effectively market monopolies that regulated trading in cities (ibid., 69). Indeed Weber says that trading in cities was the very *antithesis* of *oikos*, Friedman's household in which no trade took place at all (Weber 1978, 1213–1215). Besides, trading in cities was closed to national merchants through various local tolls designed to protect monopolies (Polanyi 1957, 65).

Friedman's explanation of the conditions for market economy is, in other words, historically flawed. There is also no justification for his extrapolation from those conditions to the macro-level description where markets suddenly become a 'self-regulating system', which is Polanyi's definition for market economy. When the focus of analysis is shifted from rural markets to trade and commerce in the cities, it becomes apparent that *markets are an institutional structure*. The step from local regulated city markets to market economy, then, is a historically complex process that emphasizes the *institutional foundation of market economy* to a much greater extent than Friedman does (Friedman 1982, 37, 41–42, 57). Hayek takes a different tack on this altogether. For him, the market is neither a natural nor a politically created structure, but it represents a spontaneous order supported by habits filtered through cultural selection processes (Dean 1999, 157). In sociological parlance, markets are *informal institutions* (Mantzavinos 2004, 101–130).

However, it is not my intention here to retrace the history of market economy. Suffice it to note that as mercantilist economic policy began to lose ground, so the boundaries of local markets began to crumble and the privileges of cities were increasingly eroded (Cameron 1989, 150–151).[11] Underlying this process were the growth of the nation state and the gradual separation of economy and politics. Without this institutional distinction, it was not possible to turn labour, land and money into commodities that could be bought and sold anonymously on the commodity markets. Initially, however, they were not commodities. Labour was only another name for human activity, land another name for nature and money merely a token of purchasing power (Polanyi 1957, 72).

The production of commodities required that segments of the population in different states were legally defined as vagrant so that they could be used as forced labour in factories. Therefore in the sixteenth and seventeenth century, European states began to enact laws that defined orders of succession and outlawed vagrancy and beggary. In order to survive the vagrant population had to start to *sell its labour power*. At the same time, it was gradually accustomed to a new regime of discipline and time use (Polanyi 1957, 86; Foucault 1977; Thompson 1983, 18–31). The *commodities* produced were then sold to this *growing number of wage earners* and to *residents of garrison towns*. This, however, required the *payment of wages in cash*; and that, in turn, required mechanisms to *regulate the amount of money* circulating in the markets and above all to *guarantee its value*. The only institution that could do that was the state.

The growth and expansion of commodity production required new investment. It was only rarely that that investment could be financed solely from the profits earned in production. For these purposes and for foreign trade in particular, it was necessary to have an effective *credit institution*. Again, that was not possible without the support and assistance of the state. Besides, in continental Europe the state guaranteed or invested directly in business in order to meet the competition of the English (Cameron 1993, 150–151). *The state-created institutions that laid the foundation for labour markets, commodity markets and capital markets.*

In order to function properly these newly created markets demanded that the state enact *legislation guaranteeing private property* and protecting the capital that had accumulated in banks, global trading companies and industrial enterprises. Furthermore, the markets required legal protection for private interests vis-à-vis the state. This concerned *state taxation* in particular, which had a tendency to keep rising because of recurring wars and the growing costs of running armies. If any country thought it was at a disadvantage in world trade, decisions on *protective duties* were also for the state to make, as was the establishment and implementation of an economic policy that safeguarded the nation's economic development (see Cameron 1993, 150–152).

This, then, was how, from around the sixteenth century onwards, through the medium of the state, *a huge institutional framework was created without which the markets could not have developed or functioned*. Nor would they function without that framework even today, for it is these state-created institutions that give the markets their predictability. Besides, the operation of the markets would be limited at best if it were not for the ability of the state to intervene and iron out social conflicts or to maintain social order (Scott 1996, 94, 105, and to engineer the autonomous operation of markets (Smart 2003, 43). Political economy had already lost sight of these facts, and they disappeared altogether in marginalist economics, says sociologist of industrial society Daniel Bell (1990, 219). Economistic models detached from real-world institutions evolved instead into a symbolic world aiming to describe people's actions in the economic realm. Historical analysis shows, however, that these models did injustice to reality by excluding the institutions that maintained the markets. This was no coincidence, as we soon shall see. Economic and other thinking 'has more to do with intervening than with representing' (Douglas 1986, 50).

Inevitably, then, our conclusion is that, in contrast to what neo-liberal economics would have us believe, *it is necessary for the state to intervene in the economy to ensure that the markets work efficiently.* This is precisely what the state has long been doing in the Western world (Polanyi 1957, 140), even in neo-liberal countries par excellence. US President George W. Bush, for instance, has imposed protective duties to support American manufacturing and agriculture, at the same time as he has been calling for the liberalization of global markets. And in the European Union, old members are now taking steps to prevent people from new member states moving out in search of work, despite the formal rhetoric of the free movement of labour.

Karl Polanyi (1957, 132) has accurately observed that the market econ-omy is characterized by a double movement. The currently predominant trend of movement is the economic policy line aimed at establishing self-regulating markets. At the same time, this is met by a countermove-ment that is aimed at regulating the markets by protecting people suf-fering from the injustices of wage labour and commodity markets as well as the natural environment, and by supporting economic activity when that is necessary for reasons of outside competition. Polanyi saw this countermovement as a vital corrective in the free market – and he was not alone in this view. Recently, Polanyi's argument was echoed by Nobel Prize winner in economics, Joseph H. Stiglitz (2002): 'We should have learned a long time ago that positive market regulation is neces-sary for the efficient operation of markets.'

## 2.4 Self-interested *Homo economicus* – an assumption to facilitate economic modelling

My main focus so far has been to show just how tendentious economic liberalism has been in its views about the relationship between markets and freedom. I have also tried to demonstrate that the markets cannot function without government institutions or without state intervention. Furthermore, I have already hinted that market agents are not the aso-cial and ahistorical particles that neo-liberal economic theory says they are. In order to manage in situations of uncertainty, market agents aim not just to follow old conventions and conclude contingent agreements. They are also keen to *create and maintain social networks*, which they need, among other things, to help coordinate their economic activity (Halpern 2005, 54–59). The closer we come to the present day, the more this strategy has been followed, as Manuel Castells (1996) points out in the first part of his work on network society.

However there is nothing new about networking. Even Polanyi (1957) observed that, far from being a distinct and separate sphere, the economy is closely bound up with the social ties of civil society and with the norms and customs associated with those ties. Mark Granovetter later elaborated on Polanyi's idea by trying to erase the contrast between *Homo economicus*, the undersocialized type of human being, and *Homo sociologicus*, the oversocialized human being. According to Granovetter, it is their very membership of different social networks and their numerous social contacts that give economic agents their capacity for rational calculated decision-making. The key decisive factor in decision-making is these agents' position within these networks and the extent of these networks (Granovetter 1973, 1360–1380; 1985, 3; Callon 1998, 9). In other words, by focusing on the network structure it is possible to describe different types of agents within the same network as well as their disparate interests. These interests are not fixed because the relationships between the networks and their members are in constant flux.

Granovetter's approach is true to present-day reality, if we are to believe network research. Its implications for neo-liberal economic theory are profound. That theory is based on the assumption of calculating and mutually independent market agents. In the network-society model, on the other hand, it is this very premise that requires explanation (Callon 1999, 186). *How does this calculating anonymous agent come about – what motives drive this agent?* In the search for an answer it must be borne in mind that there is no clear and straightforward association between the actions of the network member and network position, as Ronald Burt (1993, 63–103) observes in his studies of the windows of opportunity offered by the network. That association will largely depend on the nature of the social ties within the network (loyalty, trust, pursuit of self-interest).

Furthermore, the degree to which network members' actions are driven by self-interest varies from one situation to the next. Sometimes they may go about their business without any specific interests at all, especially in situations that involve a strong sense of trust and loyalty towards other network members. The reciprocity of interaction among network members, then, changes the situation in ways that are easier to explain by reference to the principles of gift economy rather than market economy (Carrier 1997, 9; Callon 1998, 13–14). With clients and customers, for example, the aim is to create lasting relationships (see Carrier 1997, 9; Pahl 2000, 149). For these and other reasons, it is more appropriate in the context of economic activity to talk not about rationality as such, but as Herbert Simon (1945) does, about *bounded rationality*.

In bounded rationality, economic agents turn to their social networks. This is really their only option because they are interested in maximizing the profits of the economic unit of which they are in control but they don't know how best to achieve this. The network brings together diverse expectations and compiles interpretations out of them. When the final choice is made between those interpretations, the decision-maker's moral and social criteria (e.g. loyalty) are often at least as influential a decision factor as calculation and intuition (Chapman & Buckley 1997, 241).[12] Bounded rationality, investment in networks and related trust, has the effect of pushing up transaction costs, as does the lack of trust, which is manifested in corruption. However, these factors are often missing both from economics' models and from understandings of the markets (Smart 1999, 175–176). Even in the stock exchange, where money knows no morality, investment decisions are based on ritualistic customs and interpretations of information gathered from social networks. Decisions are made not by testing the validity of those interpretations in the stock market but by looking at which interpretation is supported by the majority of network members (Abolafia 1998, 75).[13] The aim of the decision is obviously not to achieve a Pareto optimum at the overall level of the national economy, but to keep the decision-makers, in one way or another, involved in the market game (Beckert 1996, 821).

In referring to market agents I have made no distinction here between business decision-makers, on the one hand, and consumers of business products, on the other. There are clear reasons for this. It is not just business companies that are networked; consumers too, interact with one another. Friendships, for instance, have assumed increasing importance in consumers' decision-making. And not only that, consumption is largely steered and shaped not only by price relations but also by social mechanisms (see Chapter 7). These are not individual, but collective phenomena that economic theory seems unable to understand (Ilmonen 2001a). Let me take just a couple of examples. In many countries consumers are now able to choose their gas and electricity supplier but they can rarely be bothered to compare prices even though this could save them considerable sums. They also like to go to the same familiar dentist and hairdresser even when that does not make financial sense.

## 2.5   Neo-liberal economic theory and how it shapes the economy

The markets are not an essential phenomenon, but rather a legal, historical, sociological and economic frame of thinking. The same goes for *Homo economicus*. The assumption in neo-liberal economic theory of the existence of an anonymous self-interested economic agent is not only problematic but itself calls for an explanation. The same goes for the notion of *calculation* as espoused by economic theory: it requires elaboration. A common criticism against this thinking is that market agents rarely have such an intimate knowledge of the markets that they are able to conduct rational calculation. Besides, the accuracy of those calculations declines in direct proportion to increasing uncertainty. Formal economic theory has sought to redress this point by taking account of the costs of information acquisition and the uncertainty of information. I am not in the position to say how successful these efforts have been, but judging by the difficulties that formal economic theory continues to have with predicting the future, it seems clear that this issue has not yet been resolved (Sorjonen 2004, 5).[14] However, I do not want to dwell any further on this standard critique of economic theory (see e.g. Callon 1998, 4). Instead, like Callon, I would like to draw attention to the externalities that are omitted from economic calculations, to the aspects that are embarrassments to neo-liberal economic theory and that it therefore wants to exclude from the economy and the market. At the same time, this is how it comes to define *what is more and what is less important in the economy.*

Economists developed the concept of externalities to describe those economic interconnections (e.g. state subsidies for economic institutions) and those social relations (e.g. social contacts in networks) and environmental impacts (e.g. climate warming) of economic activity that are not included in economic models. In fact a large part of the economy (household work, social care) is excluded from these models. The existence of externalities means that the optimal-efficiency representations offered by economic models are always biased in one respect or another. The degree of bias depends in part on the nature of the externality. Externalities may be either negative or positive. A *negative externality* refers to *economic costs that are not accounted for in the model and that are assumed will be borne by the state, for instance.* Products are therefore underpriced, oversupplied and overconsumed. A *positive externality,* then, refers to a situation where consumers or producers do not derive full benefit from their actions. This, too, is reflected in products. They are overpriced, undersupplied and underconsumed (Callon 1998, 248; Aldridge 2005, 70–71). An example is provided by energy and the wholesale pricing of energy. When a coal plant, for instance, uses its allocated emissions' rights to generate power, it adds the price of those rights to its costs even though it does not have to pay anything to get those rights. The energy company can also decide not to generate power, to sell its emissions' rights and to make money that way.

Recognizing the existence of externalities also implies both acknowledging that the markets function imperfectly and admitting that the efficient operation of the markets has its limits. The concept of externalities allows for simplification of the model but also detracts from its power of prediction. This simplification, then, means that a framework is created within which the model works. For instance, the model acknowledges the existence of separate market agents, the goods they sell, production costs, distribution and the benefit-seeking consumer. Everything else that belongs to this process is left aside, the assertion being that this is how things work 'in my world' (i.e. in my model). The model is a representation of the markets, but given all its flaws and shortcomings it is of course little more than a pale reflection of the 'reality' constituted by the markets.[15] However, the model can be improved by taking account of externalities, i.e. by reframing it. According to Ronald Coase's theorem, however, this will create new kinds of externalities (Callon 1999, 186). An economic model, whether it is grounded in neo-liberal or some other premises, can never be more than an approximate survey of the terrain because it always includes more or less justified externalities. The same obviously goes for scientific modelling and theorizing in general.

As the above implies, it is more than credible that economics might not always even be trying to create models that reflect reality and to use them to make realistic predictions. Instead what it is doing is to use its baseline assumptions and models to demonstrate how the economy can be made to work in the way it thinks it should work and to shape the economy accordingly (Dean 1999, 58). Of course, this is no novel discovery. In his historical analysis of the archaeology of sciences, Michel Foucault (1970) observes that man who is doomed to work uses the forms of production by which his existence is governed to provide himself with representations of economics. These appear in a *position of duplication*. Not only do they *reflect economic reality*, but they also impact the way that *the economy works* (Foucault 1970, 353–354). They contribute to producing reality by influencing economic policy and business decision-making (see Smart 2003, 5).

The discipline of economics and the economy are so closely related that it is 'meaningless to distinguish between an existing reality (economy) and the analytical discourse explaining it (economics). Social science [and economics, KI]...actively participates in shaping the thing it describes' (Callon 1998, 29). In this shaping process, economics provides a way of framing the economy (through its models and forecasts) and helps it work in its intended manner. This is achieved through the medium of the calculation methods applied by economics: hence the connection between the economy and the markets with economics (ibid., 22–23, 27–28). And this is precisely what neo-liberal economics is all about: it uses its models to produce a concept of market that doesn't even exist without these models.

All in all it seems that many of the basic assumptions of neo-liberal economic theory are just plain wrong. The relationship between the markets and freedom is problematic, especially with the growing significance of global business in the world economy and with the deepening of economic globalization. Markets do not exist in a state of nature. They struggle to cope without regulated and state-maintained institutions (Mantzavinos 2004, 166; Slater & Tonkiss 2001, 199–201). What is more, the businesses that operate in the markets are not separate from one another but, on the contrary, connected in many ways and indeed committed to further cement these connections with other companies and clients working in the same field. In an environment of increasing economic uncertainty, these connections are the only safety net available to businesses, but at the same time questions are raised about the ability of the markets to compile relevant information so that businesses can engage in rational economic calculation. The ultimate objectives may be known but the means applied in order to achieve them are based on conventions rather than rational decision-making. This ordinarily means that decision-making at the business and state level involves a political normative element. Therefore, although it likes to give the impression that it can offer a generous choice of alternatives, neo-liberal economic policy in fact does the exact opposite. *It is, in the proper sense of the word, an economic policy of state intervention in the markets,* which at the macro level certainly does not yield the optimal solution for all.

When the 'invisible hand' is made visible it becomes clear that the interests of some market agents are promoted more vigorously than those of others.

However, it would be wrong to draw the conclusion from the above that we ought to dispense with the market economy. The markets do promote one kind of freedom, as should have become clear in the text. They give consumers and entrepreneurs greater freedom of choice and enhance their freedom of action. When they work properly, the markets get rid of inefficient businesses and bolster the national economy more effectively than any other alternative. These conclusions are borne out by the history of the markets. But then there is the reverse side of the coin. The history of the markets is at once a history of unequal distribution of welfare, inhumanity and subordination, inclusion and exclusion. Yes, we do need the markets. For all their faults they are the most flexible way forward, even though progress may sometimes be rather erratic in what is an increasingly uncertain and complex world. But unaided, the markets cannot work effectively for very long, all the time increasing the nation's wealth. In order for the markets to become a stooge for an efficient economy they need to be supported by both state subsidies and state intervention. This is apparent at least when the operation of the markets threatens to marginalize increasing segments of the population and when they become a threat to themselves.

In this chapter I have referred, as consistently as possible, to 'the markets' in the plural. The reason for this is that although neo-liberal economic theory wants us to believe that only one ideal model of a market exists, that ideal doesn't in fact exist outside the imagination of these theorists. The application of this model seems to highlight certain negative features and effects of the markets. Keynes wrote in the mid-1920s that the single biggest political problem faced by humanity is how to combine economic efficiency, social justice and individual freedom. Neo-liberal thinking puts all its weight behind economic efficiency at the expense of everything else. It is hard to see what good can follow from ignoring the two other major themes identified by Keynes. Economic efficiency is only a necessary, but not yet a sufficient condition for the achievement of a good society.

This should be borne in mind in all economic theorizing. Historically, there has never existed any one abstract 'market'. There are always several markets, which can be approached from a variety of different angles. One way to study them is based on the number of market agents; in this case we refer to multilateral, oligarchic and monopolistic markets. These, in turn, vary in terms of their extent. There are global, national and local markets. Markets also vary according to the kind of goods that are traded. There are land, labour, money (or capital) and goods markets. The following ignores the former three and focuses on the goods circulating in the markets.

# 3
# Commodities and Consumption: General and Specific Features

As we have seen, markets are artificially maintained structures. They support the movement of various kinds of things and agents, most notably money (capital) and commodities, as well as people who are selling their labour power and earning wages and consumers who are living on income transfers. In this chapter my focus is on the core cell of the markets, i.e. the commodity. By commodity, I mean both tangible products and more or less intangible services. The reason for subsuming *both services and goods under the heading of commodity* is simple enough. Increasingly, services today are sold in standardized packages; this applies equally to adventure holidays and hotel services. For instance, when I check in at a hotel I receive the same anonymous and efficient reception as all other guests – although when I get to my room I discover that I'm not quite that anonymous after all as I receive a second personalized welcome via the television screen. The next morning I can look forward to my standardized breakfast package.

## 3.1   Aspects of commodity and consumption

Commodities, as is well known, have both use value and exchange value. Use value and exchange value are closely interconnected. Exchange value cannot exist without use value, but the opposite is also true. Without exchange, the product cannot become a commodity; its use value ceases to exist, other than as a theoretical possibility. In the best case it will become a museum item, in the worst case just plain rubbish. On the other hand, as soon as the commodity is put to use, its exchange value usually begins to fall. This means that its use value declines as well, until such point as it becomes disposable waste and loses all its original value. This means that exchange value and use value not only presuppose each other, they are also diametrically opposed to each other (Haug 1982a, 118).

The economic side of commodity is reflected in its price. In Marx's words, price reflects its being the 'product of labour'. Price anchors commodity and consumption from one end to the economy. Consumption, in other words, always has an *economic side* to it. In the national accounts it is reflected in consumer demand, for individual citizens it is reflected in the relationship between incomes and commodity prices.

However, there can be no demand for commodities unless they are perceived by consumers as objects of their needs, as use values. The use value of a commodity, whether real or imaginary, can only be harnessed to the consumer's purposes after exchange has taken place. It follows that use value is not an economic category in the first place, but it attaches consumption to civil society – its everyday activities and varied social microspace. Consumption represents the point of intersection between the economy and everyday life.

Consumers put a commodity to use when they have picked it up and put it in their shopping bag. This can mean many different things depending on whether the main emphasis is on the use of the technical or symbolic properties of the commodity. This is a conceptual rather than an empirical distinction and provides a means to analyse the commodity's use value. When the functional and material sides of consumption take centre stage, we may refer to the *technical/functional* aspect of consumption. This, in Aristotelian terms, combines the final and formal reasons of the product. While economics is chiefly interested in the economic aspect of consumption, the main concern for engineering, physics, nutrition science and consumer policy is the technical/functional side of consumption.

The technical/functional side of consumption does not, however, cover every aspect of use value, although this is the commonsensical understanding. The use of a commodity also depends on the context of that use. That, in turn, is dependent on the cultural meaning given to the commodity. This is what Marshall Sahlins (1976, 169) had in mind when he said that use value 'is not a quality of the object but a significance of the objective qualities'. This refers to something entirely different than the physical aspect of the commodity. Therefore, describing a skirt, in Western culture, as a 'feminine' garment has little to do with what it is made of or how it is used; this is just a cultural convention of thought that has no validity in, say, Egyptian or Indian culture.

Use value is therefore also an expression of cultural meanings. When cultural meanings become entrenched as part of commodity use values, it is those meanings that give shape to the use of commodities and so constitute their use value. Because of its meanings, use value is never socially neutral, because it is integrated by social groups as part of their practical interests. They use commodities, among other things, to express their cultural membership of certain social groups, such as young people, and to set themselves apart from certain others, such as older people and children.

Social anthropologists are well familiar with this mechanism. As they have pointed out, the differences between different commodities correspond to distinctions between different social groups. Commodities are a way of creating socially and culturally meaningful networks (Douglas & Isherwood 1980, 65, 131; Bourdieu 1980; Sahlins 1976, 179–204) and breaking up the recurring cycles of everyday life into meaningful segments. Consumption has a *symbolic side*, in which the Aristotelian formal and final reasons are most clearly in evidence. This symbolic side is of particular interest to anthropology, sociology, aesthetics and semiotics.

As soon as consumers have purchased a commodity in the marketplace, its symbolic and technical/functional side begin to deteriorate, even when the commodity is not in active use. The commodity gradually loses its use value and moves outside the realm of consumption. But before that, the commodity has served a purpose. It has been used as a tool to do something, to bring about some state of affairs. A personal computer has been used to write a text, an axe to chop wood, flowers to create a pleasing arrangement.

Commodities have thus been instrumentalized in consumption and used to achieve something over and above what is reflected in the technical/functional and symbolic dimensions of consumption. For example, consumers may buy different foodstuffs and test them in virtually endless combinations to create new taste and smell sensations and aesthetic pleasures. In this sense consumption has a *productive aspect*, too. This concept refers to *creative consumption* as discussed above, to exploring the possible range of uses that commodities can offer. This aspect of commodity thus links consumption to production and to the economic dimension of commodity.

All four aspects of consumption are usually present in the same commodity, overlapping in a positive relationship with one another. As Edmund Leach (1968, 523) observes, 'almost every human activity that takes place in culturally defined surroundings...has a technical aspect which does something and an aesthetic, communicative aspect which says something'. Take a Stradivarius. This is an expensive, technically first rate, symbolically highly valued instrument that, in the hands of the most expert violonists, is used to push the boundaries of violin play-ing. When the main weight of emphasis is on the positive extremes of all dimensions of the commodity, the commodity in question is usually a luxury item, something that is effectively 'timeless'. However, the dif-ferent aspects of consumption may also diverge in the same commod-ity, stand in a negative relationship to one another and thus create a contradictory commodity. As a consequence, the technical/functional, symbolic, productive and economic ages of the commodity will diverge from each other (Lefebvre 1971, 82).

This is precisely what happens with collectibles and fashion items, in which the symbolic aspect rises above all others and begins to deter-mine those other aspects. Since the symbolic value of fashion items falls very rapidly, the same applies to its economic value, even if there are no changes in its technical/functional qualities. Collectibles follow the exact opposite path. Even if they have no remaining productive func-tions and their technical/functional qualities continue to decline, their value just keeps rising.

The multiple dimensions of commodity, and by the same token, of con-sumption, are reflected in the consumer's position through the various stages of the consumption event. Initially, consumption is approached from an economic aspect, in the role of *clients* or *consumers*. The technical/functional aspect of consumption gains prominence when the material and functional properties of the commodity are put to use. This implies the position of *user*. The symbolic aspect of consumption, then, is pre-dominant when people position themselves in society by means of com-modities, when they use commodities to express their social identity and their personal preferences. Now, they become *communicators* of differ-ent meanings invested in them by commodities. Finally, the productive aspect of consumption is most prominent when the commodity is sub-sumed to serve some external purpose – when it is used to create some-thing new. This entails the role of *producer* or 'consumption worker'.

The multiple layers of commodity and consumption are illustrated in Figure 3.1. The figure applies equally to individual commodities and to consumption more generally. Furthermore, it can be used to describe not only consumption, but also perhaps the historical stages in the devel-opment of whole societies. In the latter instance it is necessary to give special consideration to how the different dimensions of commodity and consumption are related to one another. Without empirical analy-sis it is difficult to formulate more than assumptions about this, but I would be surprised if I were completely wrong in suggesting that tradi-tional consumption has tended to emphasize the relationship between the economic and technical/functional aspects of consumption over

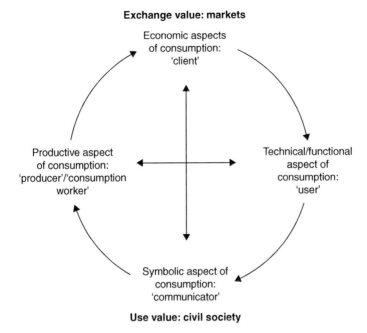

*Figure 3.1*   The dimensions of consumption and the consumer's positions

others: after all, it is against this relationship that the price and quality of the commodity are weighed. The market price of a commodity is assumed to reflect its technical/functional properties.

This view is perhaps no longer as dominant as it used to be. The closer we come to the present day, the more deeply the world of commodities has become saturated in meaning (through branding and advertising, for instance), and the greater the prominence of the relationship between the economic and symbolic aspect of consumption. People today tend to think that the quality of a commodity is conveyed by its symbolic dimension. This is reflected in pricing: products that are perceived as new and fashionable are priced highly, whereas symbolically outdated products will be marked down and sold at a clearance.

At the same time as the relationship between the symbolic and economic aspect gains prominence, so it also draws other aspects of commodity towards itself. The technical/functional dimension is put into the service of the symbolic dimension of consumption. Seeds are sprinkled on bread to create the impression that this is healthy eating. Fibres are woven into clothes that make them look like silk and feel softer. And the marketing of various foodstuffs such as pasta, rice and butter uses images of meals that can be prepared with these ingredients, taking advantage of the good-food reputation of certain countries.

## 3.2   The decommodification of products

Although marketing mixes and matches different aspects of commodities and so makes it harder to make comparisons, one thing is clear: the economic aspect of commodity is general by nature, a *communality*, whereas all its use-value aspects are specific. They are usually in evidence in all commodities. But there are exceptions. During the course of its circulation a commodity may lose some aspect or aspects of its use value. This ordinarily causes the product to lose its status as a commodity, which most typically happens through the *singularization* of a commodity (Kopytoff 1988, 73–74).

The singularization of a commodity usually happens through the *condensation of all four aspects of the commodity into its symbolic aspect*. The essential here is that the commodity is withdrawn from the market. In this process it is stripped of its economic dimension and appropriated by making it meaningful to its owner, either by dressing up the product and putting the owner's stamp on it (by pasting an *ex libris* sticker inside the front cover of a book, initialling a CD, hanging fluffy dice on a car windscreen) or by adapting and adjusting it to suit the owner's purposes (by decorating a flat, breaking in a pair of shoes, pinning a brooch on a blouse). This labelling helps the owner personalize the product according to his or her own needs and purposes – to build up the owner's social identity or to turn the commodity into a gift.

Singularization can take place either before the commodity enters the circle of market exchange or afterwards by removing it from the market. A typical form of advance singularization is where the object is prevented from entering the market in the first place. This happens most typically with products around which a special aura is created even before they have entered production by elevating them to the status of distinctive emblems for social groups or entire nations or symbols of collective identity. These will usually be entirely unique objects or artefacts. Furthermore, they are considered irreplaceable in the sense that they have no external point of reference, and therefore they can also have no price (Kopytoff 1988, 75). Good examples of such singular objects include the crown jewels and national treasures of art.

Subsequent singularization can also be a collective process, although usually it is individual. In this instance singularization involves removing the commodity from the circle of exchange and reserving it exclusively for private use. Sometimes it can even be removed from use after it has been acquired. An example of the former is the practice of *gift-giving*; an example of the latter is *private collecting*.

Collecting is the reverse side of gift-giving. It is a special case of consumption proper (Benjamin 2003 [1939]). The collector's passion is to remove a commodity from its cycle of circulation and turn it into an item freed of its technical/functional use value. However, the item is not fully exempted from all utility requirements; for the collector wants to place the item on display alongside other similar items and in that sense use it as an ornament. Collectors thus use the items they have collected to create magical circles of commodities, exceptional interiors that are pleasing to the eye and to the mind. They are the collector's way of leaving a mark of themselves, both to present and future generations.

However, this use of collectibles to create specific interiors or milieus does not mean to say that these items lose their independence when they are added to an existing collection – even though the collection no doubt increases in significance with each new addition to the items that have some common cultural denominator. Each and every collectible is special in the sense that the collector invests strong emotional commitments in the item and elevates it from the realm of mundane use value to a symbolic pedestal of adoration (Benjamin 2003 [1939]). From that high position, collectibles can of course flirt with consumers and re-enter the marketplace, but only once the owner's commitment (or finances) has dried up.

It is clear from this vacillation between commodity and non-commodity status that the biographic course of the commodity is even more complex than might be deduced from the differential degradation of its four dimensions (technical/functional, symbolic, productive and economic). Our world is not only becoming increasingly commodified, filled with more and more commodities, but a parallel process of decommodification is also taking place as commodities are purchased in the marketplace and set apart as something special. In these cases commodities are always invested with strong emotions. This has happened not only to national treasures and to gifts and collectibles, but also to items that have assumed a more prominent place than others on the horizon of our physical existence and our thinking. Examples from recent history include such superitems as the automobile, radio, television and furniture sets (Löfgren 1990, 15–27).

## 3.3   The multiple dimensions of commodity: methodological implications

The multiple dimensions of commodity greatly complicate the task of investigating consumption and present some specific requirements with regard to the choice of research method. It is not my intention in this book to provide an in-depth discussion of methods' issues around the sociology of consumption. However, so profound are the methods' implications of the multidimensionality and the movement of commodity for the rest of this book that they cannot be ignored.

The first methodological comment relates to analyses that are concerned with 'consumption in general' and that often make sweeping generalizations about consumption and society as a whole. These summary generalizations are rather problematic in that the only conclusions that can be drawn from consumption concern the national economy. When consumption is considered at a general level, the objects of consumption, i.e. commodities, lose all their specific dimensions. All that remains is the one aspect that is shared in common by all objects of consumption, their exchange value. In other words, any analysis of *consumption as such* is focused exclusively on the *economic aspect* of consumption.

Analyses of the economic aspect of consumption do not yet allow us to draw conclusions about consumption as a whole without doing injustice to use value. Unless it is the express purpose to limit the focus to the economic aspect of consumption, to its communality, we must start from the premise that consumption comprises many different categories of commodity. The use-value structures in these categories vary widely and produce different historical routes of circulation for the commodity (from communality to singularity and vice versa) and different types of relationships between use value and exchange value. The description of the use of a PC or a shirt or a beer as abstract 'consumption' prevents us from seeing the specificity of the use of these commodities and its association with their economic aspect.

Henri Lefebvre's idea of *sub-systems of everyday life* offers one way to avoid this reduction of consumption to a single dimension. By these sub-systems, Lefebvre refers to all those compendiums of meanings that parcel out the flow of everyday routines and that clearly stand out of that flow. However, these sub-systems are not created all by themselves, but as a result of a determined and deliberate effort. They require special measures to make these compendiums of meanings meaningful in the eyes of the community (Lefebvre 1971, 98).

Sub-systems of everyday life cannot be created out of just anything. For the production and maintenance of such a system at least three conditions must be met. Firstly, in order to extract something out of the flow of the everyday, it must be possible to demarcate its *symbolic boundaries,* as has been done in the cases of wine, golf or the motor car, for instance. Secondly, these sub-systems are not sustained all by themselves, but it is necessary to have *social organizations and interest groups* to support and legitimize them. Thirdly, something that is elevated to the status of a sub-system must have access to its *own text* that guarantees its publicity.

These conditions are met by such social spheres as art, literature, religion and the labour market, but there are also some commodities and consumption habits that have attained the status of a sub-system. Lefebvre himself includes in this list culinarism and cooking, fashion, tourism, sex-industry products (pornography) and the motor car. These, he says, are sub-systems that have developed a specific social hierarchy and their own rules (Lefebvre 1971, 98–100). But these are only indicative examples. It is easy to extend this list today; we could add to it at least housing (interior decoration and gardening), television (listings magazines, *Idols* and other reality-competition shows), health (lifestyle magazines and markets and health products), and various sports (tennis, golf, skiing and corresponding products and publicity).

If the focus of interest in anthropology and the sociology of consumption is on the different dimensions of use value, it is important to stress that consumption research must still not disregard the economic aspect. Even though this means that the attention must be turned to the general aspects of consumption, that focus has relevance in two particular respects. On the one hand, the general perspective is important in macro-level research, particularly in studies concerned with the conditions for consumption and with how those conditions are distributed in the population. On the other hand, an economic approach to studying consumption can also be defended in micro-level analysis, especially when the main concern is with the selection process – which after all is initially very much focused on economic considerations. The acquisition of a commodity involves a process of weighing its price against its presumed technical/functional, symbolic and productive properties.

However, it is not possible to single out any one primary way in which to approach consumption. This has not always been the accepted way of thinking. On the contrary, that has been to assume that the dominant aspect of consumption is its economic side. However, since consumption happens at the crossroads between the economy and civil society, it cannot be exhaustively understood solely from this economic vantage point. It is true that even when it is fully immersed in civil society, consumption continues to serve economic purposes, such as the reproduction of capital and labour power. But it does more. Once it has moved over into the realm of life-world, consumption helps to build up people's everyday life and to express its different sides, to maintain social ties, to make social distinctions and to build up one's own social-psychological self.

All in all then, consumption and commodities play a critical role in the process where people produce themselves in society, both physically and socially. Consumption and its fair and equitable distribution among different population groups are also among the trump cards that society's power elites use to justify their own actions and to guarantee social peace and stability. It is therefore no exaggeration to say, as Lefebvre does, that consumption and commodities are the cement of society.

The fourth methodological comment is related to the previous one. Even when consumption is approached as a collection of sub-systems of everyday life, those sub-systems must not be separated from one another or from their other social contexts. To do that is to risk losing sight of how those sub-systems work together, how society as a whole works together – which has happened all too often in research into markets and leisure (Clarke & Critcher 1985, 13–46; Rojek 1985, 179–180). As I have tried to show above, consumption can only take place in its historical, social, economic and ecological contexts. These contexts impose limits on consumption, at the same time as each sub-system of everyday life adapts and adjusts the socio-economic impacts entering their sphere to bring them in line with their own rules.

# 4
# Want, Need and Commodity

Markets cannot exist without productive capital, which is needed, among other things, to organize human labour and non-human operating systems, technological circuits and logistics. These inputs result in an influx of commodities into the marketplace. In the absence of demand for these commodities, the system will suffocate. Its existence is dependent both on human needs and wants, on access to the economic means to purchase goods and on manufacturers' powers of persuasion. My focus in this chapter is on the role of needs and wants in the regulation of consumption demand.

## 4.1 Need as a universal category

Nature imposes its own conditions on people's everyday activities, including production and consumption, but it does not dictate the form of these processes nor (at least so far) their overall level. Market-driven supply continued to rise very sharply throughout the twentieth century. This, however, would not have been possible without a corresponding escalation of individual needs. For this reason it is necessary to examine what it is in us as consumers that lies behind the constant growth and expansion of consumption.

Before we start to unravel this web of questions, it is useful to recall that our relationship to products of labour has become externalized with the commodification of need satisfaction. When products are created as commodities, they do not reach the consumer until in the marketplace. This means there is always the possibility that no one really notices them – and therefore every effort must be invested in attracting the attention of consumers to the newly launched commodity. This is understandable because attracting attention is the first and most fundamental requirement for the exchange of commodities. It is only once they have entered the consumer's sphere of consciousness that they can attract any interest.

The consumer's interest in commodities is grounded in individual needs and *driven by use values*, albeit mediated by *money*. Our perspective on the commodity is thus mediated through the economic side of consumption and focused on that particular use-value aspect that happens to be of most interest to us at that particular time. This sounds simple enough, but the situation is complicated by the diversity of the consumer's use-value oriented perspective. That perspective combines the commodity's 'true' use value and the consumer's perception of that value. The latter, in turn, is influenced by the consumer's assessment of how the commodity will help satisfy his or her current needs. Furthermore, the consumer's position will be influenced by his or her previous experiences of the commodity and interpretation of the needs that those experiences help to express (Ilmonen 1985, 58).

From the consumer's use-value oriented point of view, then, the presumed and real properties of the commodity, the way those properties are experienced and current needs *at each moment in time* are condensed in commodities. It is only when the consumer's needs fall squarely in line with the presumed use-value qualities of the commodity that a purchase becomes likely. Once a connection has been created between the commodity and needs, it will tend to become cemented. Consumers become loyal to certain brands. The depth of this loyalty varies, of course, because the novelties flooding into the market and marketing will have done their utmost to break existing bonds between consumers and commodities. If they have succeeded in doing that, the consumer's experiences of commodities will have been curtailed and the consumer's use-value centred perspective will have lost its firm foundation.

When consumers lose contact with commodities and have less first-hand experience of them, it seems that the safest and most straightforward compass for our consumption behaviour is provided by needs. This notion is probably grounded in the traditional understanding that, in conditions of scarcity, needs are sharply contoured phenomena cemented by biology. This idea has no doubt been fostered by the special status afforded in the social sciences and psychology to needs. By appealing to needs it has been possible to explain just about any political or human action (see Heller 1979, 49).

On closer inspection, however, it transpires that needs are rather difficult to unravel. One reason for this is that in moral discourses so-called basic needs, in particular, are represented as universal elements of our existence. To refer to basic needs means little more than to state what is constant in human life and therefore morally defensible. We need air to breathe, something to eat and drink, clothes, physical protection and rest. Stating all this means nothing more than to state the fundamental condition of human existence. This realization does not, however, trigger human action. It is only when these universals are *targeted* at something outside of ourselves that action is triggered. But of course by that point we are no longer dealing with needs per se, but with *specific needs that are dependent on their objects*. These needs with external objects I call *wants*. Wants are needs that have grown out of conditions of needs (for instance, we no longer want just something to drink, but a certain type of beverage, coffee, tea etc.), and they are historically variable, which greatly complicates the task of analysing needs.

## 4.2   Need and activity

The view that needs develop historically has not been the received opinion. In fact there is still a strong body of opinion which believes that needs constitute the immutable core of human nature. This position appears in a plethora of variants from behavioural psychology through to sociobiological theories of society. Without doing any injustice to them, all these variants can be subsumed under the concept of *need naturalism*.

The most common form of need naturalism is the classification of human needs into two categories: *basic* and *derived* needs. Basic needs are those that are associated most closely with what is necessary for human physiological existence – the universal elements that were mentioned above. They are considered more important than other needs because they must be met in order for people to live and survive. It is thought that providing for these needs requires political decision-making. Derived needs, then, are biologically and morally secondary in this respect, for failure to satisfy them is not considered a threat to human existence.

Need naturalism is open to many criticisms (see Ilmonen 1985, 17–23) which I shall not repeat here. Suffice it to highlight two points. The first has to do with the notion of *basic* or *fundamental* needs, which is problematic in many ways. If it is used to refer to the physiological boundary-line that separates human life from death, the concept is no doubt defendable based on physiological measurements. These will demonstrate the exact amount of nutrition, liquid and oxygen that is necessary for the continued existence of human life in extreme

conditions. But as soon as we move away from those conditions, qualitative dimensions of existence enter the picture. They impose moral,
economic and aesthetic requirements for needs and need satisfaction
that may be fateful. Thus, for instance, nationalism and extreme forms
of religion (fundamentalism) have called upon supporters to sacrifice
their physical existence for a more 'fundamental' cause, such as independence or freedom. When the criteria for the fundamentality of
needs begin to waver, when they can no longer be anchored directly
to biology, then it becomes clear there is a *political agenda* behind the
definition of the fundamentality of needs (Berry 1994, 38, 86).

Another problem with need naturalism is that it fails to make a *distinction between* a) *the condition of need and a specific need, i.e. want* and
b) *need and need satisfaction*. These distinctions correspond to those
between hunger, appetite and eating. These are bodily conditions that
are inherently associated with one another, but nonetheless analytically and in reality separate phenomena. A condition of need is a biological condition of lack of fullness. There is no biologically determined
association from this condition to the eruption of some specific need
(want). From the existence of this condition, it is not yet possible to
predict how exactly it will be satisfied. The condition of need, a specific need (want) and its satisfaction do not immediately determine one
another (Ilmonen 1985, 18). It is easy to think of everyday examples of
how some external event can ruin our appetite, despite a definite sense
of hunger. Likewise, it is impossible to infer from having an appetite
how it will be satisfied.

These food examples go to show that the condition of need has both a
physiological and psycho-social aspect (see Mennell 1985, 21; Mennell
1991, 127). It is physiological in the sense that the condition of need is
grounded in biological and physiological processes (for instance, the
development of a shortage of energy or liquid). Its outward manifestation, on the other hand, is mainly determined by psycho-social factors.
We have no gut mechanism that urges us to ingest vitamin B1 after
a heavy meal or drinking bout. Nor does our bodily biology explain
why in some communities certain foods are respected and others are
avoided. Personal experience and individual memory in general are significant at the level of the psyche, whereas customs, morals and (e.g.
Islamic or Jewish) law and corresponding forms of collective memory
are examples of ways in which the community regulates the manifestation and satisfaction of needs.

It is also impossible to understand need simply by analysing the physiological and psychological processes occurring within the individual, for

*it is impossible to understand need without its object.* A condition of need (say a feeling of hunger) does not yet imply a specific need or want. It is a relative concept, just as is its external counterpart, the object of want. That object and want are linked together by human activity. That, however, does not yet draw us automatically towards the object, because as was just discussed, the object of need, for humans, is not determined in advance. On the contrary, it only unfolds in the course of action, just as the need itself. Since our needs are *interwoven* with one another, they only become crystallized with activity – and even then they require *interpretation*. It is only then that it is possible to identify the object of need (Leontiev 1978; Galperin 1979, 63; Eskola 1982, 218–219; Joas 1996). Once the interpretation has been made, the need becomes specific and it turns into a want, *especially if the object of need remains unachieved.* A child might take a fancy to a toy. No matter what is offered in its place, absolutely no other toy will do. A man or woman who has fallen in love will only be content when re-united with the object of their love; absolutely no one else will do.

The identification of a need and its object may be a surprisingly complex process. People behave in a more or less straightforward fashion, guided by their biology, only under extreme duress. The seemingly innocuous qualifier 'only' is particularly noteworthy here. That is, in situations of extreme duress people may, for instance, eat a lot of things that they would not normally put near their mouth. But even then there are nutritionally acceptable raw materials that will be deemed inedible. This is obviously more apparent the less pressing the situation is. The choice of food will pass through a sieve that at one end is rather crude, and proceed to the other end where distinctions are very fine indeed. A rough distinction is first made between edible and inedible *nutrition*; then, on a slightly more specific level, a distinction is made between desirable and non-desirable *food*; and finally, between a desirable and undesirable *meal*.

The baseline situation in need satisfaction, then, may be so unstructured that even the object of need is not yet clear. It is only when the individual becomes aware of the condition of need that the internal tension is created which is needed to trigger activity. However at this stage the focus and direction of this activity still remains unclear, for the conditions of need and the wants emanating from those conditions are still too vague. Retail trade has long taken advantage of this by coaxing shoppers into making impulse purchases. People who go shopping without a shopping list are most likely to fall victim. In this case it is the activity, the wandering around the shops, that filters out objects of want and entices the shopper to pick them up.

Once the object of want has crystallized, activity will commence to quench the want, unless there are internal or external obstacles (cf. Heller 1979, 49; von Wright 1985, 40–41). As a result of satisfaction, the condition of need will change. The internal tension within the individual is released and new emerging conditions of need take their place. Someone who has had a good meal may feel like they need a nap, or something else may happen. The outcome is an endless carousel of needs that drives the individual to engage in ever-new activities and points out well-established trails for activity, but also fresh new directions.

Part of the reason why activity tends to become routinized lies in the circular recursive movement of need and activity. Activity is an expending of resources that creates new needs. As those resources are depleted, people will seek to find new modes of activity and new objects to restore them (rest, play, entertainment etc.). Once their resources have been restored, people return to the activities and objects of those activities that deplete their resources (going to work, going for a run etc.)

The circular movement of need and activity is not only recursive, however. Activity also moves in new directions. This is because in the course of activity, people accumulate new cognitive capacities, new skills and new knowledge. They think up new ways of satisfying their wants, and even create new wants. Conditions of need are enriched into multiple wants and their circle expands (consider the proliferation of cookery books in recent years). They swim off and enter a cycle of historical movement. *At the same time the relationship between need and activity may be inversed.* Activity begins in itself to create new conditions of needs and new wants. Someone who has taken up running may feel that jogging around the block has become rather boring; they want more, perhaps to go out in the woods with a map and a compass. Lucien Sève is one of the psychologists who has drawn attention to this phenomenon. He observes that because of the inversion of the relationship between need and activity, people do not just live in order to eat, but they begin to eat in order to create something new in their lives (see Sève 1975, 47–49, 388).

## 4.3   Interpretation, tradition and symbolic value

As we have seen then, the object of need is not recognized as such an object until it has been so *interpreted*. This, of course, does not happen in a vacuum without a frame of reference. It usually consists of numerous different elements. The most important among them are probably

a) the agent's earlier experiences and the memory traces they have left, b) the agent's socialization, c) collective memory and d) commodities striving to become objects of needs. The following touches only very briefly on individual experiences, socialization and collective memory. The main focus is on the role of commodities as interpreters of our needs.

But let me start with individual experience. That does obviously not accumulate lying down on the couch, but through action. People do not gain experience about the objects of their needs other than by turning them into *objects for themselves*, into wants. This, in turn, only happens by working these objects so as to make them suit one's needs. Wild mushrooms may be recognized as nutrition based on what one has read, but they are not considered suitable for one's own use until they have been tasted or processed. The only way one can really learn about wild mushrooms, to combine them with other ingredients and develop recipes, is to work with them, to boil them and fry them and ultimately taste them. Seen from this point of view, these activities are mainly recollections of personal experience gained of these ingredients and different ways of combining them. They help us to get in contact with sensory experiences, to prepare the same meal again, perhaps even tweak the recipe to make it even better.

Once we have succeeded in creating what we feel is a good recipe, whether for food, music or clothing, we may want to share our experience. We decide to submit the recipe to a food magazine, a record company or a DIY sewing website. If it is accepted for publication and indeed if it attracts attention, it will become collective property and stored in the collective memory. Collective memory is passed on through socialization, education and symbolic representations from one generation to the next. In the pre-modern world, it was the single most significant factor steering interpretations of objects of needs (e.g. Halbwachs 1992, 188). Even today its influence cannot be underestimated. Personal experience is really only a source of variation within the framework created by collective memory.

The family, school and church have of course been the most important institutions previously responsible for the handing down of collective memory and for children's socialization (Halbwachs 1992, 59; Misztal 2003, 91–97). In particular, the family has passed on traditions and customs from one generation to the next and in general looked after the education of new generations. Other people in the immediate community have obviously had a significant role, too. However, this is not particularly relevant for the present analysis, for regardless of whether it is the family or other people who pass on the understanding that something is an object of needs, this process is always based on the recipients of the tradition identifying themselves with the people representing that tradition and adopting their traditional frame of reference.

Thorstein Veblen developed one of the first classics on the sociology of consumption to draw attention to this. Veblen and George Herbert Mead are the names most commonly cited when sociologists talk about the *reference group*. This concept refers to the transfer through socialization of collective rules and values within or across generations (see Piaget 1974, 39). In cases where the reference-group effect operates through family generations, traditions are handed down diachronically. In this instance young people adopt their parents' consumption habits, for instance. David Riesman has used the term *anticipatory socialization* to describe this phenomenon. When the reference-group effect operates within the same generation, say within a circle of friends, Riesman speaks of retrospective socialization (Riesman 1969, 109–110). For me, however, *simultaneous socialization* would better emphasize the point that socialization happens within one or two generations synchronically, through the interaction of the members of those generations.

It is only rarely that anticipatory and simultaneous socialization co-exist side by side. When they have clashed in pre-modern society, it is usually anticipatory socialization that has come out on top. In modern society their relationship has become more complex still. Anticipatory socialization continues to wield its influence through the family institution.[1] However, it no longer affects young people's consumption behaviour as a whole in the same way as it used to. Instead, friends and the media have become an increasingly important socializing factor due to the erosion of the extended family, i.e. with the ever-dwindling presence of significant adults in children's lives. In some areas of consumption, such as popular music and literature, this has led to the emergence of marked generational differences in tastes and preferences. Simultaneous socialization has become an increasingly significant factor affecting entire generations (Misztal 2003, 83–90).

Simultaneous socialization has gained increasing significance with the continued expansion of capitalist commodity markets. This has decayed the social cement that holds together one aspect of collective memory, i.e. old traditions. The bonds created by these traditions have connected certain needs with certain predefined objects. This connection has prevented the expansion of commodity markets, and therefore it has had to be severed. This has been successful inasmuch as the prototype of modern markets, the young and beautiful woman or man, has also become the ideal type. That, in turn, has profoundly affected traditional conceptions of generational authority. In Western society parenthood and authority, for instance, are no longer associated in the same taken-for-granted way as in, say, Japan – although even there things are now apparently changing. For this reason parents are no longer in the position to play as prominent a role in anticipatory socialization as they did just a few generations ago. In fact there are signs now that parents are beginning to copy young people's consumption habits and to accommodate themselves to *retrospective socialization* (see e.g. Lasch 1980, 209–217). Social scientists talk about the 'culture of simultaneity', which is characterized by an abstract idealization of youth. Every generation wants to make the same consumption choices as young people.

The shift from anticipatory to simultaneous socialization is thus based on the loss of family influence over the interpretation of needs. Increasingly, that influence has been superseded by commodity. As such there is nothing curious about this, for the use-value dimensions of a commodity can be seen precisely as interpretations of our needs. Indeed this is the very starting point from which Wolfgang F. Haug has set out to develop his theory of *commodity aesthetics* (Haug 1982b; 1986).

Commodity aesthetics is an ambiguous concept. Contrary to intuitive impressions, it has not so much to do with commodities as with the relationship between commodities and needs. The theory of commodity aesthetics has it that because of their needs, consumers are interested in the use value of commodities. However, they cannot feel it in advance, nor can they appropriate it until after they have made the purchase (Haug 1982b, 38). It is therefore not the use value that instigates the purchase; the decision to purchase is triggered by the *promise of use value*. The basic law of commodity aesthetics, as formulated by Haug, is the condition that not use value but rather use-value promise triggers the act of exchange or purchase (ibid., 40).

Haug makes a distinction then between use value and the promise of value. Furthermore, he divides the use-value promise into two parts, i.e. the objective and subjective. The former is reflected in the visible surface of the commodity, its 'sensory aestheticism', which is consciously shaped as a separate element of the commodity, the 'commodity's aesthetic abstraction'. The 'raw core' of the commodity is wrapped under another surface, which consists of the packaging, the outer covering, design and image advertising. Together, these make up the *objective use-value promise*, which becomes an integral part of the commodity.

The *subjective use-value promise*, then, is associated with the consumer. More specifically, it reflects the ability of commodity aesthetics to influence consumers in such a way that they *persuade themselves to make the purchase* and *justify* this action by reference to the commodity's *objective use-value promise*. The task of persuasion is obviously the easiest to accomplish when the purchase most closely matches the consumer's current wants (Haug 1982b, 246). The closer this match is, the more likely it is that the consumer will adopt the perspective of the commodity's provider (Bourdieu 2005, 170). In this way commodity aesthetics and the consumer, Haug says, become interconnected into a 'functional circuit of commodity aesthetics'. This lays the foundation for the 'sensory reshaping' of people (Haug 1982b, 47). What Haug means by this rather curious expression is that commodity aesthetics take part in reshaping people's wants.

Haug's theory of commodity has some problems that I have addressed elsewhere (Ilmonen 1993, 83–88). Therefore, for the remainder of this discussion, I will drop the concept of commodity aesthetics and refer instead to the symbolic side of the commodity, because I do not want to challenge Haug's view of commodities as interpreters of our wants. His idea is also consistent with empirical reality that we make promises to ourselves about the use value of commodities. These promises reflect the way that wants work and at the same time describe our own interpretations of our wants. More accurately, *the subjective promise of use value combines both the interpretation of commodities and our wants*. It is this that makes Haug's 'functional circuit' of commodities and wants a workable concept. It is also the most important link in the chain of events that makes the world of commodities such a powerful system of socialization (Haug 1982b, 110; see also Campbell 1987; Miller 1987).

The socializing power of commodities is based on their ability to convince us that they are the only proper interpretations of our needs. Those interpretations do not of course come about by themselves, but they are the end result of a complex process that weaves together sales talk, advertising, symbolic language and mutual interaction among different consumer groups. How to get this process started and how to keep it going have been key problems in commodity production and exchange ever since the creation of the capitalist sector of the economy. Attracting consumer interest in merchandise continues to remain one of the biggest make-or-break issues for commodity manufacturing. One of the strategies adopted has been to try and increase the appeal and attraction of commodities, or their 'valence'. The easiest way to do this is to work the symbolic side of the commodity so that it sits comfortably with our cultural practices (e.g. the gender division). In this sense it might perhaps be said that the *intensification* of the use of symbolic language is an exchange-value element of commodities that has historically added to their use value, and that this element has subsequently had an ever-greater impact on consumers' relationship with the world of commodities and ultimately with one another.

Once commodities have achieved their goal and been selected as objects of our wants, those wants become fixed to commodities. Commodities now turn into motives for our activity, and they create images that at once shape the condition of needs. Commodities therefore occupy a very prominent place in our everyday life. From this, however, we cannot yet draw the conclusion that our wants and needs are fully controlled by commodities, as Theodor W. Adorno and Herbert Marcuse have suggested (Marcuse 1964, 30–35; Rose 1978, 49).

Indeed, this is not possible in the first place, for wants and commodities are never fully reducible to each other. If they were, the degree of need satisfaction would depend solely on the ownership of commodities. However, practice teaches us that the number of commodities we possess does not in itself make us happy. Need satisfaction additionally requires moral, emotional and cognitive characteristics that cannot be reached through the world of commodities alone. Those characteristics should therefore not be sought in the commodity, but rather in ourselves and in our relationships with other people. For this reason commodities do not provide a sound enough basis for a theory of needs.

## 4.4 The historicity of desires: an empirical and conceptual analysis

Above I have sketched an answer to the question of what mechanism it is in the consumer that responds to the commodity-flooded markets. However, that answer remains rather general and fails to explain the shape and form assumed today by the satisfaction of needs and wants. To make progress towards a fuller explanation, we need to examine a) the process in which consumer needs and wants evolve and become refined and b) the mechanisms governing the realization or direction of wants (cf. Falk 1990, 113). Let me start with the former question.

My treatment here of the relationship between needs and wants has so far been at a fairly general level. I have made no attempt to address the mechanism through which conditions of need are transformed, at the individual level, into wants. I have, however, stressed that human activity and the human ability to creatively resolve problems thrown up by conditions of need are central to the definition of our current wants and to ranking them in one way or another. Furthermore, referring to Haug, I have described how the subjective promise of use value connects wants and commodities with each other. However, it is not always possible to achieve the object of our needs. Our need satisfaction may be hampered by nature, other people, cultural conventions, time and place restrictions and financial restraints. In fact there is always quite a high risk that the object of our need, whether that is a commodity or something else, remains unattained, at least temporarily.

When the activity leading to a certain object of need is prevented and the object remains beyond our reach, the need does not cease to exist. Instead, the need and the drive to achieve the object remain latently within us. This creates an internal state of tension. Once that tension has formed, it begins to lead an independent existence and to try and find an outlet. In doing so it first breaks the tie with the original object of need and then with the need itself. A new condition of the human mind is created. In the words of Sigmund Freud (2004, 7): 'One portion (in quantitative terms) of an attitude, of an instinctual impulse, has remained unchanged, while another has developed further.' Jacques Lacan, Freud's successor, only calls this new form a *desire* (Lacan 1982, 265, 311). Desiring, according to this idea, becomes a permanent personality trait. As Freud (2004, 43) puts it: 'Some of these drives are used up in such a way that in their place something appears that in an individual we describe as a character trait.'

In a nutshell, the Lacanian–Freudian theory of desire says that *desire and need cannot be equated*, for they have different dynamics. Need seeks satisfaction. Once it has achieved that, it will be quenched and replaced by another need. When a need is not satisfied, a specific need, i.e. a *desire* arises. Once it has broken away from the initial need, it sinks into the subconscious, and it cannot be retracted other than in alienated form, in the shape of personal and social wishes. Those wishes can be fulfilled, but that will not quench the desire. On the contrary, desire is like a magician. It keeps conjuring up new desires out of nowhere, until the original starting point of the desire, the object of need, is reached. The satisfaction of wishes is therefore just ersatz satisfaction. Desire is the black hole of personality that sucks in any and all objects of wishes, including commodities (Lacan 1982, 286–287).[2]

Lacan's view on the psychological foundation of our existence is highly sophisticated, but just as hard to verify as it is to disprove. On the other hand, it provides an elegant explanation for the historical expansion of needs, showing that, even though they assume historically variable manifestations, their satisfaction does not lead to a generalization of the circle of consumption. Rather, that is achieved by unsatisfied needs, desires, and their multiple manifestations, *wishes*. When wishes are fulfilled, that does not satisfy desires, but merely leads to a constant search for something new – to a constant longing. That longing is the surest guarantee of the stability of 'consumer society' in its present shape.

So for Lacan, desire is typical of the human species. We have all been there, of course, felt the disappointment that follows when our need satisfaction is thwarted. Lacan's theory allows us to explain the possibility of consumer society by suggesting that consumer society has its equivalent in the structures of the human psyche. However for that possibility to turn into reality it is still necessary to solve the problem as to why human desires and wishes turn to outside objects, to commodities. That is a question to which Lacan's idea of desire offers no solution and which calls for something other than a psychological explanation – and probably a return to my own way of understanding desire simply in terms of an object-focused concept.

Lacanian theory of desire is also open to further criticisms. One of the critics of the theory is French philosopher Jean-François Lyotard, who says that the meaning given by Lacan to desires rests largely on taking absence as the foundation of our being. For Lyotard, this is a religious thought-form. Given the weight he attaches to absence, Lyotard maintains, Lacan elevates deprivation as his unattainable god and in this way reduces desire to a matter of mere faith (see Krause-Jensen 1983, 79). Indeed, that is exactly the impression one gets reading Lacan.

The third point of criticism against Lacanian theory of desire is that it is historically detached. This is partly due to the nature of the theory. Grounded in Freud's psychodynamic theory, its ambitious goal is to identify those characteristics of the human species that are independent of historical development, its so-called anthropological constants, as well as their interactions. Social scientists, however, have been rather sceptical about the existence of such constants. The argument developed here shares this scepticism, although I do accept that there exist certain biological *conditions of need* that are independent of time and place and that we share with creation. On the other hand, specific needs, i.e. desires, are clearly not historical constants.

Norbert Elias takes this same position in his study on the civilizing process, where he sets out to demonstrate how Freud's topology of personality – id, superego and ego – has evolved over time, with the adoption and assimilation of customs. At the individual level, this process has led to the phenomenon of superego, which has *meant a strengthening of self-discipline and a distanciation from personal needs and emotions.* Elias, therefore, concludes that the characteristics of self-discipline and self-control that Freud saw in his patients and that he called superego, were not universal human qualities after all, but rather an outcome of European social development and the incorporation of that development in human activity (Elias 1982, 229–336; Mennel 1989, 45–138).

The extent to which the individual him- or herself stands as an obstacle to need satisfaction, then, depends on the level of self-discipline. Customs, for Elias, are an external social mechanism that serves to delay or even limit immediate need satisfaction. Customs are not, of course, the only external constraint to need satisfaction. Others include traditions and religious and political prohibitions, variations in climate conditions and household financial resources.

The same applies to the Lacanian notion of desire as to Freudian superego. Desire and the outlet for its satisfaction are historically shaped. It is noteworthy that the search for objects of desires may in principle take one of two directions, *quantification* or *qualification*. This choice is not so much an individual as a community matter, and it depends crucially on how closely community life is governed and regulated by tradition (cf. Shils 1981).

The role of tradition in maintaining social continuity has received extensive study in classical sociological texts. In societies where tradition has a firm grip on the community, it has been able to give individuals both permissible objects of desire and point them towards ways of releasing the tension pent up by desire. This is typical of pre-modern or religiously and politically regulated modern society, where consumption assumes a specific shape. This is clearly reflected in individual consumption choices.

The impact of tradition on consumption has also attracted the attention of David Riesman, who classifies not societies but individuals based on how heavily they are influenced by tradition. Riesman describes the individual who is deeply conscious of tradition as *tradition-directed*. For a tradition-directed person, the idea of consumption constantly changing shape is an abomination. Wherever possible, this person will prefer to stick to familiar objects of desire and ways of satisfying those desires. For a tradition-directed person, what exists right now is 'everything there is' (Riesman 1969, 382–396). Any new needs and desires are completely alien to these people, even condemnable (see also Durkheim 1951 [1897]).[3] For this reason, in a tradition-directed world the only conceivable ways of releasing tensions brought about by desires are those that lead to the quantification of need satisfaction (Mennell 1991, 139–141).

In the feudal era this was still considered a moral problem. Indeed in medieval Aristotelian thinking the approach that quantified needs and sought their satisfaction in increasing quantities was largely condemned. The normative standard was the condition of shortage and the need arising from that condition. The satisfaction of those needs (*eudaimonia*) was a morally justified objective when that choice was made purely based on those needs themselves; that implied living a *virtuous* life, the way that people were supposed to live their lives (Aristotle 1992). When the desire for food grew out of a lack of energy it was right to quench it. If, on the other hand, the desire for food continued beyond the quenching of the sense of hunger then something had gone amiss. In this instance men are 'intent upon living only, and not upon living well' (Aristotle 1992). Life became a travesty of virtue, geared to the satisfaction of lust (*epithumia*). Early Christian thinking further added to this the concept of *sin*. Man possessed by lust was a man of sin (Berry 1994, 88).

The Aristotelian view began to recede in the sixteenth century. Thomas Hobbes (1991, 70) was one of the first modern thinkers to discredit this view and the associated moral standard that defined the satisfaction of desires as a virtue and the satisfaction of lust as a trampling on virtue. Bypassing the moral framework was associated with the reassessment of secular life (Berry 1994, 114). Underlying this was first of all the growth of long-distance trade from the seventeenth century onwards and the *introduction of various exotic luxury goods* (coffee, tea, sugar, silk, peppers etc.) *into the marketplace*. Another distinctive characteristic was the reassessment of secular life and the *reduction of necessities to just one: food*. All other needs were derived or volitional, and were considered boundless. One of the most fervent champions of world trade in the late seventeenth century, Nicholas Barbon, was among the first advocates of this way of thinking (ibid., 111–116). However, it was his contemporary John Houghton who provided perhaps the most succinct expression of this view when he said that the nation's wealth is created by those 'guilty of Prodigality, Pride, Vanity and Luxury' (ibid., 108–111).

With the expansion of capitalist markets and the acceleration of tradition-breaking social development in the eighteenth century, there was also a growing inclination to reassess secular life and at the same time to give increasing prominence to desires as an engine of development. A good example is Bernard Mandeville's *The Fable of the Bees*. To the present day Mandeville's text is known for its ridicule of the

Aristotelian view, which stirred up quite a scandal. His contemporaries regarded the work as an outright attack against thinking in terms of virtues. They were right. As far as Mandeville was concerned, all supporters of virtues' thinking were hypocrites. They never practised what they preached, but indulged in every possible pleasure. Mandeville wanted others to be able to share in these pleasures and aimed to identify in human practices what it was in them that really advanced real pleasure. He sought to locate what was out of this world and sensuous rather than what was claimed in moral commentaries to produce pleasure (Mandeville 1988, 166). Real pleasure could be learned through experience. That, in turn, taught us to appreciate the satisfaction of desires and, in general, the comforts of life (ibid., 169).

However, the quantitative satisfaction of desires led only to a dead end, as Aristotle had anticipated.[4] It promoted real pleasure and at the same time the nation's economic welfare only to a certain limit. For instance, no consumer could consume more than their fill of coffee, spices or other stimulants, although by present-day standards the quantities consumed in European courts in the sixteenth to eighteenth century were quite phenomenal. When the consumption of stimulants began to spread from courts to wealthy merchants, landowners and captains of industry, imports shot up (Mintz 1985, 63–64, 73). But again, the limits were soon reached. By the seventeenth century, in the highest classes of society, the constant quantitative satisfaction of desires began to transform into a fear of boredom (Englund 2004, 33).

The new visionaries who emerged with the expansion of capitalist markets, utopian socialists and classical economists, thus came to think about desires in a whole new way. These two groups differed sharply both politically and in terms of their economic motives. However both shared the view that the growth of social wealth implied *an enrichment of desires* (Carlsen, Schanz, Schmidt & Thomsen 1980, 30–34). They maintained that acting within the confines of existing desires and their quantitative satisfaction alone could no longer be socially meaningful objectives.

The harbingers of a new age also heralded the ability to take pleasure in the satisfaction of desires within the limits of existing opportunities as well as new ways of varying and developing need satisfaction. One of the utopian socialists, Charles Fourier, went so far as to install creative consumption as the central principle of his utopian community. According to Fourier it was possible, through the art of cooking, to transform crude gluttony into culinary pleasures that even children could enjoy. The same was true of artistic and even sexual pleasures (Fourier 1983, 101–175; Ilmonen 1986, 203–206). This, of course, required abandoning the idea that uses of the objects of desires were established in advance and the recognition that they had latent and unused dimensions. It was just a matter of learning how to discover them.

Even Fourier acknowledged that the art of enjoying culinary pleasures was not something that could be picked up in a matter of days, but required much learning. Above all, this involved *seeing the objects of consumption in a new light*. And that, as is the case with learning in general, required the unlearning of something else – in this case the meanings ascribed by tradition to old objects of consumption. They had to be replaced by new meanings and new experiences. At the same time, need satisfaction had to break away from its former emphasis on quantity and turn instead to subtle nuances of satisfaction – to developing the experiences it afforded. This required that traditions loosened their grip, or at least that a decision was made as to which tradition was to be followed in which instance.

The view taken by classical economists and utopian socialists on the sphere of desires betrayed an ambition to break loose from the traditional anchorage of need satisfaction. This, however, was not possible without good enough alternatives. As Wolfgang Schivelbusch observes, tradition cannot be overturned unless it is replaced with something else that is equally valuable (Schivelbusch 1992, 39). For the substitute to attract attention it must at the very least wet people's curiosity. This is something that new goods, 'novelties' with strong social appeal, have been able to achieve. This was the case with the new stimulants that began to spread to Europe with the growth of world trade, as well as with fashion and style and other new consumption mechanisms that gathered momentum with the rise of the capitalist economy. Together, all these mechanisms have begun to break down the strong influence of tradition over consumption.

The main difference between traditional attitudes to desires and objects of consumption and those inspired by new consumption patterns lies in the extent to which consumption behaviour has been constrained in advance. The traditional understanding of needs is essentially the same in the naturalist theory of needs. Needs have been regarded as given historically invariable universals and need satisfaction is supposed to have taken place within the safe harbour of tradition. Any deviation has been denounced as improper surrender to desires and often as socially reprehensible conduct (see e.g. Durkheim 1951 [1897]).

In the new way of thinking needs are, by contrast, understood as variable and malleable, as phenomena characterized by desire. Therefore it has been possible, indeed even desirable to have other than just quantitative variation in need satisfaction. Greater weight has been placed instead on the quality of need satisfaction, on the experiences derived from need satisfaction. However, this new attitude to consumption has not ousted the old one. Both these attitudes may co-exist, even in the same person, who may switch from one to the other at will.

## 4.5   Traditional and modern hedonism

The picture I have painted of two different attitudes to desires and at the same time to consumption still remains rather sketchy. The Aristotelian–Christian notion of virtuous consumption in which all excess was viewed as depraved lust, naturally had the effect of suppressing the growth of production and consumption. It did not, however, have any bearing on the goings-on in high ecclesiastical circles and in European courts. Among the elite of the Catholic Church, for instance, it was the rule rather than the exception for centuries that popes and their legates indulged in food, wine and sex (see Rinaldi & Vicini 2000). It was this very contrast between preaching a virtuous life and the sheer indulgence in lusts that Mandeville attacked in his *Fable of the Bees*. Another point that he raised was that adherence to the principles of a virtuous life also made no economic sense. For the nation to prosper economically and to feed a growing population, it had to accept an expansion of desires (Mandeville 1988, 184–185, 206).

However Mandeville was only partly in the right. Even though the expansion of desires and at the same time consumption was accepted, this was initially understood chiefly in the traditional way, in terms of a quantitative increase in the satisfaction of desires. Consumption accelerated rapidly as increasing numbers of people gained the financial resources they needed to spend on consumption, as our earlier example of stimulants illustrated (Mintz 1985, 63–65, 73). However, this soon reached saturation point and consumption stagnated. The only solution to this problem was to approach desires and consumption in an entirely new light. Instead of concentrating on sheer quantity, the focus had to be shifted to quality, to the cultivation and refinement of desires. This paved the way to creating variation even within one and the same specific need.

I move on now to examine the historical and conceptual shift in Europe from the emphasis on the quantitative aspect of desires to their qualitative cultivation. For this purpose I draw on Colin Campbell's influential analysis (which in turn leans heavily on David Hume's essay *On Refinement in the Arts*) on the differences between *traditional and modern hedonism*. First, however, it is necessary to point out that the distinction between traditional and modern hedonism is similar to many other classic distinctions in sociology, such as that between *Gemeinschaft* (community) and *Gesellschaft* (society) (Tönnies 1920, 8–81) or between mechanical and organic solidarity (Durkheim 1997 [1893]). All of these are ideal-type constructs, ways of perceiving reality, and they do not do full justice to the complexity of historical reality (Asplund 1991, 39).[5]

The shift from the *Gemeinschaft* type to the *Gesellschaft* type, for instance, has never completely eradicated the *Gemeinschaft* style of living. On the contrary, both of these styles have long co-existed; indeed the new *Gesellschaft* style would never have been able to survive without the rigorous support of *Gemeinschaft*. As Fred Hirsch points out, capitalism is fundamentally unstable and could never have sustained its triumphal march had it not been for the indirect support of those inherently alien solidaristic elements that alleviated some of the inequalities produced by the capitalist economy (Hirsch 1977, 11–12, 120; see also Polanyi 1957).

The same goes for Campbell's distinction between traditional and modern hedonism: it is not an absolute and categorical historical transition. Even in conditions that are conducive to modern hedonism, forms of traditional hedonism still remain rife, including debauchery in food, drink and sex. Indeed all of this is so common today that one might well ask is it not the other way round; is it not traditional hedonism that is modern (cf. Latour 1991)? However it seems that Campbell is not interested in the social and social-psychological situations that lead to this 'eternal return' (Nietzsche, Eliade) – and the same goes for us here. Campbell is mainly interested in describing the chain of events in which pure traditional hedonism is 'refined' or 'tamed' into modern hedonism.

Campbell takes a Mandevillean approach to exploring the transition to modern hedonism. According to Campbell, the use of an object of desire elicits in man a sense of satisfaction, which engenders pleasure. The traditional hedonist wants to maximize this pleasure by collecting as many objects of desire as possible that can deliver this sense and by indulging in them. From this, Campbell draws the conclusion that the traditional hedonist does not seek *pleasure, but pleasures* (Campbell 1987, 66). These, traditionally, include eating, drinking, sexual intercourse, dancing and singing.

The only difficulty with indulgence is that over time, with repetition, the sense of pleasure begins to wane. Excessive indulgence can blunt the pleasure altogether, eventually turning the experience into one of numbness and boredom. Pontiffs and the great despots of history have all had this feeling. It is most aptly illustrated by the words attributed to the Persian king Xerxes: 'I will offer one thousand gold pieces to any man who can show me a new pleasure' (Campbell 1987, 66–67).

Modern hedonism, Campbell says, differs from its traditional counterpart in that instead of pleasures it is characterized by the *pleasure-seeking*. It requires a completely different strategy than the traditional hedonist's need satisfaction. First of all, the modern hedonist does not necessarily need any concrete object of pleasure at all; he can enjoy things in his mind's eye – *imagine endless pleasures derived from the objects of desire* – as Barbon realized (Berry 1994, 116). For the modern hedonist, then, the mere imagination of something desirable or beautiful is enough to elicit a sense of pleasure (Campbell 1987, 61).[6]

Secondly, if in the search of pleasure the modern hedonist turns not to his imagination but to concrete objects, then his attention will be drawn to the *type of experience* that can be derived from using them. What matters is not just the physical sensory experience (taste, aesthetics, smell etc.) that comes from the satisfaction of desires. All need satisfaction involves the movement of senses, the gaining of experiences. The true modern hedonist justifies his existence by the Romantic idea according to which the most important thing in the world is self-realization. He therefore educates his senses to become theoreticians in their own right (Marx), who respect both the sensory quality of the satisfaction of desires and the emotional experiences it engenders. He seeks to extract every ounce of pleasure out of every moment (Campbell 1987, 69).

However, this focus on the quality of experience requires a special set of skills. Learning those skills has *required a historical and cultural transition* in which attitudes to objects of consumption have changed. Most significantly, this transition has brought a shift in emphasis from the material enjoyment of the object of consumption to *an emotional experience*. Underlying this transition is another more fundamental realization that the source of pleasure lies not in the object, *but in the individual and the individual's emotions.* Even the most delicious food can bring no sense of pleasure if the individual does not enjoy the experience of eating that food.

For the modern hedonist the experience of pleasure requires no explanation. It is taken as given. This is beyond the traditional hedonist, for whom the only possible source of pleasure is the object of need. The traditional hedonist is entirely dependent on that source. For the modern hedonist, on the other hand, even imaginary objects elicited by desires will do, for 'the act of consuming is as much an act of the imagination (fictitious) as a real act' (see Lefebvre 1971, 90).[7] However, in this instance the attainment of pleasure requires strict emotional discipline on the part of the hedonist.[8] Feelings must be subordinated to will. *The degree to which the individual can decide on the nature and strength of his own feelings, Campbell maintains, is the very foundation of modern hedonism* (Campbell 1987, 70).

However, before emotions can be shaped and steered at will, it must be understood that they are volitional. This has not always been the case, and still isn't. On the contrary, even in the Middle Ages emotions were still likened to natural forces, regarded as phenomena beyond the individual's control. They were located outside individuals, within their living environment. The forest has been perceived as threatening, the mountains as frightening. In other words, it has been thought that emotions move from the reality outside into people without their having any control over this. It was only since around the sixteenth century that this thinking began to change. The living environment has become emotionally neutral, de-emotionalized, and emotions have been relocated within individuals (Heller 1979, 199; Campbell 1987, 72).

This ideational relocation of emotions has paved the way to a new concept of nature and man, which is closely linked to the growth of *self-consciousness.* One of the results of this has been the separation of perceptions of the world and self. The world has become an object that can be shaped, the self a subject doing that shaping. At the same time, however, with the world and the self now understood as fundamentally separate entities, modern thinking also began to treat the self as an object. This led to new words appearing in the English language. 'Self-confidence', 'self-pity' and 'self-love', for instance, only became established in the seventeenth and eighteenth centuries (Campbell 1987, 73).

Since the introjection of emotions into the individual, outside stimuli have no longer been understood as mechanical forces with a causal effect. This has had two important consequences. The first is the realization that the individual's response to external stimuli is mediated through consciousness. This means the individual is free to choose that response, even though it is culturally conditioned (see Menand 2002, 330). Maurice Merleau-Ponty expresses this same idea by saying that physical stimuli provide causes or opportunities for individual responses rather than being the actual causes of those responses. The attitude taken to stimuli depends in turn on the *meanings* people assign, in their consciousness, to those stimuli rather than on the stimuli in themselves (Merleau-Ponty 1963, 161). This leads to another ideational innovation: it is possible to circumscribe and control emotions as one pleases.

The mere notion that emotions can be controlled does not, of course, necessarily lead to their being controlled. That requires compelling outside reasons. The most important among these reasons have included the growth of wage labour and the development of customs. The latter process was initially driven by the nobility, then by the bourgeoisie. Embourgeoisement and the associated thought-forms, modern rationality (formal rationality), individuality and the Protestant Ethic (people are judged based on their acts) have had a significant role in shaping emotions and emotional expression (Foucault 1978, 125–127; Elias 1978b, 169–203; Campbell 1987, 74; Schivelbusch 1992).

The development of human emotional life as we know it today has obviously been a long and complex process. I confine my attention here to just one link in this chain, i.e. the nobility's code of conduct and Protestantism. One of their most distinctive characteristics is a general hostility towards direct, 'genuine' expression of emotions. We are urged, initially by the nobility's code of conduct and later by Protestantism, to observe our emotions and where necessary to conceal them, to show a 'poker face' (especially in the case of emotions that have to do with selfishness and sexuality) (Elias 1982, 235–250). In his *Essays*, Michel de Montaigne describes this as mere playacting, pretending, cheating and lying. No doubt this was part of what was going on, but on the other side of the coin there was also the desire and intention to get along, in a civilized way, with fellow human beings. To do this, it was necessary to focus attention on one's own as well as others' behaviour and their motives (Elias 1978b, 78–82).

As a result of this self-reflection, our comprehensive 'world-embracing' emotions are fragmented into more analytical feelings. As philosopher Agnes Heller says, 'I am in a bad mood' breaks down into 'I am sad', 'I am suffering', 'I am down', 'I feel hopeless' (Heller 1979, 124).

The hiding of emotions, then, has primarily meant hiding from others what kind of relationship one has with objects, events and people in the environment. What happens here is that the individual ceases to react on the basis of immediate emotional impulses. The hiding of emotions thus causes the *separation of emotion and action*. Consequently, the individual's action will no longer necessarily betray the nature of the underlying emotion. This opens up a whole new potential for action: seeking to consciously influence others by manipulating one's own emotions.

The refinement of emotions and emotional manipulation put a drain on human vitality. I call these activities *emotional management*, one of the most perplexing phenomena of our day that has a decisive impact on our needs. Emotions, as we have seen, are largely based on conditions of needs and desires (cf. Heller 1979, 67). When emotional expression is controlled, that reflects back onto desires and the way they are satisfied. At the level of needs, the regulation of emotional expression is manifested in restraint. It curbs need satisfaction and triggers a Lacanian dynamic of desire. *The emergence of desire as the psychological engine of human activity is thus an outcome of emotional management* and in this sense a relatively modern phenomenon (see Ilmonen 1999, 303).

The emergence of desire is followed by modern *hedonism*. That, too, is grounded in self-reflexive human action, in 'despotic' control of one's emotions (Campbell 1986). As people learn the art of emotional management they begin to engage in self-realization by mastering the physical stimuli they have experienced. However, whereas in traditional hedonism they are processed by sensory means, they are now received at the emotional level, where work is begun to elaborate or vary their meanings. This happens within the individual's mind, at an imaginary level. That of course would open up endless opportunities for pleasure, unless limits were imposed on the imagination. Indeed new meanings are elicited precisely by virtue of emotional management, which provides emotions with a 'rationalized form'. It is this *rationality of emotions* that, according to Campbell, is the other main characteristic of modern hedonism (Campbell 1987, 76).

The rational nature of emotions elicited by the exercise of imagination is most clearly apparent in *day-dreams*. Day-dreams do not wander off into just anything between heaven and earth, but the imagination is deliberately kept within the bounds of the possible. This is the only way we can make-believe that the day-dreams really are achievable, which adds to the pleasure that can be derived from the imagination. Indeed Campbell suggests that day-dreaming can be defined as the process where the individual intervenes to make adjustments to imagery in order to make the imagined scene more pleasant to contemplate (Campbell 1987, 83).

The imaginative anticipation of just anything will not, however, suffice to produce a sense of pleasure. After all, the event may also arouse fear and apprehension. So in order that a day-dream can give pleasure, there are still some further conditions it has to meet. According to Campbell the day-dream must first of all assume the form of *longing*. But even that is not enough to guarantee pleasure. That will only be aroused when the sense of longing is attached to something unknown (Campbell 1987, 86). However, Campbell's reasoning is not entirely convincing.

One of Campbell's aims is to explain the constant expansion of the sphere of consumption, the 'hunger for novelties' by reference to the characteristics of the modern hedonist. It is understandable, therefore, that he says pleasure is only elicited by the longing for something new and unknown. However, Campbell does not offer any persuasive explanation as to why this should be the case. Surely the exact opposite can be equally true; surely the longing for something old and familiar can arouse just the same sense of pleasure? During a long hike the expectation of a hot bath gives added spring to the step. During a period of separation lovers look forward to seeing each other again.

It is not hard to imagine other examples. Insofar as they can be generalized, one might well presume that dreaming about something vague, some unknown novelty, will not yet elicit a sense of pleasure. Rather it is more credible that we need to have at least some rudimentary notion of the object of our longing before it can begin to engender a sense of pleasure. This usually means an emphasis on the ideal characteristics of the object of longing. Even then, the sense of pleasure is only elicited once the ideal is so finalized that the individual begins to desire what it is he has imagined. The theory of activity I have used, or indeed the Lacanian concept of desire, might provide a useful complement to Campbell's philosophizing, for what else could more easily elicit pleasure in day-dreams than the imagination of something that on account of emotional management has long been hampered.

However, Campbell fails to elaborate his thinking in either of these directions. The choice not to resort to Lacanian thinking is understandable in the sense that it rests so heavily on Freudian assumptions. A more problematic omission is that in emphasizing imaginary satisfaction, Campbell's theory ignores our *activity* in the world of commodities. As I have stressed, conditions of needs are not translated within our minds directly into specific needs. The latter only become clear to us once our daily activities and their complexities bring various needs to our minds.

Without the action preceding the satisfaction of our desires, we would not have the experience from which to draw in the imaginary satisfaction of desires, in refining that experience in the concrete use of different goods, in improving food recipes or in introducing elements of playfulness in our acts of love. Without concrete action, Campbell's theory of modern hedonism is unable to demonstrate how consumption is grounded in activity. Campbell does offer convincing evidence of the central role of imagination in modern consumption, but he fails to show how and why the modern hedonist proceeds to use concrete objects of consumption, as Falk has pointed out (Falk 1990, 118–119; Campbell 1987, 90).

For imaginary consumption to transform into concrete actions we have to assume the existence of some external or internal mechanism that compels the consumer to give real shape to the imaginary. Exclusive focus on external mechanisms has usually led to such theories as the *manipulation thesis.* Consumers are turned into buyers because advertising and other marketing, the whole mechanism of commodity aesthetics, has been so honed and refined that consumers have no other option but to buy. Explanations that focus exclusively on internal mechanisms, on the other hand, draw upon the concept of *addiction.* Consumers buy because they have no option; they have an internal compulsion to do so (Scherhorn 1990, 38; but see also Sulkunen 2004). The former focus leaves open the question as to why consumers do not object to being manipulated. The latter explanation is problematic because addiction is usually very specific. It fails to provide a satisfactory explanation of how a shopping addiction, say the compulsive desire to buy shoes or perfumes, expands to encompass consumption as a whole.

The easiest way to overcome the shortcomings of the manipulation thesis and the shopping addiction as explanations for modern consumption is to look at the consumption process as a whole – both the forces that drive the modern hedonist and the buying stimuli to which they are exposed at one and the same time. In practice this means that three different elements have to be bundled together, i.e. desires and the imagined (symbolism) and real object of consumption. For this we can borrow some useful elements from the theory of desire as well as from Campbell's and Haug's theories, complemented with some sociological variables.

Imagination is unquestionably a central pillar of modern consumerism (Campbell 1987, 88–89). It sets the scene for the imaginary consumption event and only occurs at the symbolic level of imagination. No attempt would ever be made to turn it into reality were it not for the action-elicited desire that underlies the longing and that is seeking for an outlet of satisfaction. It makes the modern consumer turn to objects in the real world and to think about the imaginary satisfaction they yield. This is where Haug's distinction between use value and the subjective promise of use value enters the scene.

As we recall from the discussion earlier, use value is a characteristic inherent in the commodity, while the subjective promise of use value is the consumer's own act. The consumer attaches such characteristics to the object of consumption that correspond to the ideal produced by the desire and the imaginary pleasure of satisfaction that it promises. However, when that promise is put to the test in the event of consumption, the actual use value may not necessarily live up to the promise. It does not quench the desire; and even if the desire were quenched, that would only happen momentarily, until boredom sets it. Once it becomes too familiar the initial object of our longing loses all its attraction. The search will therefore resume and desire will turn our attention to the novelties flooding into the marketplace.

But this search for market novelties is highly selective, as any manufacturer and marketing team will testify from bitter experience. Most novelties are liable to cause economic setbacks (cf. new mobile-phone peripheral functions). Therefore desire and novelty do not yet, in themselves, suffice to explain modern consumption, other than at a rather abstract level. In order to gain a concrete understanding of consumption, we must furthermore assume the existence of mechanisms that give a shape to desires and above all to their manifestation – the subjective use-value promise. Such mechanisms include routines, styles and fashions (see Chapter 7).

Since the subjective use-value promise plays such a crucial mediating role between need and concrete consumption and since it only appears in people's imagination, it is understandable that so much effort is invested on the supply side to find a representation that appeals to it. The subjective promise must be located at the level that corresponds to imagination. Furthermore, it must assume the same ideal features that arise from mechanisms shaping the subjective use-value promise. This is one reason why the symbolic aspect of objects of consumption has continued to gain in significance. This is at once a feature that distinguishes modern from traditional consumption and that separates it from need-centred satisfaction that is fixed and settled in advance. From this it follows that a study of needs will not yet lead us to the secrets of modern consumption.

From conditions of need we have arrived now via the action triggered by those conditions at desires. Desires correspond in us to the growth of commodity markets. In principle, our desires are boundless. For that reason the direction they assume is unclear and impossible to deduce from conditions of need. And even an exploration of desires will not help us any further in establishing that direction. We must also be able to trace the promise of use value that goods themselves have given us as well as the disappointments caused by this promise. Because of those disappointments, manufacturers have to go back to the drawing board and improve their products and develop new ones. However, novelties do not necessarily become objects of our consumption. As modern hedonists, we may content ourselves with using our old stuff, insisting that it has qualities that are missing from new products. We continue to listen to our LPs, even though digitally remastered CD versions produce a much better quality of sound. In order to find out what course consumption will take in the future, therefore, we need to take account of pleasure-seeking. But for that purpose it is not enough to have just some abstract imaginary object. We must also know what is on offer and how well commodities reflect and interpret our desires.

There is also another reason why needs are an unreliable guide to understanding the form of consumption. No matter what the functional mechanism of consumption, it does not yet resolve the thirst for novelty. *Ease of access* to objects of desire, especially in social circles who can afford them, returns the consumer to Xerxes's situation. He is overcome by boredom, a problem that neared epidemic proportions among the self-confessed upper-class hedonists of the nineteenth century (Englund 2004, 33), and that shared surprising similarities with 1980s narcissism.

Narcissism was regarded as an 'illness of our time'. The boredom that followed deprived life of all meaning. Life became empty and meaningless. In the nineteenth century Charles Baudelaire coined the concept of 'spleen' to describe this feeling – a sense of total absence of desires (see Baudelaire 2006 [1869]; Englund 2004, 39). A huge entertainment industry has grown up to combat this ailment, but that in itself has become self-repetitive to the point of becoming boring. Indeed, Immanuel Kant's diagnosis of boredom probably remains valid to the present day. Entertainment is not so much a cure as part of the illness (Englund

2004, 41). Even the modern hedonist has to work hard to overcome the feeling. But this is an uphill battle with recurring setbacks. It involves recurring 'regressions' to traditional hedonism, gluttony and excessive shopping. These are followed by an intense sense of guilt, which is expiated by reverting to disciplined modern hedonism.

# 5
# Consumption and the Necessary Economic Conditions for Consumption

Even the modern hedonist cannot participate in the markets without money. Money is a major determinant of both the external conditions for production and consumption and the relationship between those conditions. In the national economy the ceiling for consumption is determined by the total volume of income (and assets). The income distribution among population groups, in turn, regulates the balance between production and consumption and draws the limit for the satisfaction of needs and desires. It is important, therefore, that the sociology of consumption does not ignore the economic dimension of consumption.

One of the main conditions that determine how consumers approach the markets is the *amount of income at their disposal*. This does not, however, determine how that money is actually used. Disposable income does not translate automatically into consumption. Much also depends on savings' propensity and on the receipt of income in the form of money. Money is itself a commodity that is given different meanings. It depends on these meanings as to how prepared people are to give up their disposable income and how they want to invest it.

## 5.1  Income and consumption

The transition from income to consumption is far from straightforward. The money that people own is not always at their immediate disposal. On the one hand, part of their income is earmarked in advance for a specific purpose. This requires that they save money for that purpose

(Zelizer 1990). The savings rate varies over time and from one society and social group to another. However, since saving can justifiably be considered a form of delayed consumption, I shall pay no further attention to it here. On the other hand, people spend part of their income in advance by taking out consumer loans and using credit cards. Unfortunately, I have to leave this issue aside as well because there is not enough research on this increasingly important subject. We know that in the United States, for instance, the bulk of consumption is now based on credit.

## 5.2   Income, consumer-choice theory and Engel's Law

There is no direct path from the amount and distribution of income in society to the shape of consumption. Gender, social class and status as well as the individual's life situation and life stage have all been shown to have a bearing on consumer behaviour (e.g. Crompton 2002; Raijas 2000). However, none of this detracts from the importance of studying consumption from the vantage point of income. This is made amply clear by one of the earliest approaches to explain consumption on an economic basis, i.e. consumer-choice theory.

Consumer-choice theory is a variant of the theory of rational choice. It is committed to the viewpoint known as methodological individualism (*Homo clausus*). Here, consumption is viewed as an individual act unaffected by the burden of past or present social relations. In other words, the theory has it that choice is not affected by any external factors. Each consumer weighs the choices before him and arrives at one by rational judgement. In the context of consumer-choice theory this means, more or less, that the consumer will go for the option that, given the income at his or her disposal, will yield the highest perceived need satisfaction. However, it is not thought that this rational calculation is biologically grounded; rather it is a form of *economic rationality* that compares disposable income to the prices of goods. The theory has received much criticism (which I will not repeat here. Instead it might be useful to look at the purposes for which choice theory has been used and to explore its limits.

The development of choice theory in the nineteenth century grew out of concerns about economically irrational consumer behaviour, and particularly working-class lifestyles. Therefore the focus of the theory was to determine the level of costs necessary for the reproduction of the working population. Since in those days food represented the single biggest expense item for the working classes, the challenge was to find foodstuffs that would most effectively restore the population's labour power.

However these concerns about the reproduction of the population's labour power were just one of the social reasons behind the building of the theory of consumer choice. Another at least equally important factor was the fear of social unrest, particularly in the aftermath of the French Revolution in 1848. Poverty was now seen in a new light. It was no longer considered sacred but nor was it considered a disgrace: it was understood as a social problem that could possibly be solved, in part at least, through the rational use of the working people's wage income.

From the mid nineteenth century onwards a solution to this new problem was sought in both economics and nutrition. The problem was addressed both scientifically and on an ideological and educational basis. On the one hand, the aim was to determine the price of labour power for wage-policy purposes. On the other hand, the task was undertaken to root out the working class's 'irrational' consumption behaviour. These challenges effectively marked the beginning of empirical research in the social sciences. The necessary methodological tools were already in place thanks to the statistical work by Pierre-Simon Laplace, Antoine Cournot, Adolphe Quételet and Carl Friedrich Gauss. Those tools were now to be put to the empirical test. The first concrete statistical consumption surveys were conducted in the spirit of Quételet's moral statistics (Töttö 2000, 164, 171). Frédéric Le Play and Ernst Engel conducted detailed studies of family income spending or budget analyses. Le Play published his results in 1855, Engel two years later. In Britain, Edward Smith conducted a similar survey in 1863 (Sellerberg 1978, 17, 31–33).

The main focus of these household budget analyses was on the *ratio of income to food expenditure*. The assumption was that households are flexible in all other aspects of consumption but not in their expenditure on food. Therefore, it was thought that that consumption remained relatively constant even with rising household income. This assumption was corroborated by Engel's cross-sectional analyses. He consequently proceeded to elaborate the *statistical regularity* he had observed into what has become known as *Engel's Law*: *As income rises, the proportion of income spent on food falls*. At the time that Engel conducted his studies that proportion in households he had defined as poor was 60 per cent, and even in middle-income households as high as one-half (Stigler 1954, 95).

This line of work that was initiated by Le Play and Engel has continued across Europe to the present day. Notable examples include the household surveys in the UK and the Nordic countries. They serve a variety of purposes, including the construction of the consumer price index and national accounting, but one of the most obvious reasons for their continued popularity is their ability to predict the proportion of food expenditure regardless of variation in income levels (Ilmonen & Pantzar 1985, 4–5). Indeed, comparative studies between European countries and North America have shown a remarkably *constant relationship* between the *growth of income and consumption* and the *structure of consumption*. For instance, H. S. Houthakker proposed the rule of thumb that a 10 per cent increase in national income leads to an increase of 6 per cent in food expenditure (income elasticity 0.6), 8 per cent in housing expenditure (income elasticity 0.8) and 12 per cent in clothing expenses (income elasticity 1.2) (Houthakker 1957, 546–547). Income elasticities are not independent of time and place, but they lend further evidence to Engel's Law that the proportion of food expenditure falls with rising income levels (see also Deaton & Muellbauer 1986, 193–195).

More than 50 years have passed since Houthakker published his figures, but they continue to remain more or less accurate – which is quite amazing in view of the vast changes that have happened since in the supply of food and clothes and in our consumption habits (see e.g. Ilmonen 1991a). One might well expect that the proportion of income spent on food and clothes would have increased, but not so. This again lends support to the idea that there is no other association between fluctuations in income levels and main categories of consumption than the regularity observed by Engel. The most plausible explanation is that the changes that have happened have not greatly affected the relationships between the main categories (nutrition, housing, clothing etc.) as much as expense items within those categories (in food, for instance, the relationship between semi-finished and other foods).

The statistical regularity observed by Engel and Houthakker's calculations that support it provide us with a rule of thumb that allows us to assess trends in the material standard of living of any given country: *the smaller the proportion of the national income spent on food, the higher the country's material welfare.*

## 5.3    Engel's Law and income groups

However, Engel's Law can be used not only for assessing the level of material wealth in different countries. It also allows us to analyse the relative position of income groups within a country and to make comparisons across different countries, since the corollary of the Law says that *the larger the share of national income that one social group can appropriate, the less money it spends on food,* even if the volume of food consumption increased and its quality changed.

## 5.4 On the limits of consumer-choice theory

Engel's Law serves as a measure not only of a nation's material development but also of the level of material welfare within income groups. It describes in general terms how income is related to consumption structure. It makes sense to expand on Engel's analysis and to try and see whether it is possible to establish more detailed associations between income and the internal structure of different consumption categories (food, transport etc.); in other words, whether it is possible to identify regularities in the relationship between income level and specific consumption choices. In the case of food consumption, for instance, could it be possible to discover associations between specific items similar to those established in Engel's Law? The question has been raised before and consumer-choice studies have sought to find an answer as early as the 1950s when Merrill K. Bennett proposed a generalization of the association between income level and the consumption of different foodstuffs (Bennett 1954, 114).

Bennett concluded that as income levels rise, a) the proportion of cereals and cereal products in the food basket falls, b) the proportion of fats and oils initially increases but then starts to fall, c) the proportion of sugar, milk and dairy products in the basket increases and d) the proportion of fruit and vegetables first rises slowly, then more rapidly. Bennett believes that his projection has wider relevance, for it reflects the modernization of our eating habits (see Ilmonen & Pantzar 1985). To put this idea to the test it is interesting to compare these results with recent statistics on food consumption in the Nordic countries.

In this comparison at least, Bennett's projections are reasonably accurate. The share of cereal products (flour), milk, butter and fats, potatoes, sugar, coffee and tea in the food basket increased in the Nordic countries in the first half of the twentieth century. In Finland, for example, the consumption of these strategic foodstuffs peaked in the 1950s (Laurila 1985, 95); elsewhere in the Nordic countries the peak in the consumption of these foods came earlier in the 1930s, in the aftermath of the Great Depression. This is consistent with other data (income, population growth etc.) which demonstrate Finland's economic backwardness compared to the other Nordic countries.

Following these peaks in consumption the share of these foodstuffs in the Nordic food basket has rapidly declined – but here the picture of consistency begins to break down. In Sweden, for instance, the share of cereal consumption has continued to rise, in contrast to Bennett's predictions (Konsumentverket 1986, 28; Laurila 1985, 98). On the other hand, the trends for fat and oil consumption are still consistent with Bennett's results, falling in all of the Nordic countries after a peak period. The share of meat and meat products as well as fruit and vegetables, then, has increased in keeping with Bennett's predictions, but in the 1980s there are signs of a drop in meat consumption. The trends for milk and sugar consumption in the Nordic countries are also at variance with Bennett's predictions: their shares have long been falling, even though some dairy products, notably cheese and ice cream, have continued to contribute a larger share to the food basket (Konsumentverket 1986, 3, 25; Laurila 1985, 95, 98). All in all then it seems that the regularities observed within the consumption of food are not as strong as predicted by Engel's Law. Instead, what the above observations from the Nordic countries possibly reflect is the fact that low income does not fully overlap with low consumption. For instance, low income groups may choose to purchase brands that are the cheapest in that product category, which leaves them with more disposable income for other consumption.

Be this as it may, Bennett's partial failure can be explained by him repeating one of the fundamental mistakes of consumer-choice theory. As consumer-choice theory is committed to methodological individualism and focused on individual choice it is easy to forget that income does not automatically lead to rational action and a careful weighing of the choices available. Instead, consumer choices are steered by supraindividual preferences and social mechanisms such as publicity, fashion or style. Finances only set the general framework in which these mechanisms work. In other words, a theory that sees food choices merely as a function of income will be unable to explain why people in the same income bracket can differ systematically in their eating behaviour (Bourdieu 1986, 299, 303).

Another point that Bennett's projection seems to miss is that, even if we accept the individuality of consumer preferences, it is very rarely that the consumer can follow up those preferences. Apart from economic rationality, the consumer is steered and influenced by customs, ethical obligations, cognitive and aesthetic preferences, tastes and emotional impulses (Boudon 1981, 156) – themes that constitute the social in society and that are the necessary conditions for sociology. For example, the fall in the share of sugar and oils in the food basket probably has more than a little to do with nutrition education and media coverage of the adverse health and other effects of these foods.

The critique levelled against Bennett is typical of sociological criticisms against economic micro theory. It can also be extended to Engel's Law. This law might hold true at an historical juncture where a national economy is breaking away from a culture of poverty and moving towards a culture of material wealth. However, it is possible that as welfare continues to grow, Engel's Law will reach its limits. Since the 1960s there have been signs in a number of European countries that the regularity discovered by Engel has ever more limited applicability (Ilmonen & Pantzar 1986, 100–104).

It is hardly surprising that Engel's empirical generalization is beginning to lose some of its validity. It is, after all, in essence a rather mechanical law and based on an assumption about the association between income growth and different consumption items, which states that food expenditure is the least flexible of all household expense items. In other words, the theory is grounded in the assumption that if they have to tighten their belts on spending, consumers will always and everywhere cut their food expenditure last. However, under conditions of constant welfare, there are bound to be changes in people's cultural preferences. As a result it is possible that spending on housing, electronics and transport, for instance, may become just as inflexible or even less flexible than food expenditure. Having said that, this only happens when the growth of income slows or stagnates. In practice, this means that under these conditions, people are prepared to compromise on the quality and types of food they consume so that they don't have to make any other quality-of-life compromises. Necessity is a historically variable category.

My criticism becomes easier to understand when we recall that in formulating his law Engel specified one fundamental condition. In assuming that consumers were rational in their choices, he limited his focus to the nutritional aspects of food, to the energy that can be obtained from food. However, nutritional value is just one of the factors that govern food choice, albeit a very significant one (see e.g. Ilmonen 1990). With rising income it is likely that growing attention is paid to considerations other than energy intake, most notably the health effects, aesthetic values and other symbolic and cultural meanings of food. In this situation people may in fact be more concerned about whether they are eating too much rather than about whether they are getting enough nutrition.

What is more, it seems that this likelihood increases further as food is turned into a commodity like any other and when it is couched in eloquent language. In other words, as soon as standardized production and consumption have satisfied needs, as soon as need satisfaction assumes institutional characteristics, the function of need satisfaction can no longer be separated from the signs of that function. This applies equally to clothing and to food (Barthes 1979, 168). It follows from this confluence of functions and their meanings that the relationship between income and consumption is not mechanical, as Engel suggests, but confounded by all the possible meanings that are associated with food items. Those meanings always intervene between income and final consumption choices. Their impact is multiplied with the commodification of the supply of food and the branding of different foodstuffs – a process that has accelerated with the growth of self-service.

## 5.5   Consumer choices and prices

One further point that must be raised in our discussion of Engel's Law is that it only describes the proportion of food expenditure as income falls or rises. It does not bring us any closer to solving the mysteries surrounding the choice of individual food items. Nor indeed can it, for all Engel-inspired consumption studies are focused on the aggregate or macro level. The same goes for those analyses in which the focus has been shifted from income to commodity prices. This has not produced any clear results of the kind put forward in Engel's Law. Analysis of the impact of prices on food choices has proved too complex and difficult, both for statistical reasons and because of the inherent complexity of the choice process.

Despite the difficulties involved in analysing the impact of price changes on the choice of food, this subject has motivated a number of short-term assessments. The findings lend some support to the view that sharp fluctuations in food price either increase or decrease the demand – at least for some foodstuffs.

There are plenty of examples of how demand is impacted by rising prices. It seems that *this impact is usually short-lived*. There is no evidence of any fundamental shifts in consumer choices. For this reason it is surely not unreasonable to suggest that the choice of food should be examined in its economic, historical and social context so that we can gain a broader understanding of the impacts of prices and income on consumption (cf. Tigerstedt & Törrönen 2005, 46).

The conclusion we can draw from economic-consumption research is that production does not transform itself into consumption without the reflecting prism of social order, history and culture (Lévi-Strauss 1969, 129–135; Sahlins 1976, 57–63; Siikala 1985, 131–132). The economy, income and prices are no exception to this rule. As Marshall Sahlins has pointed out, economic factors have no determined social impacts. Even the most rigorous demand analysis that emulates special offers cannot demonstrate why people pick one out of a range of special offers. It is equally impossible to deduce the shape of consumption (say the content of a food basket) directly from a rising income level, although economists have tried to do that, too. What we can infer from income level is more or less what proportion of income is spent on food. Income level also sets the limit to how much people can spend on leisure and other similar forms of consumption. Its content, by contrast, is dependent on the structure of society (e.g. need for communication media), individual preferences (e.g. self-catering or hotel accommodation), family decision-making (to what extent do children have a say), expert opinions (health) and other similar factors.

# 6
# The Use and Meanings of Money

No discussion of the economic conditions for consumption and their distribution in society can avoid dealing with the peculiar thing that lies at the heart of those economic conditions, i.e. money. Money is, of course, itself a commodity that circulates in the market as payment for consumer goods. However, it is not just any commodity but has unique distinctive characteristics. It mediates between production and consumption, or goods and our desires. Money has been given this function because it is necessary to have a common measure of exchange value that is 'pure', an 'abstraction' that is independent of other commodities (Simmel 1978, 165).

Money has not always been such a commodity, and still isn't in all places, even though efforts to create a unified national monetary system in Europe gathered momentum as early as the sixteenth century. The decisive turning point in the development of money came with the expansion of world trade and the growth of wage labour and its counterpart, consumerism, i.e. with the marketization of a large part of consumption. This created the need to have a general means of exchange. However, the proliferation of money instruments has been a very slow process. In Canada, for instance, it was not until the 1950s that banknotes issued by private banks were replaced by Federal Bank notes. In Afghanistan, the heads of warring factions are still printing competing currencies to the present day. The same is true in many African countries (Ingham 2004, 76–77; Gilbert 2005, 375). In Western economies, financial instruments known as derivatives, which are based on expectations of the future value of money, gained increasing popularity in the late 1990s. In other words, these economies have two different kinds of money: money whose current value is known and money whose value is not yet known but only assumed. Both types of money are used for trading on the money market. Furthermore, businesses sometimes use certificates of deposit as a means of payment, many employees have lunch vouchers and shoppers may use discount or gift vouchers in the supermarket (e.g. Dodd 2005, 560).

So even today, money is still not an unambiguous entity marked with state emblems, and it is not always clear what its value is based on and why it is accepted as tender. It is not even clear that money is just an abstract value and an expression of purchasing power. I shall attempt to shed some light on these questions below.

## 6.1   Money as value and symbol

Money is an old invention that has been used since the beginning of recorded history. Originally it was associated with loans and coins (Ingham 2004, 93–105). However, never before has money held such a central and taken-for-granted position as it does in the capitalist market economy today. This, ultimately, is because while in the pre-modern world money was regarded as an intrinsic value, as *a measure of wealth*, in capitalism it has increasingly become *a general symbol of value*. In this capacity it serves more purposes than ever before. In contrast to earlier forms of society, market economy uses money for every possible purpose known to economics: as a measure and store of value and as a means of exchange and indicator of wealth (Polanyi 1957, 51–52, 72; Dalton 1971, 67; Turner 1986, 109; Godelier 1987, 154; Fine & Lapavitsas 2000, 266). Through these roles, the markets and money steer civil society and its institutions, whereas in more archaic societies the economic system and the markets were the 'social function' of these institutions (Polanyi 1957, 44, 49, 52).

In archaic kingdoms, money was in fact not only stored as a treasure, but also used for other purposes. It was needed to pay taxes and the wages of public administration officials, although they were partly paid in kind. In Europe this principle continued into the feudal age (Polanyi 1957, 53). The increased use of money, then, was a result of the collection of taxes in money, the consequent need to produce food for sale in the market and the growth of wage labour. From the sixteenth century onwards it gathered rapid momentum as European nation-states desperately needed money to maintain their permanent armies and to finance the indulgences of their courts.

More recently, the continued growth of the use of money has been associated with the separation of money from its material properties, such as gold and silver, with the printing of paper money. At the same time, however, money has continued to represent some of those material properties and, in principle at least, it has therefore been possible to convert it back to those properties. In the latter half of the twentieth century, however, even this last link has been severed and money has been reduced to a mere *fictive quantity*. One of its aspects, the intrinsic dimension of money, has been impoverished. Money no longer has any material value (as gold, silver etc.). Nonetheless it must still be 'real' money in order to serve its function as a means of exchange. It must be printed by the government and have the government's official approval. This has caused huge problems in establishing fictive money, for two main reasons.

The first source of difficulty has been that in contrast to bartering the burden of trust in money-based trading is on a third party, i.e. the printer of money. This allows two parties who have only limited trust in each other to engage in trade. Both of them must, however, trust that the means of payment used is 'real' money. In fact there are two necessary sides to this trust. Firstly, users of money must be able to trust that the fictive money corresponds to its value. Secondly, they must also trust that others have trust in the value of money (see Ilmonen & Jokinen 2002, 50). Without such *reciprocal trust* the circulation of money would not be possible and commodities would have to be directly bartered. That would cause untold difficulty because of differences in the use values of goods and because of the temporal and spatial distances involved in present-day trading. Money and trust in money help overcome the future risks related to the circulation of goods, its spatial and temporal delays.

Another reason why reciprocal trust is so important is because all money is ultimately based on relations of debt and compensation. For its user, money appears as means of compensation, whereas for the printer of money it represents debt. The latter must pledge to take the money back after releasing it into circulation. It is this that lies at the heart of the requirement of trust. If this trust breaks down, as happened in Germany in the 1920s, in the final stages of the Soviet collapse and in Argentina in the 1990s, the national money system will collapse. Since this is a real risk, why do we still use money? Because the market economy needs a common indicator of purchasing power. That, however, cannot be created without creating a relationship of debt. What is a receivable to the user of money is debt to its printer. As Geoffrey Ingham (2004, 72) puts it, money cannot be created without the creation of debt. (Paradoxically, without debt there would also be no money!) For money to be accepted in everyday use the printer must give assurances that this debt will be repaid. This also applies to credit cards. They, too, involve a three-way relationship of trust between the card holder, the recipient of payment and the credit institution that vouches for the validity of the credit card.

The debt relationship as a source of money and the promise to honour the debt involve two things. First, the issuer of debt must have large reserves that guarantee the repayment of the debt. As a rule the only entity with large enough assets to realistically be able to do this is the state.[1] In fact, even the state would not be in the position to do this were it not for its exclusive right to levy taxes. Second, it is the very promise of debt repayment that gives money its value. This, however, does not yet guarantee the future value of money. That, at the very least, is a matter of negotiation, which is resolved politically as a result of conflicting pressures from various interest groups. As Max Weber suggests, as long as money is money, its value is based on conflicts of interest. It is these conflicts rather than accounting that steer the world (Weber 1978, 79). However, the value of money is not determined by conflicts of interest alone. Money constitutes its own autonomous region within the economy. It is subject to expectations that are governed as best as they can be by central banks and other major economic agents. These expectations also have the effect of regulating the value of money (Ingham 2004, 81–82). Currency speculation in the late 1990s and early 2000s has shown how deep an impact it can have on the value of international currencies and particularly on the US dollar, the preferred currency of international trade.

Secondly, there is always a symbolic dimension to money that is significant for its approval. For this reason the symbols that appear on money are usually national icons that enjoy the approval of the masses. For instance, the American one-dollar coin that pictured Susan B. Anthony, feminist and social reformer, was never accepted as legal tender (Gilbert 2005, 374). And the British pound sterling, despite its long history, only became legal tender after the First World War; prior to that, only large notes were printed. The one-pound and ten-shilling coins were introduced later. However, it was not until 1960 that the reigning monarch's portrait first appeared on the one-pound note, presumably reflecting the acceptance of Queen Elizabeth II as a symbol representing and uniting the nation as an 'imaginary community'. When the euro was launched, all the nations in the monetary union were allowed to choose their own symbols for their coins and banknotes (Dodd 2005, 564). Likewise, following the liberation of African colonies, money was used both for purposes of state-building and to strengthen the unity of the nation.

This, however, has not happened entirely without conflict. In Kenya, for instance, the Mau Mau movement challenged the symbols used on the national currency and tried to push through its own preferences (Gilbert 2005, 375–377).

As the use of money has continued to increase and the uses of money have become more diversified, so our dependence on money has continued to grow. That in turn has strengthened individuals' vertical ties to society. Therefore, in this direction, the increasing use of money has increased social integration in society. This point was highlighted by Karl Marx in his *Economic and Philosophical Manuscripts* of 1844: 'If money is the bond binding me to *human* life...is not money the bond of all bonds?' (Marx 1959, emphasis in the original). Yes, the answer is, it must be, for money is indeed one of the most important factors guaranteeing social order. However, it can only guarantee social order so long as people retain their trust in the value of money, i.e. so long as inflation and devaluations remain within tolerable limits. When money begins to lose its value on virtually a daily basis, under conditions of hyperinflation, people's trust in money will break down and there will be problems maintaining social cohesion. This is what happened in Germany in the 1920s and in Yugoslavia and the Soviet Union in the late 1980s.[2]

The increased dependence on money at the individual level and the integrative effect of money at the community level have combined to make money a central means of exchange and interaction in modern society. This, coupled with the symbolism of money and the tendency of money to become separated from its material content and to transform into a 'pure' commodity, has generated a theoretical debate on the role of money in which *money is seen as only a symbolic quantity and a means of communication*. This theoretical position has also been described as Chartalism, whose early representatives included Baron de Montesquieu, Charles Dutot and Louis de Jaucourt. They suggested that the value of money does not derive from money itself, but from the outside, starting from the meanings associated with money (e.g. nationality and wealth) (Foucault 1970, 181; Smelt 1980, 205–206; Ganssman 1988, 285–289).

From early on, Chartalism met with opposition from Metallists, including such names as Joseph Paris-Duverney, Étienne de Condillac and Destutt de Tracy. They maintained that money has intrinsic or independent value, or more specifically, value based on the social relations it reflects (Foucault 1970, 181; Smelt 1980, 205–206; Ganssman 1988, 285–289). The latter perspective is prominent in the labour-value theories of David Ricardo and Karl Marx, according to whom the value of all commodities is determined by the number of hours invested in manufacturing. Money is simply an indicator of that ultimate value.

Metallism no doubt opens an important perspective on money in regarding it as a reflection of social relations. It helps us understand why money is always so closely interwoven with relations of power and governance in society. However, the automatic coupling of the value of money with the value of labour is problematic. In the former Eastern Bloc, for instance, labour surely never ceased, yet in the last years of the Soviet Union the Russian rouble lost virtually all its value as it was no longer considered real money. Its purchasing power went out of the window. In other words, money is useless unless it is acknowledged and recognized as money.

Besides, Metallism cannot deny the existence of fictional paper money. The value of that money is not dependent on the number of hours of labour put in but rather on currency speculation and on what the central banks are doing and on expectations related to the value of money. Different economic interest groups may therefore have different relationships to this money, but that is not dependent only on the amount of labour, but it is also influenced by non-economic, cultural (attitudes to different currencies), psychological (inflation expectations) and other similar factors. It is these factors that lie behind the sharp fluctuations in the value of the euro since its introduction, since the value of this currency cannot be understood based on the number of hours worked in the eurozone.

On the other hand, it is not entirely tenable to view money simply as a symbolic system, or as a language, as Parsons would have it. For money to serve as a symbolic means or 'message', it must all the time have a physical form. Nowadays, however, money is very much an accounting unit that neither 'circulates' nor 'flows', even though these misleading words are still commonly used (Giddens 1990, 25). It would be impossible to say what exactly this kind of accounting unit symbolizes. Another reason why this view is problematic is that money is understood as a 'shared symbolic language' (see Parsons & Smelser 1956, 140). This concept refers to the understanding of language as an abstract structure of rules. Language, however, only has meaning in its specific context, as speech that is always something specific (e.g. Wittgenstein 1969). The symbolism of money only reveals its message when it is put to concrete use.

However, Parsons suggests that money is precisely a symbol and measure of economic value. But this is a problematic position, for how can a symbol measure what it is said to represent? For money to serve as a measure of value it should be fundamentally similar to the goods with which it is exchanged. In other words, it should be useful. This, however, conflicts with the understanding of money as only a symbol (Ganssman 1988, 291).

We run into similar difficulties if we think of money as a symbolic means of obtaining what it symbolizes. That would be tantamount to saying that whoever wears the crown is king or whoever wears a doctoral gown is a doctor. This, however, is to ignore all the social practices that make the king 'king' and that make a doctor a doctor and that provide the justification for their carrying those symbols, the crown or the gown. The king will only be coronated once that person's legitimacy to the throne has been established. The same applies to money.

Money that is understood in symbolic terms only cannot be used as a means of exchange, as compensation for the value of other commodities, for that would be the same as to argue that by stealing the king's crown one could become king, as Heiner Ganssman (1988, 392) points out. For money to be useful as a means of exchange and measure of value it must be backed up by institutional arrangements (e.g. a banking system). It must itself become an institution that is supported by the state with its economic and political resources. This requires generally accepted symbolism – national references that convey the dignity required by trust. It is only through this that the 'chips' become real, are turned into means of exchange and measures of value that command trust.

Money, therefore, cannot be understood only as a symbol of value with no intrinsic value. It must have intrinsic value in order to be accepted as a means of exchange. Public trust that money will be redeemed at face value cannot be maintained by institutional arrangements alone – this requires other guarantees as well. Money must be tied to some specific economic reserves, as is made clear by the Estonian case. When Estonia wanted its own currency following independence in 1991 it had to put up the country's forest reserves as guarantee. However, the intrinsic value of money lies not only in money itself and in the underlying social wealth but also in the meanings given to money outside the realm of the economy. In this sense money has to be understood as a dualistic and contradictory entity whose value is determined through its material shape, symbolic meaning and immaterial content – invisible expectations based on economic success (see also Smelt 1980, 207–209).

What applies to paper money also goes for credit and other cards. They are aestheticized on the basis of separate economic interests and with a view to appealing to specific customer groups. Customer loyalty cards issued by shops aim to capture key elements of their wider marketing communications but also of their membership. The same can be said of credit cards. As Simon Smelt (1980, 221) observes, 'The American Express Card says more about you than cash ever can'.

Since my purpose here is not to consider the determination of the value of money or to deal with money as a general rather than a specific cultural quantity, the focus in the following is on the symbolic and sociological meaning of money. However, rather than seeing it as an abstract structure comparable to language, I approach it as a message growing out of everyday situations and conveying social relations and as a discourse that articulates different meanings. This is a justified approach in that by the end of the twentieth century, the value of money has become completely severed from the real economy. Its value is increasingly determined based on expectations attached to money and on related currency speculation (see, however, Thrift 2005).

## 6.2   Profane and sacred money

Money that has intrinsic value is one of modern society's *hyperobjects*. It is the ultimate commodity that has come to occupy centre stage in our thought horizon. It is almost as if our earth-centred world view had given way to a money-centred world view. Money radiates its influence into the tiniest cells of our social life, reducing everything in our environment to something measurable in money terms (Simmel 1978). We dream about money. Money excites constant hopes of a fortunate coincidence such as winning the lottery (see Falk & Mäenpää 1997, 14–30). People cheat and lie for money – they even kill for money. Stories about big money have been turned into books and films. Money invites value judgements that brand both money itself and its users in this world (see Godelier 1987, 16). Regardless of the amounts of money involved, this gives qualities to money that are hard to determine out of hand (Simmel 1978, 259). Yet this is not a task we can leave aside if we want to better understand the communicative properties of money. This is therefore what I want to do next.

It is easiest to appreciate the depth and diversity of all the meanings given to money when its scarcity does not limit our focus to the quantitative dimensions alone, i.e. when we have enough money to squander. Money that is left over after all basic 'necessities' have been met is our 'own' money, money that we can, in principle, spend as we please. It is good to stress the 'in principle' because even the way we spend our own money is regulated by community attitudes and practices. A useful tool for the analysis of the former is provided by Émile Durkheim's (1995, 81) distinction in his study of the elementary forms of religious life between the *profane* and *sacred*.

This distinction borrows from anthropological thinking but Durkheim's application of these concepts is original to say the least. According to this distinction there is, on the one hand, 'pure' reality, the realm of godliness, which is set apart from the wretched secular world (Douglas 1984, 8–9). The concern of all major world religions is with the realm of sacred. They want to keep it clean and uncontaminated, protected against the constant threat posed by the profane; its very existence is a threat, for it deprives the sacred of its other-worldly halo, contaminates it. And when that happens, the sacred loses its hold over people.

To prevent this from happening, it is necessary to constantly invest in 'emotional work', but that is very difficult without advance agreement on the most appropriate forms. For this purpose it is necessary to have *rituals*. Rituals are a way of materializing symbols of the sacred, of giving them a shape. The performance of rituals renews faith in the sacred, in the world view it entails and in the frame of mind it requires. At the same time, rituals prescribe how people are to conduct themselves when confronted with sacred things (Douglas 1966; Ilmonen 1991b, 23; Bell 1992, 31; Durkheim 1995, 34). In other words, rituals are a way of dealing with the sacred. However, they are also a way of making the sacred present in the secular world.

The church, however, is not the only institution, nor is religion the only sphere of life that supports the sacred. Durkheim goes so far as to suggest that anything or any institution can in principle be made to support the sacred. Indeed, it is unlikely that there exists a community or society where the sacred does not exist in some sphere of activity. Take the most 'secular' and atheistic societies you can think of such as the former Soviet Union and present-day North Korea: even though they have prohibited all other religions except Confucianism and the 'Juche Idea', the sphere of the sacred has never been completely obliterated. On the contrary, it has been purposely exploited by announcing that some basic texts and political leaders are sacred. The reason this has been possible is that sacredness is not attributable to the inherent qualities of any particular thing but it is a quality ascribed to something. Some things are simply labelled as sacred. *Sacred is nothing other than a classification or attitude* that, once it has been around long enough, is supported by institutional arrangements. It is a way of viewing things and as such it must have the support of the community in order to hold sway and influence.

In Durkheim's language, sacred is a *collective representation* that makes us *see things in a particular light* (1995, 229–230). More precisely, the sacred is a vehicle through which the citizens of a given country assume a relationship to an object labelled as sacred – the totem. The representation transfers it into the world of myths, which helps to legitimize the power relations concealed by the sacred and to reproduce them unbeknownst to collective and individual consciousness (Godelier 1999, 169–172).

Although it is possible, in principle, to sacralize anything or any sphere of life, not everything lends itself to carrying the aura of the sacred. It is always difficult to move something into the realm of the sacred. In addition, having to remove the phenomenon from the sphere of mundane reality and elevate it through transition rites to a state of supermundane purity, it is also necessary to obtain collective approval for these moves. This task is made much easier if the community, in thinking about 'the things of its own experience' finds that one of them is in some respect more significant than others (Durkheim 1995, 436). As we have seen above, money is one such thing. As the old anthropological wisdom goes, 'Money is to the West what kinship is to the rest'.

## 6.3 Blessed, cursed and profane money

Given the vast importance of money in modern capitalist countries, these countries should be well placed to elevate money to the realm of the sacred. The positive attitude taken by Christianity and Islam towards earning money has at least done no harm to this endeavour. It hardly comes as a surprise, therefore, that in the Western sphere of life money has time and again been raised to the throne of the sacred. However, its position on the throne has been less than stable – not least because money seems to have a very special place among all things sacred.

As all phenomena within the sphere of the sacred are divided into two categories, the benevolent and the malevolent sacred, these qualities are also found in money, often simultaneously. William Shakespeare draws our attention to this in *Timon of Athens*, where he says that money is at once the source of good and evil (Shakespeare 1971, Act IV Scene III). This is, in fact, a reiteration of the pre-Christian view according to which the love of money is the root of all evil. On the other hand, affection for money is also a basic pillar of our civilization. There is still strong faith in the blessed effects of money (MacFarlane 1987, 118–119).

However, not all money is sacred but just ordinary worldly mammon that provides an important means of exchange for people living in large cities and that spreads the typical attitude of indifference to human relations (Simmel 1981, 212–214; Simmel 2005, 49). So how does one tell the difference between sacred and profane money? In the end one doesn't, because as Durkheim points out, sacred is not a quality of any 'thing', but rather the community's outlook on that thing. This, in principle, means that the same pot of money can be both sacred and profane, but not simultaneously – except when two different groups of people take a different view of that pot of money.

If, however, we ignore those situations where different social groups are looking at the same pot of money, there still remains the possibility that attitudes to money vary over time according to the purpose for which it is used. In this case it is obvious that at least money elevated to the realm of the sacred will not be accepted as a means of exchange and speculation. Such uses would be interpreted quite simply as sacrilegious. The only kind of money suitable for these purposes is 'status-free', money that is intended for 'general use', as Karl Polanyi has observed (1971, 303; see also Belk & Wallendorf 1988, 8).

So in what situations is there a tendency to regard money as sacred? According to one answer, this ordinarily happens in situations where mythical meanings are given to money by referring to the divine or imperial origin of money. The US dollar with Abraham Lincoln's portrait and 'In God we Trust' inscription is an interesting example. This idea was once, and probably still is, one way of sacralizing the dollar (and withholding help from those in need) in the US Bible Belt. The extent to which this view is shared and accepted is a different matter. As the dollar has become the currency of choice in world trade, its sanctity has become secularized ('In cash we trust').

According to another answer, money is regarded as sacred in cultures where it is considered a primary quality of human identity. This, at least, is the view of psychoanalyst David Krueger. In American society and elsewhere where personal income is a central building block and manifestation of people's social identity, it is not considered proper to talk about money as any other ordinary everyday matter. On the contrary, the subject is surrounded by numerous taboos, and even when it is a permissible subject, it is strictly regulated by rituals (Krueger 1986, 3–16). The sacrality of money is also reflected in the respectful attitude shown to wealth (Belk & Wallendorf 1988, 8–10).

The interpretation of owned money as sacred on grounds that it is not appropriate to talk about money and wealth in our culture is supported by Christianity's ambivalent attitude towards money. Christian belief has it that enterprise will always be richly rewarded in material wealth. On the other hand, representatives of Christian faith consider money itself a manifestation of evil, as something coming from Satan himself. As the medieval songs of the Carmina Burana say, money sends the world spinning and turns on their head all the values that the church regards as sacred (Alho 1988, 80–89). It turns people's attention away from manifestations of glory, from God and Jesus and their adoration to matters secular, above all to the soul-corrupting temptations of the world. To Christian faith, therefore, mammon represents the malevolent sacred.

These Christian ways of thinking about money have slipped unnoticed into our everyday thinking. Where money is accumulated into huge piles of wealth, we admire and respect, but nevertheless condemn it behind its back. How can this be explained? My own interpretation of Christianity's ambivalent attitude to money, to its blessedness and cursedness, depends on the perspective from which the circulation of money is approached. The respect given to money has to do with the *earning of money* that has the blessing of the Protestant Ethic, with ascetic enterprise. The condemnation of money, then, has to do with the extravagant use of money, with *waste,* which is censured by Protestantism. On this basis it may be assumed that ways of earning and spending money are more generally associated with the meanings given to money. I shall here ignore the aspect of earning money (see, however, Ilmonen 1993, Chapter 6) and concentrate instead on ways of using money.

## 6.4 Use of money and ways of sacralizing it

Money, then, is worldly mammon that is useful as a general means of circulation and exchange. However, it does not necessarily remain within this category all the time, but it can be elevated to the category of sacred. This requires a transitional stage followed by ritualism that *singularizes* general money as money that has meaning only to its owner. In this case a 'special purpose' is designated for money (Zelizer 1990, 349; Zelizer 1997, 1–36, 60–64; see also Thomas & Znaniecki 1958, 164–165 and Polanyi 1957).[3] In a society where economic growth has turned consumption into a virtue, the sacralization of money is largely associated with the ways in which it is earned and acquired, but nowadays this can just as well be achieved through the use of money.

The use of money can be sacralized both collectively and individually. Whichever route is chosen, the purpose is to objectify the sacred by exchanging profane money for a thing or object reflecting the sacred, a totem (cf. Durkheim 1995, 190).

In American society, Russell Belk and Melanie Wallendorf (1988, 16) have identified four different types of object that, they suggest, have totemic qualities and the acquisition of which sacralizes profane money. Their views have wider relevance and therefore deserve to be introduced here. The objects mentioned by Belk and Wallendorf are *souvenirs, lucky charms, gifts and collectibles*. Furthermore, they consider investments in charity as comparable to these objects.

Souvenirs, lucky charms and gifts are regarded by Belk and Wallendorf as incarnations of sacred experiences. Souvenirs and lucky charms are particularly significant in this respect. In contrast to gifts, they are always fundamentally personal in the sense that their element of totemism speaks only to their owners. Souvenirs and lucky charms are intended not only to remind their owners of some of the highlights of their life but also to allow them to relive these moments again and again and ensure they will be able to relive them in the future. They, so to speak, re-create past events in the present and in this sense resemble the type of collective ritual that Paul Connerton describes as *commemorative ceremony* (Connerton 1989, 50, 61).

Commemorative ceremony provides a way for nations or social groups to pick out from the flow of history events and moments that bring to mind sacralized experiences. When it succeeds in doing that, commemorative ceremony contributes to the maintenance of collective identity. Souvenirs and lucky charms in particular work in the same way. Not only do they give material shape to their owners' most cherished experiences but they also become incorporated as part of their identity. For this reason the desecration of lucky charms and even a disrespectful attitude is always seen as a threat. It may be a sign of an impending accident, which can only be avoided by restoring acts of ritual adoration (cf. the Muddy Waters song 'Got my Mojo Working'; mojo means lucky charm).

Any object can be a souvenir or lucky charm, so long as this is the meaning it is given by the people who collect them. Not so with gifts. Giving gifts is a social institution. Even though it is generally assumed that a gift is personal in the sense that it should say something about the person who is giving the gift, the way in which it is given is regulated by norms and often requires a gift in return, which does not necessarily have to be anything material. The anthropological under-standing is that anyone who gives a valuable gift usually expects in return increased esteem in the eyes of the community (cf. Bourdieu 1986, 31; Mauss 1990; Graeber 2001).

In modern societies where at least part of people's property serves as capital assets, the gift institution, in the form it appeared in the Potlatch parties of the Berbers or the Indians of the Great Plains, no longer has meaning. However, the ultimate purpose of gift-giving in modern soci-ety still remains unchanged. For us, giving gifts is a system of social integration and expression of solidarity. In exchange for a gift people expect anything from loyalty to a material countergift. The principle, however, is that the countergift should in some respect be equally as valuable as or more valuable than the original gift in both an economic and moral sense. Insofar as this is true, a gift can be considered an investment, a way of elevating the value of profane money, of making it sacred money.

Charity and donations can also be regarded as one variant of the modern gift institution. In these cases money is formally used to enhance the well-being of others rather than oneself but in exchange the benefactor expects to receive the community's moral approval. This is no doubt what has motivated Bill Gates in his philanthropy. When he donates money for medical research he wants to show the world that he is using his immense wealth to benefit other people, too. He probably expects that this will legitimize both his wealth and its con-tinued growth by further strengthening his monopoly position in the computer software market. In many countries this expectation is legally recognized among other things through tax laws which say that charity donations are tax deductible.

The third way of sacralizing profane money has to do with the col-lection of goods and commodities. For this purpose, however, not just any goods will do; collectibles must be objects already sacralized by society and its history. Examples include items made famous by his-toric figures and contemporary celebrities as well as cultural objects that have achieved cult status, from stamps and first editions to early issues of rare comic strips. The status of these items is supported by rit-ual worship, which raises their moral or aesthetic value to such heights that they are recognized as national treasures of 'immeasurable value' and that will not be sold at any price. This, however, is not entirely true, because these items do occasionally come up for sale – although the prices they fetch are so high that there are very few individuals who can afford them. Businesses, on the other hand, may purchase them both for investment purposes and with a view to enhancing their corporate image.

Despite their apparent differences, the three uses of profane money identified by Belk and Wallendorf follow the same basic pattern. The purpose is to sacralize the money earned by means of consumption. All other consumption takes place through the general function of money. As a means of exchange and measure of value, Simmel said, money is 'colourless' (1950, 414; cf. 2005, 34). By this he meant that when nothing else than quantity mattered, money lost all its nuances. Money was simply and solely a matter of 'how much'; the questions of 'how' and 'what' were ignored (Simmel 1978, 259). But not entirely. When money became a common means of exchange a new practice began to spread (Zelizer 1998, 59). This practice was to refrain from the use of money and to *sacralize part of it for special purposes* (Zelizer 1997, 1–36). This finds expression in different ways of saving money (under the mattress, in a dedicated bank account etc.) – setting aside part of one's money for special purposes. These savings are related to goods, services and acts that have a special meaning in a given culture and that require so substantial an investment that it is necessary to put aside the money in advance (Polanyi 1971, 264–266).

Significant items for which it is necessary to save up in advance include marriage endowments, school fees, wedding and funeral expenses and, in modern society, foreign holidays, cars and houses. The money that is set aside for these and other such purposes are 'earmarked funds' that in principle are untouchable, sacralized for this specific purpose. Therefore it is preferable to keep them separate from all other earned income, as William I. Thomas and Florian Znaniecki found Polish peasants did. If they were short of money they actually preferred borrowing to dipping into these earmarked funds (Thomas & Znaniecki 1958, 166). Vivian Zelizer (1997, 1–36, 71–118, 199–216; 1998, 62–63, 66) has reported similar results in her studies of recent American history.

However, these conceptions of money have not gone without critical notice. Ben Fine and Costas Lapavitsas (2000, 376–377) have accused the Polanyi school of thought, and Zelizer in particular, of confusing two things, i.e. what money is and what it represents or does. Zelizer, the critics continue, refuses to see money primarily as an economic quantity. But why should she have? Zelizer is mainly interested in how and in what connection people want to dedicate the general means of exchange that is money for special sacred purposes. She is not denying that they are put to use and that in that instance they serve the exact same function as any other money (e.g. Zelizer 2005, 584–587).

Finally, it should be stressed that there are also uses of money that are liable to negatively sacralize money, to curse it. The negative sacralization of money happens primarily in two kinds of circumstances. Firstly, when the use of money jeopardizes the existence of a social group because of the selfish actions of some member of that group, there is a high likelihood that money will be labelled as being cursed. The archetypical example of this kind of activity is *gambling* where not only the individual gambler's but possibly the whole family's finances are at stake.

Another type of activity that tends to curse money with a stamp of being contaminated is the completely self-interested purchase of other people and their services. This mainly takes the form of *corruption and bribery*. Countries that rank high on the Transparency Corruption Index are generally characterized by competent and more or less egalitarian public-service institutions. In countries where corruption is rife, people say they disapprove but nevertheless partake in corruption without too much of a conscience. But all the same bribery and corruption do put a negative stamp on money, partly because their only purpose is to advance one's own interests or at best those of some social group, and partly because Western culture traditionally makes a distinction between human beings and objects.

Humans and goods belong to two distinct spheres that must not be confused. Bribery, however, does not acknowledge this distinction, but confuses these two separate spheres of reality. Nonetheless, the domain allocated for humans is ethically superior or higher up than the domain in which objects are placed. When someone bribes a civil servant, for instance, they are applying the principles of the ethically lower to the ethically higher domain and threatening to contaminate those principles. As a consequence, the briber and bribee have to take the risk that the money exchanged is labelled as cursed.

Western thinking also holds that there is something specific about the human condition that precludes any direct comparison with an entity that is labelled under such generic term as 'commodity'. Man has a 'soul', a trait that sets us apart from other entities and that makes it very difficult to put a price on us, even though insurance companies and some sciences have occasionally tried to do so (cf. Kopytoff 1988, 84). On this basis it is easy to understand why Marx's and the Catholic Church's view that labour power must not be seen simply as a commodity used to hold much political sway. It also explains why corruption and bribery are thought to tarnish the money that is used to corrupt and to bribe. After all, it is used not only to buy the person's labour power, his body, but also what is most sacred about him, his soul (see also Durkheim 1995, 47).

## 6.5   Profane money and its uses in the household

The discussion in this chapter so far has been limited to those uses of money with which money has been elevated to the status of sacred. This is done either beforehand or afterwards by obtaining things that are already sacralized. However, these instances do not represent the principal forms of money use. In the end money is first and foremost a rational tool, a means of exchange that keeps the modern economy ticking over – and as such remains firmly in the realm of worldly mammon. This, however, does not mean that its use is governed by economic rationality alone. Money is always influenced by extra-economic, social and cultural factors (Zelizer 1990, 351). This is most clearly evident when we consider the use of money in households.

Economic research typically approaches the household as a black box, a collective spending unit (see Sen 1983). It accepts as given the internal mechanisms driving that black box and is unable to shed any light on how households arrive at their consumption decisions. This requires two sets of data. The first concerns the source of money, particularly the question of who in the household brings in the money. Research has typically addressed this question in general terms and gender-neutrally. However, we need to go beyond this level of analysis in order to properly understand the internal allocation of money within households. In modern Western culture it is customary to define the income brought by men and women into the household in different ways. Men are traditionally seen as the family's breadwinners, whereas women's earnings are usually regarded as 'extra' income. This is still very much the prevailing view and it has significant practical implications. But the implications of this view extend even further. It also impacts the use of money within the household.

The source of household income does not yet determine how that income is spent. Ultimately the decision on household spending is dependent on a) the meaning given to the money earned and b) who in the household has primary control over the income received. Historically, the situation in Western countries has been straightforward. Women's earnings from the labour market have *belonged to men* in the sense that it is they who have had full control over the use of that money and that the money brought into the household by women has mainly been regarded as *collective money* earmarked for the whole family's well-being.

Income earned by men has of course also been regarded as money for the whole family but part of that income has always been interpreted as their private assets (Zelizer 1990, 356–366). As we move closer to the present day, however, the situation becomes more complicated. Nevertheless the basic picture is very much unchanged, as Jan Pahl has discovered in his studies in the UK, which also have wider interest (Pahl 1989 and 1990).

Pahl has conducted interview studies on household spending in the UK. His results suggest that generally, decisions on household spending are made by men. However, there are clear exceptions to this rule, in three cases. The first is that when the woman in the household is better educated or comes from a higher social-status background than her husband, she will usually take control of family finances. Secondly, the likelihood of women taking control of family finances increases in proportion to their rising earnings relative to their husbands' income. Thirdly, women control family finances in typical working-class families where both spouses are in gainful employment and both are in 'unskilled' jobs (Pahl 1990, 123–124).

However, control over family income does not yet equate to control over household spending. That comes only with the actual handling of money, going out and doing the shopping, paying bills etc. In British families there is a relatively clear division of labour in this respect, which together with control over household money reveals a rather sharp gender asymmetry in the use of household money. When the woman has control over family finances, it is she who actually handles the money. When it is the husband who has control, the day-to-day handling of money still remains the wife's responsibility; he will only make the mortgage and insurance payments and look after other major expense items. Daily consumption, on the other hand, is the wife's domain. Tellingly enough, Pahl did not encounter a single family where the woman was in control of household finances and the husband was in charge of daily money flows (Pahl 1990, 125).

Control over the household's disposable income and the source of income are also connected with how that money is spent at each moment in time. This follows directly from the foregoing. When the wife controls the family finances and when she has a relatively good income compared to her husband, a larger proportion of the household income is spent on household management. In other words, *women look after the whole family's well-being* and are also prepared to dedicate a larger share of their income to that end than men (Pahl 1990, 130). From this we can draw the conclusion that the money earned by women is predominantly *general* money. Men, by contrast, are more inclined to singularize part of their income, to consider it *their own money*. This is clearly seen in the attitude of British couples to free-form consumption. According to Pahl, men take it for granted that they can use part of their income as they please, and their wives are prepared to accept this. Men feel that in their capacity as family breadwinner they are entitled to their own little freedoms. For women, on the other hand, the question of spending their own income on themselves is a difficult one. They feel that any such spending is out of the family's pocket and they therefore feel bad about it (Pahl 1990, 132–133).

It seems clear, then, that there is no direct association between the necessary conditions for consumption, on the one hand, and actual consumption, on the other. One of the reasons for this lies in the nature of the mediating factor, i.e. money. As we have seen money is not only a technical quantity. Money, in our culture, belongs to the sphere of the sacred. It must be secularized before it can be used for purposes of general circulation and consumption. Nevertheless, most money is understood beforehand as earthly mammon. But even that is not just a neutral mass; it too is cut across by various extra-economic social divisions and cultural meanings, which shape and limit our spending in at least the following ways. They a) offer direction to money users by making them sacralize their money for some specific purpose; b) provide direction for spending money on different purposes within the family, for example; c) control different types of money, e.g. general and particular money; and d) connect the sources of money with different end-uses (Zelizer 1990, 351; Zelizer 1997, 199–216; Zelizer 1998, 65).

Consumer-choice theory is ignorant of all these perspectives related to money. Yet without an in-depth analysis of them it is impossible to offer any general conclusions about the relationship between the necessary conditions for consumption, money and actual consumption, as we have already noted. The situation is further complicated by the fact that the desirability of goods pouring into the marketplace is determined by how they are valued in different cultures and by how quickly their valuation varies historically.

# 7
# Mechanisms of Consumption Choice and Their General Cultural Framework

As we have seen, disposable money is divided, firstly, into earmarked funds, which are deposited in a bank account and which are only used when the time comes; and secondly, into money that is spent on daily, weekly or monthly consumption. At this juncture I shall leave the former type of money in that bank account to accrue any interest that is paid. Instead, my focus here is exclusively on the money whose purchasing power is constantly used in the market. The use of that money is guided by specific principles that I call the *mechanisms of consumption choice*. But before we move on to consider those mechanisms it is necessary to look at the broader framework of those mechanisms. This I call the *cultural frame of reference* for consumer choices. I start out from this framework and then proceed to examine the concrete mechanisms of choice. However, there would be little point in conducting this analysis at a general level. Instead I heed to my own methodological advice in Chapter 3 and concentrate largely on one everyday system, namely food.

The reason for this is clear. As we have seen, food is a special consumption item. In conditions of scarcity it has occupied an exceptional place in need satisfaction. This is not just because access to nutrition is considered a priority concern in a culture of poverty; the reasons are much more varied. Food opens up a specific perspective both on consumption and on the distinctive cultural and social features of a given society. The very process of preparing food continues to appeal to all our senses and arouses unexpected desires.

An event that has even greater influence over the choice of food than preparing meals is the act of eating itself. At its best, it offers an incomparable source of pleasure and satisfaction. At the same time it penetrates our 'selves' – shapes our personal and social identities. Food is a major mediator of biological, psychological and social processes in our life. Eating means that those processes do not happen outside of ourselves within the confines of the biological and social conditions for our activity but within ourselves, in our body.

## 7.1  Culture as a frame of reference for food choices

Food is not just neutral mass – it has a whole range of cultural dimensions. Those dimensions define and determine food and make the choice of food a highly complex process that is difficult to unravel. However, we cannot afford to ignore this task because it is only by exploring those dimensions that we can hope to understand the actual process of food choices. An understanding of how the cultural meanings associated with food have changed will help us see why Bennett failed in his attempt to formulate regularities between the consumption of different foodstuffs à la Engel's Law. After all, the existence of such a regularity requires that despite variable external conditions, dairy products and vegetables, for instance, are always given the same cultural meanings.

Our culture infuses meanings into food only within the given boundary conditions. It is obviously impossible to give a value to something that we don't know or that is completely beyond our reach. In this regard our biology and the ecological and economic boundary conditions set the general boundaries for food choices but the range of choices available is still virtually endless. It depends on cultural factors which of those choices people go for and which of them they decide to leave aside. The relationship between boundary conditions and food choices can also be described by saying that the former set the upper limit for consumption choices. Cultural factors, for their part, steer those choices within the confines of what is possible by infusing meanings into them (cf. Lévi-Strauss 1962). However, this does not warrant the conclusion that the relationship between the boundary conditions for food choices and the cultural variables steering those choices is unidirectional. The selection process that is guided by cultural factors feeds back into the boundary conditions of food choice and shapes those conditions, either improving or worsening the future choice of food.

The crudest cultural distinction regulating the choice of food distinguishes between what is regarded as edible and inedible. This distinction is not based on any objective criteria. In Britain, for instance, meat is (for most people) a staple part of the diet but even so, not all meat is considered edible. People in Britain do not eat dogs, scorpions or snakes; instead they prefer pork, mutton or beef. But not all cuts of meat. Chops and fillets are valued more than cuts from other parts of the animal, which is reflected in the fact that they are much more expensive than, say, sweetbread or intestines or brains – which, interestingly, conflicts with economic theory in that the former are available in greater abundance than the latter.

This example goes to show how culture works. It impacts our perceptions like an internalized lens through which we look at phenomena on the outside. More precisely, culture shapes our attitude to the surrounding reality cognitively and emotionally by ascribing meanings to its different parts. This also applies to food. Culture apportions values to different foodstuffs and different meals, which then steer consumption choices by ranking these foodstuffs and value loadings. At the same time, culture builds a framework for the production and provision of nutrition.

There is no point importing or producing locally every possible foodstuff because consumers are not prepared to buy them. People will only put in their trolleys foodstuffs that are accepted in the local culture. In this sense culture is the blueprint of human activity: 'It determines the coordinates of social activity and productive activity' (McCracken 1988, 73). As noted earlier, food choices are not just the outcome of the individual consumer's deliberations nor the joint outcome of economic and ecological factors, but the supply and demand of food are impacted by historically contingent cultural ways of thinking.

By providing a set template for our thinking, culture facilitates our food choices, but at the same time it prevents us from trying new foods by giving us 'advice' on our consumption decisions. I call these decisions food *content choices* (cf. Goode, Theophano & Curtis 1984a, 212). But this is not the only way that culture impacts our food choices. That is, when we are wandering down the aisles of the supermarket, the choices we make are not haphazard and without purpose – we have in mind a certain meal we are planning to prepare. That meal will require different quantities of various foodstuffs. The rules, the recipes for how to mix those ingredients and in what proportions, are provided by culture. In doing so, culture provides guidance with respect to *choices of food forms* (ibid., 212).

Food choices therefore concern both form and content. The choice of research focus between these two aspects, then, depends on the interests of the research project. If the purpose of the research is to compare different situations of food use, say dining in different countries, then the focus will have to be on contents, for that is obviously the main area of concern in everyday dinners (ibid., 212). If, on the other hand, the research objective is to study the constancy of the food system amidst all the changes taking place in society, the focus must be turned to the rules governing the way in which meals are put together. These rules have to do not so much with the use of specific foodstuffs as with recipes; the rules of form that say how different meals are supposed to be assembled (ibid.).

When we turn our attention to choices of form it is not possible to limit the focus simply to choices of specific foods (Pantzar 1988, 12–13). On the contrary, we need to take a broader view and study the household or even larger social units. In addition, it makes sense to raise the level of analysis from the choice of specific foodstuffs to selections at the aggregate level, to dishes, meals and the food system. As Judith Goode, Janet Theophano and Karen Curtis emphasize, the rule of thumb in food research is first to identify the rules of eating in a certain social group (choices of form) and then to move on to examine how those rules are applied (choices of content) (Goode, Curtis & Theophano 1984b, 85; Whitehead 1984, 137–138).

The rule of thumb suggested by Goode, Curtis and Theophano calls for some reservations (more on this later), but for our purposes here it is instructive. When from this vantage point we set out to examine the principles of food choice, we find that there are two main types. These can be described by the dual concepts adopted by Claude Lévi-Strauss, i.e. *metaphor* and *metonym*. The *idea of metaphor* is based on *similarity or correspondence*, whereas *metonym* refers to *proximity or adjacency*. We start out from the metaphor when we want to compare meals, say lunch and dinner, and when we recognize that one part of the meal is called a starter and the other a main course. In this instance we need to focus on what it is that makes a particular course (e.g. quantity, sweetness vs. sourness). Recipes for compiling a starter and a main course, in turn, are built according to the principle of metonymy: the key is to know what foodstuffs go together (Barthes 1967, 63).

Anthropological studies comparing the rules for the content and form of foods in Western countries have found that the content elements have changed quite rapidly during the twentieth century. It is therefore difficult to specify the impact of metonymic principles on food choices. For instance, the now fashionable fusion cuisine freely combines elements from very different food cultures or ingredients that used to be considered incompatible (say raspberry and meat) and thus does not respect the old principles of metonymy. Metaphoric rules, by contrast, seem to have remained relatively unchanged. The 'themes' of meals have been passed down from generation to generation without much change. This has given rise to the *generalization* that the *meanings ascribed to foodstuffs and menus are highly resistant to change*. This, it has been suggested, may be because food has such a prominent role in determining and maintaining the identity of ethnic groups (Kalcik 1984, 39–40; Goode, Theophano & Curtis 1984a, 213).

Lévi-Strauss stresses the same point in his studies but he draws more far-reaching conclusions than anyone else. According to Lévi-Strauss, the reason why cultural themes have such staying power is that they sink from the surface of society into its collective subconscious. There, they continue to shape our thinking and everyday life as unconscious cultural codes. It is for this reason that it makes sense to argue that food is first an object of thinking and only then an object of eating (Barthes 1979, 171; Lévi-Strauss 1962; but see also Harris 1986). In other words, Lévi-Strauss suggests that we first decide what we want to eat today, and only then decide what to buy for food. Indeed this is often precisely what happens, but as I have said more than once, it is only in the course of our activity that we become clear about the object of our needs. There may be something on offer or something may be so temptingly displayed in the shop that in the end we decide to buy something entirely different than we originally intended. When we go out for dinner with friends we may also change our minds, and not just once, depending on what other members of the party decide to order.

### 7.1.1  Gustemes of everyday food choices

Whatever the grounds on which we make our food choices, we have to think about those choices in advance. That, in turn, requires that there are existing classifications of food. Lévi-Strauss and the school of structural anthropology work from the assumption that both mythical and everyday thinking about food is structured by binary conceptual oppositions. Reality is perceived not as a continuum but rather in terms of binary categories. That, naturally, does gross injustice to our thinking about food. If we have a cholesterol problem, for instance, we don't classify foods into one low-cholesterol category and one high-cholesterol category but we place them on a continuum where at one end we have foods that contain no cholesterol at all and at the other end foods with a very high cholesterol content. However, things are simplified by the fact that we follow the sociological practice of splitting this continuum into two different categories. Lévi-Strauss uses the term *gusteme* to describe these kinds of bipolar cultural classifications of food (Lévi-Strauss 1969, 115–117; Lévi-Strauss 1986, 143). Gustemes are rule-like principles governing food choices, although they are not followed slavishly in every situation. The most significant examples are the distinctions between *everyday and festive food* and *breakfast, lunch and dinner* (Douglas 1984, 15; Goode, Theophano & Curtis 1984a, 211). The following deals solely with the former distinction. Gustemes are not detached from other forms of thinking or existence and, therefore, can only be understood in their relevant context. It follows that gustemes of everyday and festive food derive their content largely from those features that distinguish the festive from the everyday. Everyday life represents the micro level of social existence. Its key functional category is routine, which has its temporal equivalent in repetition. Days unfold one after the other in a consecutive chain and closely resemble one another until such time as there occurs a radical change in the course of life (a new job, redundancy, marriage, birth of a child etc.). Once these changes have been lived out, routine and repetition set in again (e.g. Lefebvre 1971, 24, 98; Heller 1978, 305). It is consistent with this attitude to look upon food as the fuel of the 'human machine' and to view eating as an act of 'refuelling' in order to maintain the capacity for human activity (Ilmonen & Pantzar 1986, 97–98). I call this everyday attitude to food the *nutritional attitude*. It is possibly the oldest of our attitudes to food and it continues to have great influence over our everyday food choices (cf. Harris 1986, 19–46; Godelier 1987).

The nutritional attitude to food is perhaps best crystallized in the concept of *strength*. Strength is associated with food and nutrients that are thought to have a high energy content. Meat and blood and above all their combination, a blue steak, represent the ultimate of strength. Herein reside many key meanings of our culture. Blood, of course, is considered a giver of life received from God himself, the seat of all our emotions, the bond that connects family members (Douglas 1991, 270; Fiddes 1991, 65–93). Meat, then, sends our blood rushing – it is a source of courage and sexual potency (Twigg 1984, 22–24). The opposite of the blue steak is represented by fruit and vegetables, which are low in energy and which are often described as being *light*.

The nutritional attitude is nowadays increasingly associated with *ease of effort*. Many studies support the notion that as far as cooking is concerned, consumers around the world place high premium on speed and ease. On the supply side, this has accelerated the growth of semi-processed and processed foods such as hamburgers and filled sandwiches. This trend has been driven above all by producers' profit motives. However, on the demand side that trend would not have met with the intensity of response it has had it not been for the growth of women's wage employment and the accelerating pace of everyday life that followed with wage employment (Warde 1997, 154). This, however, is not yet a sufficient explanation for the growing emphasis on ease and convenience, because women's culture also includes the notion of the ideal meal that is freshly prepared from start to finish (Mäkelä 1996, 14–18; Mäkelä 2000, 12–13; Murcott 1986). However, various techniques of preserving foods have helped to make this task easier. Most of these are ancient home-made techniques such as drying, salting and smoking. Other more recent methods of preserving include pickling in vinegar, fermentation, sugaring and finally the industrial method of canning in the late eighteenth and early nineteenth century (Shephard 2000, 17–25). The use of preserved foods has not detracted from the appeal of home-made food or made it any less genuine, even though modern preservation methods are highly industrialized.

In nutrition science, the everyday nutritional attitude to food is usually converted into energy, which is measured in terms of calories or joules. Although these measures seem purely quantitative, there is more to the nutritional attitude to food than just the quantitative aspect. It also has a qualitative side to it, which might be described as *life control*. This reflects a new kind of attitude to our body. This new attitude comprises both eating and sexual acts, which are historically associated with one another in both European and other cultures (Braudel 1982, 128; Hirschman 1977, 43; Goody 1984, 114; Mennell 1991, 142–144).

The new Christian attitude was followed by a more disciplined lifestyle. That was in evidence as early as the eighteenth century in bourgeois eating habits. Many of the etiquette rulebooks and cookbooks published around that time warned people of the perils of overeating and gluttony. The recommendation was to abstain completely from certain foods and to exercise moderation in eating habits, which was regarded as conducive to good health (Elias 1978b, 84–127; Goody 1984, 129–132; Mennell 1991, 144). In the spirit of the Protestant Ethic, this has been interpreted as the training of the body (Foucault 1978, 107).

By the nineteenth century this new attitude to the body had been espoused only by the elite and the bourgeoisie; it had not yet reached the working classes and the peasantry. This was understandable in that the still-emerging working class lived in constant poverty, hovering on the brink of starvation. In these conditions it would have been absurd to reproach workers for gluttony. Even so, the nascent science of nutrition set out to address the working-class issue, which it chose to formulate as a 'stomach issue' (Hirdman 1983, 124). Nutrition science set itself the goal of improving the working-class's eating habits and to provide related consumer information (Ilmonen & Pantzar 1986, 98). This could be described as an attempt to strengthen their life control.

One key aspect in this project to enhance life control was the promotion of healthy eating habits. This eventually led to a new way of classifying food: more and more often, foods were now classified into the dual categories of *healthy* and *unhealthy*. These gustemes have no doubt been important in earlier times, too, but the surge of interest shown by women during the twentieth century has been unprecedented (see Mäkelä 2002, 26; Prättälä 2003, 213, 215). It is hardly an exaggeration to say that the distinction between healthy and unhealthy is nowadays an integral part of the life-control gustemes that support welfare-state policies.

It is a different matter entirely which foodstuffs and dishes, consumed in what quantities may be regarded as healthy or injurious to health. This has now become a fiercely contested issue in both the economic and political realm. Even nutrition science, it seems, is still standing on the fence (Gronow 1998). What does seem clear is that both nutrition science and public opinion are leaning towards the position that nutrients in the 'light' category can generally be regarded as healthy, whereas those in the 'heavier' category, at least when consumed regularly and in large quantities, are considered unhealthy. However, people are clearly reluctant to give them up, not only for reasons of tradition but also because many 'heavy' foods taste so good that people want to keep them as special treats for themselves (chocolate, ice cream, a piece of cake etc.)

Although the health effects of different foods remain controversial (one example is the on-going debate surrounding the Atkins' diet), one closely related factor, i.e. *the safety of food*, has continued to gain increasing importance. The recorded history of food knows of greater and lesser instances of forgery that since the nineteenth century have been called scandals. Right through to the present day, food has been forged in a bid to cash in some quick profits. This has prompted government interventions to monitor food imports and to test foodstuffs on a regular basis. This testing is motivated by two main reasons: firstly, in today's global market there is increasing uncertainty about food sources. Secondly, consumers are dubious about foods and brands that do not meet with general public approval. Trust in food, or at least the tendency to try and find food that is considered trusted, is one of the everyday gustemes of life control. Its antithesis is *indifference* to food or *scepticism* in the trustworthiness of food (Jacobsen & Kjaerness 2003, 245–274; Guzman 2003, 289–314).

### 7.1.2   Gustemes of feast choices

The opposite of mundane or everyday is feast. In European history, feast or celebration has always implied a different kind of behaviour than everyday life. When everyday life and everyday food culture bowed to the requirements of the Protestant Ethic, one of the agents of persuasion was modern nutrition science. Together, the Protestant Ethic and nutrition science pathologized gluttony and censured even the pleasures of eating. During festivities, however, these doctrines were happily brushed aside and all moderation was abandoned. A feast was a time of celebration, pleasure and happiness (cf. Freud 2004).

Feast and celebration is conventionally associated with eating; indeed this is one of the primary meanings of 'feast' – a sumptuous meal. A feast is not a feast without the opportunity to indulge in a meal that breaks with everyday eating habits, to immerse oneself in the pleasures of food. In fact it is more than an opportunity; there are social pressures to join in the celebrations. On the one hand, European culture has traditionally embraced the norm that during feasts and festive periods, rules of everyday eating should be broken. Meal times, for example, are different. On the other hand, the feast itself must have met at least two conditions: it must have been bigger and included different foods than everyday meals and it must have included dishes that are particularly tasty and sweet. People look forward to feasts with gusto (de Garine 1976, 151). Both these conditions have placed greater demands on the content and form of the feast compared to everyday meals.

The most immediately apparent aspect of a feast makes it clear that there is something special about its content. A feast must support its host's social status and honour. Therefore every feast must include at least some foods and dishes that are culturally revered. In Europe, examples might include truffles, caviar, oysters or foie gras. In other words, a feast must in some respect be *exceptional,* different from ordinary everyday food. Furthermore, it is generally accepted that one should not worry too much about the calories or the healthiness of the feast: after all, anything that tastes good is bound to be unhealthy anyway.

There are also certain requirements of form. A feast should have a greater number of courses than an ordinary everyday meal and those courses must be served in a strictly defined order. In somewhat more general terms, a feast must follow certain implicit rules in order to qualify as a 'proper' festive meal. But even this is not enough. It is not particularly difficult to serve up a feast if one knows the rules and has enough money. Expectations are higher than normal. A feast must be a sensuous treat for the eyes, offer surprises and include carefully thought out details that alert the guests' senses. It takes time and effort to prepare a feast but the effort is always rewarded. A good cook can transform a feast into a *refined* experience (Mennell 1985, 73–74, 114). That, however, is no easy task, but requires great experience, skill and taste. An upstart cannot but fail to impress because he or she will not have the requisite skills of refinement but instead is still captive to vulgar practices (Bourdieu 1978).

To sum up my discussion of the consumption of food, the conclusion it suggests is that the main gustemes of the feast are exceptional as opposed to ordinary, laborious as opposed to quick and easy and refined as opposed to mundane and vulgar. It is only through adherence to these rules of thumb that a feast becomes a 'proper' feast. The gustemes of everyday and feast, healthiness and unhealthiness, healthiness and disregard for healthiness and heavy and light do not cover all the different ways of thinking about food choices in Western culture. As we will soon see, there are also various other gustemes. However the gustemes shown in Figure 7.1 provide a general framework for the European way

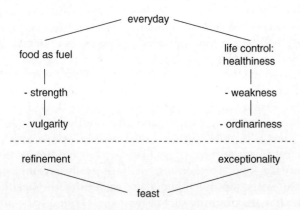

*Figure 7.1*   Basic gustemes of the everyday and feast

of thinking about food. They do not, however, provide an answer to the actual event of food choice since there is marked variation both within and between them depending on the situation and time.

## 7.2   Mechanisms of consumption choice

Cultural gustemes of food are primarily expressions of common ways of thinking in society (cf. Lévi-Strauss 1986, 80). It is just as difficult to get from cultural gustemes to concrete food choices as it is to get from social status to people's consciousness. In critiquing this kind of Lévi-Straussian analysis, Jack Goody observes quite rightly that in European science 'there is a tendency to spirit away the more concrete aspects of human life... by locating their interpretation only at the "deeper" level, which is largely a matter of privileging the "symbolic" at the expense of the more immediately communicable dimensions of social action' (Goody 1984, 25).

The cultural level reflects only the general principle of classification. It exists before the choice – but only as a possibility that does not necessarily materialize. In other words, the symbolic classification requires execution, *an event which combines cultural meaning with the action (choice)* (cf. Sahlins 2000). In human behaviour, execution connects the cognitive aspect with action, neither of which should be given precedence in analysing the process, as idealistic or materialistic interpretations of social life have done. According to the former view an event is the mere effect of a cultural meaning. This, however, is to ignore the institutions and the social forces and interests that produce and maintain meanings, as well as situational factors (e.g. the behaviour of other people and supply). According to the latter view, then, cultural meaning is the immediate effect of the objective features of the event (Godelier 1999, 22, 27). This view, is turn, fails to recognize the separation and specificity of the cultural level, which maintains historical continuity in the social world (cf. Sahlins 1985, 154; 2000, 293–304).

What makes the event so important is that neither the cultural meaning nor everyday material processes have primacy in accomplishing it. The event is a separate stage in a social-selection process that follows its own 'logic'. It is not reducible either to cultural meanings or to the material conditions of choice (income, supply, scarcity of outlets etc.). From this it follows that it is impossible to derive events directly from cultural meanings, or the other way round, to derive cultural meanings from events. Instead, insofar as they remain unchanged, events produce constant practices and ways of thinking, institutions that are liable to create their own symbolism and language.

What, then, is the mystical event that ties together the cultural meanings of food and the concrete choices of food? To find out, we need to turn to the collective modes of action that give concrete shape to food gustemes. These modes serve as filters that guide food choices by branding some foods as healthy and others as unhealthy, for instance. I call these modes of action *mechanisms of consumption choice*. They include convention and tradition, routine, style and fashion. I begin with the first two.

### 7.2.1  Convention, tradition and consumption choice

Together with routines, conventions and tradition are the oldest social mechanisms involved in transforming cultural codes into concrete food choices. As long as they govern people's lives, they are capable of resisting change in consumption choices. The objects and forms of need satisfaction are given in convention and tradition-directed communities. They are not doubted or called into question. They are repeated because this is the way things have always been done before (Riesman & Lerner 1965, 382–396). It is therefore correct to say that as conventions and traditions funnel social action into one channel, so they also cement consumer behaviour.

In France and Britain, Europe's cultural and political centres of the time, the grip of tradition and conventions remained firm through to the end of the sixteenth century. The situation began to change following the first consumer revolution, as a result of which the nobility started to develop new ways of living. These changes were most noticeably reflected in eating habits: while the poor were still eating to live, many rich people were now living to eat. The differences between the eating habits of the nobility and the working classes were no longer just quantitative, but also qualitative. By this time the nobility were eating so much that they simply couldn't have eaten any more. They had to start thinking about how they could develop and refine their meals. So while the nobility feasted on ever-more elaborate dishes and delicacies, peasants had to content themselves with a monotonous diet based mainly on bread and soup (Goody 1984, 134–135; Mennell 1991, 142).

Tradition and conventions continued to play an important part in consumption choices even after the seventeenth century, especially in rural areas and in the working classes, but they were no longer the sole mechanisms steering consumption choices. In fact it was not until the late nineteenth century that the role of tradition in consumption began significantly to recede. The reason for this was the second consumer revolution: capitalism was now gaining an ever-stronger hold over the consumer goods' markets and seeking to overcome the physical and mental obstacles in its way.

Tradition did not, however, lose all its influence in guiding consumption choices; that did not even happen in the early twentieth century after the third consumer revolution (the emergence of mass markets) or in the latter part of the twentieth century after the fourth consumer revolution (the branding of commodities and the growth of service use). It is important to underline this because sociology, in its preoccupation with dichotomies, would have us believe that modernity has consigned traditions to the rubbish heap of social history. This, as I have just pointed out, is not true. As old traditions have started to wane, so they have been revived and brought back before disappearing altogether. At the same time, new consumption-oriented traditions have been created (Valentine's Day, Mother's and Father's Day etc.) (Heelas, Lash & Morris 1996, 87–170).

Nowadays there is even talk about tradition-directed consumption. This term has been coined to salute the consumer goods and consumption habits that were central in a world that was much more dependent on natural conditions than is the case today. At the same time, the concept serves to highlight those aspects of our ancestors' consumption that are considered recommendable (spelt, wild rice). Guidebooks have been published on the Stone Age Diet, for instance, to provide guidance on how to address obesity and other phenomena associated with extravagance, and there is also a new genre of cookbooks dedicated to preserving traditional dishes (e.g. Heine 1994; Child, Bertholle & Beck 2009).

Old traditions thus continue to live on in our consciousness, even though their specific contents have changed over time. In addition, we have created a whole host of new traditions, some of which have started with the birth of the nation-state. Physical borders alone have not been able to separate one nation-state from another since they are a constant source of dispute. They have had to be supported by symbolic boundaries: national flags, monuments and annual public ceremonies (Hobsbawm 1988b, 271).

Unlike old traditions, new ceremonies are not connected to any specific social practices such as grain or wine harvests. On the contrary, they have from the outset been abstract references to a national entity, drawing heavily on such phrases as king and country and national duty. It is clear from these expressions that the new traditions are thought to have the function not only of helping to draw symbolic national boundaries, but also of culturally transcending conflicts that have developed within nation-states at the level of civil society (Hobsbawm 1988a, 10). Against this backdrop it is also easier to understand the establishment of completely new ceremonial highlights, such as Mother's Day and Father's Day, even though these might originally have had some other functions, too.

Although traditions are ordinarily understood as collective phenomena that involve the whole society, they also occur at group level in business companies, clubs, associations and families. In these contexts, traditions have evolved as recurring events that structure group activities and that are binding upon all members of the community in the same way as national traditions. In fact these in-group traditions may be even more binding than national traditions in the sense that it is much easier to control group rituals, and sanctions are readily meted out for non-conformity because that is felt to present a threat to the very existence of the group. Jewish culture, for instance, prohibits the eating of pork, hare, rabbit, conger-eel, cuttle-fish and other scaleless fish, and this rule is subject to heavy sanctions in Jewish settlements (Douglas 1966; Roden 1994, 155).

However, it is not my intention here to discuss the traditions of specific (ethnic, religious etc.) small groups, but rather to explore the nature of traditions that govern broader communities and whole societies. This is necessary so that I can move on to consider the difference between traditions and conventions. Earlier I pointed out that the development of modernity has eroded old traditions. The same goes for conventions. The changes sweeping ancient conventions have happened in fundamentally the same way as the erosion of traditions, i.e. in the wake of market expansion, urbanization, wage employment and the erosion of family ties. This means that we cannot explain the difference between traditions and conventions directly on the basis of their social connections. A more useful starting point is to look at how these mechanisms work and at how they are reproduced.

### 7.2.1.1 *Tradition and convention: differences and similarities*

Tradition and convention are both *manifestations of collective memory* that find concrete expression in repetitive behaviours that punctuate and give rhythm to everyday life. Another feature that they share in common is that it is very difficult, if not impossible to trace their origin. It is only when we turn our attention to the maintenance or reproduction of traditions and conventions that we find their first difference.

Traditions are followed publicly (Malinowski 1960, 72) and failure to conform will usually be sanctioned. Conventions, on the other hand, are not followed publicly and there is no one there to apportion sanctions (see Weber 1978, 29). They are institutional matters of course.

This difference provides a first clue as to where we need to look to see how the mechanisms of tradition and convention differ. Given that tradition and convention are forms of repetitive behaviour, is it possible that they have a different relationship to their underlying rules, as the existence of sanctions in one case and the absence of sanctions in the other give cause to assume? To find out, we need to elaborate on the picture drawn earlier of the relationship between cultural ways of thinking and food, to dwell for a while on the *nature of rule-abiding behaviour*. For this purpose I draw on the distinction applied by Paul Connerton but already made by Ludwig Wittgenstein (see e.g. 1969) between rule-governed and habitual behaviour.

According to Connerton the dividing line between rule-governed and habitual behaviour depends on whether or not a rule is followed. In order to be able to follow a rule, one must first be aware of its existence. Once the existence of a rule is recognized, it is followed even if circumstances change. In the Nordic countries it is customary to have a schnapps or a beer with Baltic herring. When this rule is not recognized, one turns to conventions. In European culture women guests are always served first, followed by male guests, and the host is always served last. This order might seem strange in Chinese culture but it may still be applied when a Chinese person travels to Europe (Connerton 1989, 30–34).

When an observer sets out in Lévi-Strauss's footsteps to analyse the eating habits of a South American Indian tribe, he might feel that he can detect an underlying 'grammar', a set of rules that says which ingredients can and cannot go together. There is nothing wrong with this unless the observer then concludes that he knows exactly how different foodstuffs are used in this culture. That is something he does not and cannot know, unless he complements the picture by information gained directly from the people living in that culture. If he does that, he will immediately realize that the rules and the application of those rules are two different things. For this reason the observer must also study the *applications* of the rules that govern the eating behaviours of the members of this culture (cf. Pike 1990; Harris 1990).

This, however, never happens in structuralist-influenced research and in French research in particular, which sees rules and grammars at every possible level of reality and then proceeds to semiotize them. It consequently fails to notice the chasm that one inevitably comes across on proceeding from the rules or grammars of eating to the application of those rules, to the preparation of meals or to language use. Knowing the recipe does not yet guarantee a good meal and knowing the grammar does not yet guarantee fluency in language use. It is only through repeated language use, when the rules of language become a habit that the accumulative effect of repetition begins to kick in. This is the point at which we no longer have to think about the rules when we are applying them and at the same time, the point of inversion between the rules and their application. Application maintains (or changes) the rule, not the other way round (Connerton 1989, 34; Wittgenstein 1969).

Both conventions and traditions are applications of rules. However, their relationship to rules is different. A convention is based on a *custom or habit* whose underlying rules remain more or less unconscious. This is quite simply because the collective applications of those rules have become embedded as part of our *bodily practices*. They are constant features of our existence which express social (gender, age, status etc.) and affective (liking, rejection etc.) attitudes.

As bodily practices, conventions become part of our social self. Our gender, for instance, is immediately apparent from our minutest body movements, from the way we shake hands, the way we sit, kneel and curtsey. In this sense bodily practices are a means of self-expression (e.g. a way of expressing politeness). But this is just one side of the matter, because they also wield power over us. A convention is not just a sign or a cultural code but *knowledge and memory within our body* (Bourdieu 1990, 166).

With the cultivation of a convention and the silent socialization that follows, we learn to 'understand' with our body, a phenomenon well known to sports' pedagogics. The inverted commas are needed to emphasize that this understanding is not a conscious process but one where memory accumulates in our body and constantly reproduces our bodily gesture-language, its social consciousness (cf. Connerton 1989, 104). It is this merging of bodily language as part of our social self that makes it so difficult both to change conventions and to consciously create them.

Tradition, then, is a form of collective remembering that is aware of the rule. In other words, it is not habitual behaviour but rule-abiding behaviour. The application of a rule allows only limited latitude because it is usually very strictly interpreted. Tradition is upheld by rituals, which are unchangeable and which largely dictate how the tradition should be lived out. To deviate from rituals is not only to break against tradition; it is also a gesture against the mythical origin that those rituals represent. Such deviation is usually sanctioned, although not necessarily in any outwardly visible manner, but in more subtle ways that cause an inner sense of disquiet or anxiety.

The threat of sanction serves as a constant reminder that in following a tradition one should try not to stray from the narrow path of rituals. It is precisely in this sense that following of tradition is more a matter of consciously abiding by the rules than following a convention. From this it follows that even though it is hard to create collective traditions, they are nonetheless easier to bring about or to shape than it is to create or change conventions. This is well understood in politics, as recent European history illustrates. Impressive examples are provided by the German Third Reich's traditionalism and ritualism and the rise of political ritualism in socialist countries. To create a tradition, all that is required is to install rituals that support a phenomenon elevated to a sacred status by some social group. Every member of the society concerned will do wisely to respect and follow those rituals if they are to avoid reproach and possibly more serious consequences (Hobsbawm 1988a, 4; see also Havel 1991).

Convention and tradition do not, however, only differ in terms of how they are related to the underlying rules; they are also differently located in *time*. Conventions are attached to daily routines and become their building blocks. Without conventions, our days would not resemble one another to the extent they do. Traditions, for their part, break down those routines. They are dates in our calendar that intersperse everyday time with sacred time. Tradition reflects collective remembering, which is interjected into the flow of social time so that all those who adhere to the tradition perform the required rituals simultaneously. This is collective remembering in the true sense of the word (see Misztal 2003, 90–98).

The following of conventions lacks the ability of traditions to synchronize social activities. On the other hand, one of the features that conventions do share in common with traditions is that they contribute to maintaining social cohesion. One of these features is that they anchor the current moment and its experiential elements to the past. Tradition and convention are used to overcome the detachedness of the current moment, drawing contents from the past to fill that moment. In this way they provide continuity to living and at the same time unwittingly *justify* current practices by reference to the past.

In a sense the execution of traditions and conventions is a cult, or in Walter Benjamin's words a *phantasmagoria*, where the primordial enters the scene (Benjamin 2003 [1939]). It brings *the past into life in the present* and reminds the people who are attached to it of their common origins. In this way tradition and convention reinforce the social identity of their supporters and by the same token mobilize their social conscience. It tells both those who are attached to the tradition and outsiders 'who we are'. Furthermore, tradition and convention transfer beliefs, value systems and behaviour patterns from generation to generation. They are also *forms of socialization* (see Misztal 1996).

The activities that are significantly promoted by traditions and conventions are central to the hierarchical power relations of any community or to the continuity of the nation-state. For this reason it is understandable that power elites in particular have placed such a heavy premium on fostering those activities. (This is at once why common people have tried to hold on to their own traditions.[1]) Because of the weight afforded to them and the elements of ritualism they involve, traditions in particular, but also national conventions have been turned into 'civic religions'. At least as far as traditions are concerned this view is defendable in the sense that the ritualism they require does not differ from religious ritualism. It is focused on what is regarded as sacred (or at least desirable), and both show how people are expected to act in relation to that sacred (or desirable) matter.

Not all traditions and conventions, of course, maintain the three social functions mentioned at the same time. However there are certain areas of social activity where prevailing traditions and conventions can combine these functions. Examples include at least language and food. They are also particularly relevant building blocks for our social self. For this reason it comes as no surprise that through the ritualism required by traditions and the conventionalization entailed by conventions, food and language have so effectively resisted the pressures of change from modernity.

### 7.2.1.2   Convention, tradition, everyday and feast

When food choices are guided solely by tradition and conventions, it is easy for each member of the community to apply the basic gustemes of food, say to tell the difference between everyday meals and feasts on special occasions. In pre-modern communities, this distinction has further been facilitated by the division of labour between convention and tradition in relation to the everyday and feast. Ordinary *everyday meals* have largely been governed by *conventions*. Preparations for a feast, on the other hand, have been governed by *traditions*. These manifestations of habit systems have thus been associated with different dishes and

foodstuffs, particularly in conditions of scarcity, where for their everyday meals people have had to resort to weak carbohydrate-containing
foods and to set stronger high-protein foods aside for festive occasions.

In European thinking, heavy (strong) foods are traditionally considered to originate in the animal kingdom. These foods have been held
in greater respect than other foods. This is still the thinking today,
although it has begun to break down with the growing popularity of
rice, pasta, vegetables and fruits, all foods that fall in the 'weak' category (Twigg 1984, 121).

The gustemes of light have been important in European meals not
only because they have been associated with variation in social practices, the everyday and feast and conventions and traditions, but also
because they have been associated with social divisions, particularly
with the gender division. Strong has been regarded as a male attribute
(Twigg 1984, 123–124; Sahlins 1976, 171; Fiddes 1991, 28–29; Prättälä
2003, 213). Vegetables, on the other hand, have been regarded as feminine foods. This probably goes some way towards explaining why it
has been so hard for men in Western cultures to become vegetarians
(Prättälä 2003, 213).

The gustemes of heavy and light are historically anchored to the
class structure, too. Since the seventeenth century the nobility and the
emerging bourgeois class have sought to detach 'strong' foods from
feast, for instance, to turn meat dishes into everyday food. Peasants and
members of the rapidly growing working class, on the other hand, have
had to content themselves with vegetables and grain products (Goody
1984, 134–135; Mennell 1985, 48). The situation remained the same
through to the twentieth century.

It is only since the Second World War that things have begun to
change, as scarcity has become a thing of the past (for the most modern
parts of Europe at least) and as the redefinition of the basic gusteme
of life control, healthy vs. unhealthy, has obscured the connection
of meat with the upper classes. While it was previously thought too
good for 'us', meat is now blamed for many diseases. As a result, the
upper and middle classes in many European countries have decided to
'lighten' their diets and have begun to eat more vegetables, especially
in day-to-day meals (see e.g. Bourdieu 1984, 181–182, 188–189). In the
working class, on the other hand, the consumption of meat has continued to increase.

Although the contents of old everyday and feast gustemes have
changed radically over the past 50 years, convention and tradition have
not lost their significance in guiding food choices. They have retained

their influence over food choices, even though European meals have been swept along by the tide of internationalization and even though the consumption of semi-processed and processed foods has increased sharply since the 1960s (Ilmonen 1991a, 170–171). Convention has guaranteed the continuity of everyday eating, particularly its contents, which indeed are more closely tied to conventions than form.

Tradition, then, regulates choices of form rather than content of food, recipes rather than their detailed applications. Even though the trends discussed above, the Europeanization of eating habits and the increased use of processed foods, such as frozen shrimps and canned mussels and tomatoes, have begun to filter through to affect people's choices of food content at festive occasions, there have been no major changes in form. The same tendency to hold on to the old and familiar ways of eating that is evident among American-Italians, for instance, is also evident in European eating habits. New ingredients are used in accordance with old rules and recipes. As Goode, Curtis and Theophano (1984b, 211) observe in their studies of Italian meal habits in America: 'the major locus of continuity in the food system is not the frequency of pasta or tomato sauce, but the rules for constructing and timing foods based on sauces'.

In other words, the internationalization of national cuisines has not dramatically affected day-to-day eating habits, even though there have been some changes in content. The same applies to foods served on festive occasions: there have been some changes in content, but the form of meals, the way they are prepared and their timing, have all remained unchanged. There is nothing really surprising about this. After all, it is primarily over the form of eating that tradition wields its power. It does not allow for unexpected deviations or for endless variation. Therefore *traditional and non-traditional* and *conventional and unconventional* are important gustemes in the selection of food. They are interwoven with other gustemes, too, such as those of strong and light, but independent of the categories of everyday and feast. Both everyday and festive meals can be traditional and conventional.

### 7.2.2   Routines and consumption

In the latter half of the 1990s studies in the sociology of consumption have largely focused on themes and issues raised under the banner of post-modernism (e.g. Bauman 1992, 48–49; see also Featherstone 1991; Lash 1990). One of the main lines of research has been concerned with consumers as *reflexive agents*, a trend which started in ethnological consumption studies. The notion was brought into sociology by Anthony

Giddens, who gave it arguably its most influential formulation in his opus magnum *The Constitution of Society* (1984). In this pioneering work, Giddens argues for a reflexive agent who is doomed to forever making choices in his life and who can, at will, choose to do otherwise. This idea of the agent is crucial to understanding why the sociology of consumption has concentrated so much – quite legitimately so – on questions of fashion, style and other such phenomena.

However, not all types of consumption fit in with Giddens' idea of agent. As we interact with commodities, consumption, just as any other activity, eventually becomes habitualized (see Weber 1964, 372). Through habits, 'we inhabit the world. It becomes a home, and the home is part of our everyday experience'. It is not as easy to change this 'home' as agency theory claims. Therefore it is also necessary to look more closely at the consumption mechanism that does not fit in with that theory. I call this mechanism *consumption routine*. It works on the principle of repetition, without referring to any specific events in the past. Consumption routines are ways of living in the here and now (cf. Heidegger 1977). Choices are made as before, without any particular reason.

### 7.2.2.1   Action and behaviour

The sociology of consumption is to a large extent grounded, either implicitly or explicitly, in the concept of agent. This is understandable if we bear in mind that this discipline has developed as a reaction to the critical theory view of consumers as weak, manipulated marionettes of production and mass marketing. In stressing the role of agency, the sociology of consumption takes for granted the agent's power to choose to do otherwise. This is surprising since the accomplishment of action is inherently problematic. As Campbell suggests, 'individuals do not always succeed in their attempts to implement their decisions'. Failures inevitably happen because of opposition from other people and structural obstacles, such as infrastructure limitations, but also because people simply are unable to do what they set out to (e.g. to lose weight) or because they are reluctant to 'implement their will and therefore "to act"' (Campbell 1996, 157).

Campbell thus makes a distinction between action and non-action, acts that do not fit into the concept of action. The former has to do with willing or will power and its practical application. Action must therefore be defined as *voluntary and subjectively meaningful conduct* (Campbell 1996, 25). Non-action, then, consists of *involuntary reactive responses and conduct*. This may also be called *behaviour*, which is characterized by repetitive practices. However, neither the individual concerned nor out-side observers can immediately identify the underlying principles.

Campbell is not the first sociologist to make this distinction between action and behaviour. Max Weber (1964, 372), for example, described the routinization of action as 'one of the principal continually-operating forces in everyday life'. Alfred Schutz and William Thomas and Florian Znaniecki have also applied the dichotomy of action and behaviour in their theories.

The distinction between action and behaviour is not of course abso-lute and watertight. Weber, too, assumed that these two different modes of conduct cannot be mutually exclusive. On the contrary, he suggested that behaviour 'shades over' into action (Weber 1964, 116). What he wanted to convey with this expression is that human conduct is always a mixture of action and behaviour. If this is accepted, the implication is that action doesn't really exist at all in the proper sense of the word. However, there is no need to accept such an extreme standpoint even when we apply Weberian action theory. That is, it is also possible to fol-low the thinking of Durkheim and more recently Campbell and work from the assumption that behaviour consists merely of ' "decayed" ver-sions of earlier "true" actions' (Campbell 1996, 57; Durkheim 1983, 38, 79, 83). There are good grounds, therefore, to treat these categories as analytically distinct.

### 7.2.2.2   *Forms of behaviour and circumstances*

It is possible that during our primary socialization we pick up behav-iours of which we are not aware and which therefore never translate into action. If, however, we assume that behaviour starts out as ordinary action and only later develops into behaviour, two questions need to be asked. Firstly, what are the social situations or circumstances that are most likely to lead to the translation of action into behaviour? Secondly, we also need to know how behaviour changes and what form it assumes as a result of this change.

To answer the first question, it is useful to try and identify the cir-cumstances that are most conducive to ideal-type agency (cf. Camic 1986, 1047). In addition, it is useful to try and find out in what kinds of circumstances our conduct is dominated by repetitive unmoti-vated performance (cf. Giddens 1979, 218). Micro-economic theory and economics in general, leans on the assumption of one ideal type of action, i.e. rational decision-making.[2] The discipline that has devoted the most attention to repetitive behaviours is anthro-pology. It is useful, therefore, to see how these two approaches can contribute to our understanding of the interaction between action and behaviour.

According to economics, rational action (decision-making) is bound up with epistemological issues or in Giddens' terms, with knowledge-ability. Keynes is one of the best-known representatives of this view. If the probability of a certain outcome is relatively high, in other words if all relevant aspects of that outcome are well known, then the conditions are favourable for rational agency and for the individual to become a true agent of his own economic future. However, when uncertainty increases, when the probability is unknown, the situation changes in ways that are well reflected in investment decisions. How do investors arrive at their decisions in situations of high uncertainty? In his *General Theory*, Keynes emphasizes the importance of 'devices' in making investment decisions under conditions of uncertainty. Such devices include conventions, mimesis, fashion and habits. They allow behaviour that 'saves our faces as rational, economic men' (Keynes 1964, 114–117, 152).

Anthropology deals with repetitive behaviour or ritualism in two different contexts. In the Durkheimian tradition, ritualism is seen as a way of strengthening group solidarity and by the same token social order. Bronislaw Malinowski does not deny this, but he underlines the specific nature of the situation in which ritualism commonly occurs. According to Malinowski, rituals are common when a particular outcome is important but individuals have no control over that outcome (Malinowski 1960, 79–81). Ritualism is connected with magic; it is what people resort to when they begin to run out of options. In fact, Malinowski assigns rituals the same role as Keynes assigns to 'devices'. This is hardly a coincidence, since Malinowski was very much influenced by neo-classical economics. New-generation anthropologists have had no objections in this regard for they, too, have seen rituals as a way of coping in contingent circumstances, as a way of reducing the anxiety caused by difficult decisions taken under conditions of uncertainty.

But rituals are of course not the only 'device' that can facilitate decision-making. As we just saw, Keynes also refers to fashion, mimesis, habits and conventions. However, he was clearly less than analytical in compiling this list. Fashion and mimesis do not really belong to the category of 'device' if they are understood as forms of behaviour. Old memories can be recalled and used creatively in new situations ('to do otherwise'), and fashion can be blindly followed, but this is not necessarily always the case. When old memories and recollections are applied to a new situation and when fashion is followed reflexively, the individual begins to approximate the position of an agent. This is the position in which the decision is made on whether or not to apply old experiences and whether or not to follow fashion. Habits and conventions are consciously reflected upon only in exceptional circumstances where our adherence to them can no longer be taken for granted. Once the situation has cleared up, habits and conventions return to govern our behaviour (Durkheim 1983, 83; see also Bell 1992, 87). They become mere routine.

Although they both represent repetitive behaviour, routinized habitual actions and routinized rituals are different from each other. In the Malinowskian tradition, rituals are associated with magic. People resort to magic whenever they enter into action that involves high risks. Magical rituals must be skilfully executed, in strict adherence to old customs, because otherwise the magical powers will not lend their support. Rituals therefore are formal by nature, easily controllable. In this respect they differ from routines, which are constantly evolving and unfolding (for instance in the workplace) and which are an important way of living out everyday life. Routines are not formalized nor are they actively reflected upon. It suffices for routines to make everyday life orderly and predictable.

Rituals are for the most part forms of collective action. Routines, on the other hand, are primarily recurring patterns of behaviour (e.g. do you put on you left or right shoe first, do you brush your teeth first thing in the morning or after breakfast?). In this regard they resemble individual superstition, which requires rituals for the desired outcome to be achieved. However, it is important to keep these two forms of behaviour apart. Whereas personal superstition uses rituals (e.g. wearing certain clothes or carrying a lucky charm) to try and control the future, routines lack such a dimension. Routines are just established ways of making our everyday life easier and more manageable. We are not, however, particularly aware of this function of routines nor indeed do routines always make our everyday life any easier. In fact, to an outsider they might seem to do quite the opposite; but routines are hard to change. They come as second nature to us, they are too close up to be noticed. One reason why routines tend to go unnoticed is that over time, routine behaviour becomes embedded in body gestures, ways of walking, sitting, choosing paths etc. They become internalized, corporeal knowledge that is welded as part of our everyday self.

Although routines are mainly individual practices of action, they still produce conformity at a general level. Outsiders become aware of our routines, for instance, through Gallup polls and begin to follow them.

This leads to collective time rhythms, the viewing of TV news at a certain time of day, lunchtimes etc. Adhering to those rhythms is a way of persuading ourselves and others that we are *normal*: it is this sense of normalcy created by routines that is the most common way in which people relate to the world around and at once the most obvious frame of reference for attitudes of general trust (Misztal 1996, 108). Even in the extreme uncertainty that prevailed in concentration camps, eyewitness accounts say that people still tried to maintain a sense of normalcy by repeating their daily routines, as if nothing untoward had happened (Frankl 1978). However, this sense of normalcy does not come without a cost. Routines also limit our scope of action.

To help make our everyday life more manageable, routines come down to the level of *practical consciousness*, as Giddens suggests. Practical consciousness is closely related to Edmund Husserl's and Alfred Schutz's concept of natural attitude, by which they refer to the frame of reference that is used in observing and interpreting the everyday world. In this process of observation and interpretation, however, the agent is not aware of that frame of reference (Schutz 1962, 299). Giddens (1979) echoes this view by saying that practical consciousness refers to recall of which the agent is unaware and which cannot be verbally expressed.

Practical consciousness is perhaps the most central concept in Giddens' theory of structuration (1979).[3] The reason for this is that according to Giddens, the reflexive monitoring of our action takes place at this level of practical consciousness, which is at once the dominant mode of consciousness. The predominance of practical consciousness is explained by the fact that is corresponds to the dominant form of everyday action, i.e. routine. Indeed, routine is the second conceptual cornerstone of the theory of structuration.

'Corresponds to' is in fact not quite accurate. More correctly, we ought to say that routines materialize practical consciousness. In effect, the execution of routines means 'to have a particular kind of mental cause operating' (Turner 1994, 16). Routines incorporate the contents of practical consciousness. Giddens himself might not subscribe to this, but for me some of Bourdieu's thoughts about sport are well suited to describe the relationship between practical consciousness (mental reason) and routines (action). According to Bourdieu, training in sport is entirely about the cultivation of the body. Once the athlete has reached a certain level of training he learns to 'understand' with his body. In other words, training is about teaching and learning as a body. The athletic performance, then, is repeating what has been learned (Bourdieu 1990, 166).[4]

'Understand' is placed in inverted commas to emphasize that this understanding is not a conscious act but a form of memory that is incorporated in our thoughts as given assumptions and that finds expression in permanent trajectories of our body language. This kind of 'understanding' has many advantages. Routines are not just ways of reducing uncertainty or, in Giddens' words, of strengthening ontological security, but they also *conserve energy*. They put everyday life 'in order' and, in Dewey's words, make it 'habitable'. When we follow our routines we don't have to start all over from the top every time, or constantly have to weigh options that are open to us. We can simply do what we've always done before. At the same time, this constancy creates for outsiders a suitable frame of reference in which the agent is seen as *trustworthy* (Misztal 1996, 68).

Routines thus perform many functions at the same time. They are a) a way of reducing *the complexity of decision-making* and conserving the energy it takes. In addition, they are liable to create b) a sense of a safe habitable world and a *sense of normalcy*. Furthermore, they help to make our behaviour c) *predictable* and d) create a framework within which we are perceived by outsiders as *trustworthy* (cf. the anecdote about Kant, who was said to maintain such a strict regimen that people set their clocks according to his daytime walks).

Once we have become habituated to our routines they become an integral part of our body language, of our 'character' (Camic 1986, 1052). This is why it is not as easy as Giddens implies to proceed from practical consciousness and routines to the position of agent, a position where he says people are always free to 'do otherwise'. Giddens does not take this problem seriously. This is probably the reason why, in his theory of structuration, Giddens rejected conclusions drawn on the basis of routines and instead moved towards the rational agent of micro-economic theory.

### 7.2.2.3 Routines and consumption choices

One of the most persistent trends of modern consumption has been the growth of uncertainty about consumption choices. There are many reasons for this, but I will take just a few examples. Firstly, as manufacturing processes have become ever more sophisticated, as new materials have been introduced and the markets have become ever more globalized, so our knowledge of where commodities come from, what they are made of and how they work has continued to decline. Secondly, the more volatile the (global) market prices, the more special offers there are; and the more superficial variation there is in the marketplace, the harder it is for consumers to know, let alone compare the prices of even the most common goods. The growing emphasis on design (not just in the sense of aesthetic appearance but also the manipulation of smell, for instance), image advertising and new packaging methods are also combining to make making rational calculation more difficult in consumption choices. Furthermore, since consumers themselves are increasingly involved in the finishing of products, they also have an unpredictable impact on transaction costs associated with consumption choices. For instance, it is difficult to estimate in advance the true cost of a package holiday.

For the reasons just mentioned, it would be a miracle if the consumer were capable of making a purely rational choice between competitive products. Instead, in order to minimize the sense of uncertainty in that situation and to facilitate decision-making, consumers will be likely to resort to routines they have learned. This assumption can be tested by looking more closely at the five different stages of consumption: a) the decision of what to buy, b) the decision of where to buy, c) our behaviour/ action at the place of purchase, d) the actual use of consumer goods and e) the handling of waste from consumption. I am unable here to discuss all of these stages in detail. Instead I will offer just a few examples and focus on the first four stages only – even though the fifth is also very interesting. After all, we do not just throw away used goods but we also keep them for various purposes, as Lévi-Strauss's *bricoleur* does.

*In the making of consumption choices routines find expression in the constant repetition of the same choices and in brand loyalty.* These routines are not necessarily consciously reflected upon, however. As Deborah Lupton (1996, 155) says, 'food preferences may be acted upon in a totally unthinking way, as the products of acculturation and part of the habits of everyday life'. In the context of food choices, the persistence of consumption routines is reflected in the continued popularity of many traditional dishes and underlying gustemes (strong vs. light, health vs. disregard for health). Even though food baskets everywhere have become more internationalized and even though the use of processed foods has increased since the 1960s, the range of ingredients used and the meals put on the table have shown very little change.

*Brand loyalty*, then, is reflected in a high degree of bonding with the same brand. Even though new and cheaper products are constantly being introduced in the marketplace, people are reluctant to part with their favourite brands. Market researchers have shown, however, that brand loyalty varies by type of commodity. The decisive factor, it seems, is the extent to which a given commodity elicits an emotional commitment from the consumer and how large an investment the purchase represents in relation to the consumer's income. In the case of daily consumer goods, the level of emotional commitment and brand loyalty is likely to be low; examples might include clothes' pegs, detergents, toilet paper and so on. On the other hand, in the case of expensive capital goods that are purchased more rarely or staple goods that are emotionally highly charged, brand loyalty is bound to be high. Examples of the former include cars and perfumes; and of the latter motor oils, breads, beers and popular foods (see Seies 1986, 87).

The *decision on where to buy* depends, in turn, on whether we are shopping for basic consumption goods or investment goods. Choices of the former are predominantly based on routines, whereas purchases of the latter are so rare that people never get to the stage of forming routines. Therefore, conscious reflection plays a more important part in the decision on where to buy. Purchases of perishables, on the other hand, are governed by rules which say that most of what is needed during the week is bought from the corner shop (if there still is one), pretty much regardless of price. For the weekend, people usually drive out to the supermarket and buy larger quantities at the same time. And once they have found their favourite supermarket (assuming they have a choice), people will habitually keep going to the same one.

In manufacturing and especially in services, there has been a long-standing trend to *pass on a growing share of labour costs to the consumer*. This has happened on the quiet over a longer period of time, by testing and probing, because putting consumers to work can be very risky. If consumers fail to perform the tasks they are assigned as intended the private company may be thrown into chaos. To avoid such a scenario, consumer work (which retail trade and banks call 'service') has been standardized as far as possible to guarantee that operations run smoothly and to minimize annoyance among other consumers and service employees proper.

However the main motivation for this standardization effort is to help shops and banks cut their costs. A clear indication of the importance of this cost-cutting motive is the publication of a whole range of books on how to increase the productivity of customers (Fuller & Smith 1991, 1–16). In practice, the steering of consumers is reflected in their being led along carefully planned routes through the supermarket aisles, where goods are displayed according to shopping frequencies to make sure they end up in people's shopping trolleys. The standardization of consumer behaviour has perhaps been carried furthest in McDonaldized restaurant systems, which scatter numerous clues around to maximize consumer throughput, forcing patrons to participate in the script designed for staff members (Leidner 1993, 68–74).

There is very little earlier research on the routinization of the use of purchased goods. However, sociologists of food have often pointed out that consumers prefer food that they are used to and that they have been brought up on, i.e. home-cooked meals (Lupton 1996, 49). It also seems that forms of meals are highly resistant to change. Breakfast must be different from lunch, which in turn must differ from dinner (Douglas & Gross 1981; Murcott 1982; Prättälä et al. 1993). On other areas than the consumption of food there is a continued dearth of research into the routinization of consumption but we do of course have ample first-hand experience. Take the bicycle. When we trade in our old trusty bicycle that had no gears with a new mountain bike that has 20-odd gears, it is initially quite a cumbersome ride. However, it doesn't take all that long for us to learn how to work our way through the gears; shifting gears soon becomes more or less mechanical and we can cover long distances without giving any conscious thought to the small movements with which we control our bicycle.

### 7.2.3   Style and choice of food

Style is the third important mechanism through which cultural codes materialize in consumption. Style began to emerge in Europe at around the same time and in the same places as new tradition-breaking lifestyles. Those lifestyles and the style factors aimed at shaping everyday life were indeed so closely interwoven that they virtually determined one another. Not directly, however, but through a third factor, i.e. taste.

#### *7.2.3.1   Style and the problem of taste*

In the seventeenth and eighteenth centuries style became an important social determinant as the highest strata in European societies adopted it as their social standard (Gronow 1990, 103). At the same time, style emerged as a focal point for social debate and philosophizing, attracting some of the greatest minds of the day from Voltaire to Kant and Hume. The problem of taste was laid bare but not resolved.

Taste was an important topic of debate even in antiquity. One of the conclusions then was that taste was about *immediate sensation,* which is always and necessarily *individual and subjective.* For this reason *de gustibus non est disputandum,* there is no disputing about matters of taste. As a purely subjective category, however, taste could not provide an acceptable social standard. Therefore, as early as the eighteenth century, taste was also understood as a general phenomenon, as a binding social fact that could be taken as an *educational ideal*. And that, of course, meant it was necessary to be able to discuss matters of taste whenever and as often as people wanted, for the outcome of that discussion would decide what was regarded as legitimate taste and the proper social standard. On the one hand, then, taste was not to be separated from individual sensation, but on the other hand, it was to reflect the universal principle on the basis of which social classifications were made (Schaper 1987, 39–40).

Kant tried to solve the problem of taste, the understanding of taste as a subjective experience and universal phenomenon, by looking for a space that would provide a vantage point from which to transcend the subjective within taste (Gronow 1997, 11). That space had to be necessary, universal and above all a priori. By necessary and universal, Kant meant a space that was beyond specific social interests. Only from such a vantage point would it be possible to arrive at objective statements about taste (Schaper 1987, 45, 49) and to lay down general and, at once, legitimate taste standards that were applicable to all members of society.

However, the problem was that no such space existed in empirical reality and therefore it was impossible to extract the subjective element out of taste. The only way to overcome the conflict between general and specific in matters of taste, therefore, was through the *sociologization of taste* (Gronow 1990, 103; Gronow 1997, 11). The taste adopted by one social group was represented as a universal criterion of good taste that applied to society as a whole. This is the route followed by Pierre Bourdieu (1984, 364), for example, as he elevates the taste of the upper middle classes as the legitimate taste of society. The same applies to Stephen Mennell (1985), who describes the taste of the nobility as legitimate taste.

This is problematic, however. Since the definition of a particular taste as a universal standard does not vitiate the subjective element of taste, the legitimacy of that standard cannot be firmly established. The prevailing taste can always be called into question, either by asking whether some commonly accepted practice really is in good taste or by making demeaning or derogatory comments about an acquired taste scale. Both of these strategies have long been everyday reality. For example, they were both applied by the bourgeoisie when it called into question the taste of the nobility (Mennell 1991). It is because of this questioning that we still refer to the unwritten rules of taste. If they were written, they would need to be constantly revised and updated. For the same reason it is not possible to compare taste to a norm because it does have the same kind of strong steering effect (see Noro 1991, 81). However, even in matters of taste, not just anything goes. There has always been a thin unspoken line between good taste and bad. For this reason the prevailing thinking has been that it is indeed possible to educate taste (Schaper 1987, 47).

From the seventeenth century onwards the training of taste became a major mission for the nobility in Europe's political heartland; from the eighteenth century this mission was largely taken over by the patrician class. A whole line of cookbooks was published to this end, including not just recipes but also information and advice on manners and customs (Mennell 1985, 69–101). But guides were even published on the refinement of taste, such as David Hume's *Of Refinement in the Arts* (1987 [1742]). Ultimately the purpose of this literature was to ensure that these rules of bourgeois taste were assimilated from early childhood; that they were internalized as dispositions. Dispositions provided the foundation for collective taste, or as Kant would have it, *sensus communis* (see also Maffesoli 1995, 80). Adopted dispositions had no coercive power but they guided consumption choices and life decisions, insofar as they were unconscious. When dispositions were conscious, Rousseau (1985) says they were used strategically to further one's own interests and to make social distinctions. Bourdieu has subsequently developed his sociological analysis based on this observation (Bourdieu 1980; Bourdieu 1986, 240, 300; Bourdieu 1990, 60, 131).

Taste thus became an important external and internal determinant of social group identity. What I mean by the external definition of identity is what Bourdieu had in mind when he said that taste had become a *practice of classification* that the social group aimed to establish as a visible criterion of good taste (Bourdieu 1986, 299). He has described this form of symbolic struggle as *objective* (Bourdieu 1990, 134). The definition of internal identity, then, refers to *subjective symbolic struggle*. What this means is that the purpose of taste-training is ultimately to change the way that people perceive and value the social world. The end result is a behavioural disposition that, like a convention, finds expression in bodily gestures and habitual reactions and choices. This might well explain why Bourdieu himself associates his concept of *habitus* with taste (Bourdieu 1990, 131). Taste reflects the individual's *style*.

Combining *habitus* and taste is a problematic solution. On the one hand, Bourdieu suggests that *habitus* is an 'ontological and preconscious' disposition to act in a particular way under changeable circumstances (Bourdieu 1980; Bourdieu 1978; Bourdieu 1990, 77). On this basis one might assume that once a given *habitus* has been adopted, the individual will follow the corresponding mode of conduct, and that *habitus* in this sense is comparable to a convention, adherence to which involves no conscious reflection on the underlying rule. This is confirmed by Bourdieu himself. An individual conditioned to a given *habitus* no longer makes any choices, for those choices are made in advance by the *habitus* itself (Bourdieu 1984, 474; see also Gartman 1991, 438). On the other hand, we learn that *habitus* is a form of capital –but in contrast to a convention it can be applied creatively. *Habitus* reproduces and transforms itself (Bourdieu 1980) and in that sense is indeterminate (Bourdieu 1990, 77). For *habitus* to work in this way it would need to be applied intentionally and strategically under changeable circumstances, in full awareness of the rules that govern it.

It is quite clear that because of his reluctance to use objectifying language, Bourdieu lapses into illogicalities (see Lau 2004). *Habitus* cannot be preconscious if it is at once intentionally reproduced and transformed. In a sympathetic interpretation, it seems that in his production from the 1980s onwards, Bourdieu leans towards the latter standpoint, but there are other interpretations as well (see Alexander 1995). In this frame of interpretation, *habitus* can be associated with the concept of taste, which further links it with the idea of style. My own thinking here is that taste is not a preconscious blind principle of choice but rather a *style-consciousness* that is being worked upon and that is the outcome of conscious development and refinement. However, this does not mean that taste changes constantly. On the contrary, through ritualization and habituation, it tends to become mainstreamed. Once taste has become cemented as part of the individual's *lifestyle*, any changes may require special effort.

Taste-training is not just an individual matter but a lasting theme in the social history of modern times. Queen Elizabeth I was one of the pioneers of new thinking about consumption. In the late sixteenth and early seventeenth century she made sweeping changes to the principles of financial management in her court. (The same was repeated in France and Spain.) A Protestant by conviction, she wanted to use her own as well as England's national wealth to create economic and social benefit. To this end she took advantage of the increased market supply to assert her role as leader of the country. At the same time, Elizabeth I forced the peerage to follow her lead. Peers, therefore, no longer contented themselves with stockpiling the receivables they collected from peasants but turned them into money. And that, in turn, was refined into new styles that they used in order to try and climb the court hierarchy.

This did not mean that old traditions and conventions were discarded. Indulgence and pleasure continued to characterize everyday life in European court societies. There was, however, a conscious movement away from indulgence in that new kinds of practices and new rules of behaviour were introduced that departed from old bodily practices. Slowly but surely, they became like second nature to high nobility (cf. Elias 1982). The limitations imposed by the old moral economy broke down, which prompted a dramatic surge in interest in luxury products (Braudel 1982, 178).[5]

The new habits of taste that the peerage began to develop from the seventeenth century onwards were not yet routinized, however; this was still a tentative search for novelty, a conscious shaping of the social space and an exercise in building a 'class body'. The purpose was not so much to set oneself apart from other social classes but rather to create a coherent social identity. It was therefore more about collective inclusion rather than exclusion, but from the outside it appeared as a break from other classes, including the lower nobility (cf. Burke 1983, 302–312; Thompson 1983, 219). This came to have relevance in the eighteenth and especially the nineteenth century when the bourgeoisie in European trade cities began to develop their own distinctive lifestyles that differed from old traditions and conventions.

Taste-training among the nobility started from eating and dressing. This is hardly a coincidence. On the one hand, the growth of global trade had given European courts and major cities access to foods and cloths they had never seen before and that allowed them to wage a battle over the external determinants of the standards of good taste. On the other hand, food and clothing had always been core areas of taste education in the sense that they involved a strong corporeal element. Unashamed gluttony and 'bad' dressing brought humans too close to nature for comfort. Therefore, the minimum criterion for good taste was to break cleanly away from nature. This perhaps also helps to explain the disapproving references made in the teaching of manners to the animal kingdom ('You eat like a pig').

Later, by the nineteenth century, taste began to spread as a classification practice from food and clothing to every possible sphere of life. Eventually, as it became more prevalent, it developed into a coherent *style of consumption* within a particular social group, a collective principle of consumption choices focused on *objects of consumption* (Gronow 1997, 99). One of its distinctive characteristics is that separate consumption choices refer to one another and stand as symbols for one another (Bourdieu 1986, 297–300).

As a system of consumption choices, style works according to the totemic principle: the social group uses style as a marker of its distinction in society. Since this is an aggregate-level event, it is not consciously planned or thought out but rather an indication of knowing one's own as well as others' place in society (Bourdieu 1990, 131). At the individual level, of course, choices are conscious and strategic. Individuals within social groups are keen to use these choices to set themselves apart from other groups, even from their own. This kind of approach to consumption emphasizes the social-identity model. It works as long as the quantity of goods produced and brought into the market is more or less constant. However, the situation changes when after the mid-twentieth century we enter the society of abundance that is flooded with novelties. Here, the maintenance of a consumption style at aggregate level, in other words as a characteristic of a particular social class, runs into trouble (Gronow 1997, 29), and at the same time the style-based choices made by the representatives of this group become wider.

From the 1960s onwards when people started to have more leisure time and to move around much more, when the service sector in national economies began to expand and when class boundaries began to crumble, the close connection between style and social class was severed (cf. Featherstone 1991, 110). Furthermore, as people were earning much more than before, they had greater freedom to choose their own way of life regardless of their social class. This led to a rapid diversification of lifestyles. The relationship between these new lifestyles and social class was no longer simple and straightforward. Indeed, it is reasonable to assume today that there is at least as much variation in lifestyles within modern social classes as there is between those classes.

### 7.2.3.2   *Prestige foods and trickle down*

Before the market was saturated with novelties, conscious class-based distinction could be accomplished in one of two ways: *either the prevailing good taste was disputed* and made laughable (see e.g. Bahtin 1995) or *ever-finer taste distinctions were developed* within the confines of the prevailing taste – as Baldassare Castiglione (1959) encourages people to do as early as the sixteenth century in his *The Book of the Courtier* – and new objects of consumption were acquired that differed from the old ones. The former strategies have been part of the arsenal of ethnic minorities and lower social strata in their symbolic struggles. This has often gone unnoticed in the social sciences. The latter strategies, then, have typically been applied by European elites, where people have had ready access to the two key resources required by these strategies, i.e. time and money.

Distinction through food has led, firstly, to European (as well as Chinese) elites buying specialities for their dinner tables; luxuries that others have not had the economic or legal resources to acquire (Goody 1984, 98–99; Mintz 1985, 18; Schivelbusch 1992). On the other hand, instead of indulging in gluttony, elites have begun to refine their eating habits, to create *new kinds of taste nuances and aesthetics*, to develop modern hedonism. Once the social differences appearing in consumption have become established, every possible avenue including legal action has been pursued to maintain them. Standards of dress have been specified for each social class, including the required material of clothing (e.g. velvet) and pattern and design (e.g. button arrangements), as we shall see later. By the end of the nineteenth century, however, it was necessary to discontinue legal regulation, allowing the consumption items adopted by the nobility to start trickling down to lower social strata.

It did not take long for social scientists to realize that elites wanted to set themselves apart and to assimilate ever-new consumption items. Thorstein Veblen drew attention to this in his moralizing critique of what he called 'conspicuous consumption' among the upper classes: they specifically wanted to purchase consumption items that were difficult to obtain and that they thought enhanced the prestige of the owner (Veblen 1994). These goods have subsequently been described as *status goods, positional goods* or *prestige products*.

Veblen furthermore assumed that over time both prestige goods and other aspects of upper-class consumption styles would trickle down from the highest to the lowest social classes. Georg Simmel had earlier suggested a similar view. The reason for this phenomenon, it was thought, was that every class lower down in the social hierarchy was always inclined to imitate the choices and behaviours of the classes immediately above them. C. Wright Mills referred to the middle-class's status-enhancing and competitive consumption (Mills 1976, 163; see also Feldman & Thielbar 1976).

It has been suggested that this mechanism is still applicable today. Bourdieu, for instance, approximates this view in his studies of consumption in different social classes, even though he takes critical distance from the idea of intentional conspicuous consumption (Bourdieu 1990, 133). And Bourdieu is not alone; in fact he has lots of kindred souls, even though they do not necessarily share his theoretical perspective (see Mason 1981, 67–96; McCracken 1988, 93–94).

In other words, there is still relatively broad support for the notion that consumption habits tend to converge based on imitation among social classes. And it is no doubt true that the trickle-down mechanism applies most particularly in the case of status goods that require substantial investment, such as cars, mobile phones or yachts. However, it is not quite clear what exactly it is that in this instance trickles down. Besides, there is also the question as to whether the trickle-down phenomenon occurs in food and other less capital-intensive goods. To find out, we need first of all to explore what it is that gives value to a certain food or meal.

There is no simple and unambiguous answer to this question, for it obviously varies from one culture to the next. However, Derrick B. Jelliffe is probably in the right when he makes the generalization that prestige foods are those that are reserved for special occasions (weddings, funerals etc.). Also, they are usually expensive and hard to come by, either because they are out of season or not locally available. For these reasons availability was traditionally restricted to the merchant class that was engaged in global trade or to other higher social classes (Jelliffe 1967, 279–280). Typical examples of such foods would include oysters, caviar and swan meat – a special favourite of the British Royal Family. Indeed, this gives some indication of what prestige foods are all about: they are *exceptional in terms of content* and essentially *luxury* items.

Having unusual exceptional food is a particularly important part of special occasions but impressive ingredients and foodstuffs can also be included in everyday meals. Herein lies a potential threat to prestige food: the more common and frequently used the food becomes the greater the risk that it loses its status as prestige food. This has been the fate of most spices (sugar, salt, pepper) and stimulants (tobacco, tea, cocoa, coffee). As they became daily staples from the nineteenth century onwards (Tannahill 1975, 94, 219; Schivelbusch 1992; Gronow 1997, 90; Kurlansky 2003) they were increasingly regarded as 'everyday' foods as opposed to 'valuable' foodstuffs (truffles, caviar). However, these thought categories should be regarded not only as economic but also *moral categories* (Sahlins 1976, 214).

Since there is always the possibility that prestige foods may be downgraded into ordinary everyday food consumed even by common folk, elites are under constant pressure to discover new prestige foods and so keep their distance from other social classes. This is an on-going struggle because whenever they have had the material resources to do so, the members of those other classes have been inclined to imitate the behaviours of the elite. They have not always had to use the exact same goods as the elite; counterfeit and pirate production has seen to that. However, these two tendencies, *distinction* and *imitation* have explained why the contents of the cultural categories of valuable and cheap have constantly kept changing.

The consumption of prestige foods is an external symbolic means with which members of the elite can demonstrate their unity. This, in itself, is something that is easy to imitate; but why do so? That status foods are exceptional is not reason enough to imitate the upper classes. That is, among other population groups such imitation may meet not with approval but rather with a sense of resentment. There must be a special motive for imitation. As it has turned out, one such motive is that the prestige foods favoured by high society have widely been regarded as special privileges of upper-class gourmets (Bourdieu 1986, 300–301; see also Sayer 2003, 352).

### 7.2.3.3 Limits of the trickle-down mechanism

So are there still foodstuffs in the European food basket that are considered special delicacies and that trickle down the social hierarchy? I shall attempt to unravel these two questions by first addressing the latter one.

When the trickle-down mechanism was first 'invented' (Tarde 1890, Sombart 1967, Veblen 1994, Simmel 1997), consumption across Europe and the United States had already assumed many of the forms that are familiar to us today, following the significant expansion of wage employment and consumerization, the establishment of global trade and the branding of goods. At that time strong social bonds were also eroding, although not completely disappearing (e.g. Scott 2002). Individualization gathered momentum and new lifestyles began to emerge in major cities.

In metropoles the social scene was rather different from other parts of the country in that class distinctions were less obvious and conspicuous than in rural communities. It was therefore necessary to accentuate those distinctions by means of consumption. This was done by developing an 'eye for style' and by styling public behaviour, as Simmel observed in his metropolis essay (Simmel 1981, 219–222; see also Simmel 1997 [1900] and 2005; Sennett 1976; Noro 1991). In this carousel of styles, the dazzling consumption that had characterized old society and that was previously restricted to courts and manor, now received its first public outing (cf. Mason 1981, 95). This could not but affect consumption in other social classes too, particularly as the rapid advances in technology had made it possible to imitate the elite's unique consumption items and to produce them on a mass scale (Wilson 1985, 41).

If there is undisputed empirical evidence to support the existence of a trickle-down effect in the late nineteenth and early twentieth century, the situation is completely different in the latter half of the twentieth century, which saw class structures throughout the modern world become more and more complicated and class boundaries become less distinct, at the same time as the peerage lost its monopoly to define good taste. The blurring of class boundaries is a consequence of the growth of social and geographical mobility and changes in the industrial structure, the dramatic rise in real earnings, individualization and changes sweeping the workplace. Furthermore, thanks to the latter two trends, the working class has been in the position to spend more money on optional consumption and to acquire the positional goods that used to be exclusive to the upper classes, such as expensive designer clothes and overseas' holidays.

Indeed, it is only on rare occasions now that the concept of *positionality*, in the sense of being related to social status, can be associated with commodities. Within the terrain covered by this concept there has been movement in two different directions, firstly from the class bond to the quality of goods and their moral value, and secondly back to their owners. Consumption in the upper classes has first of all labelled some products as 'high class'. Secondly, it is assumed that the people using them are consequently 'of a higher class' than others (Sayer 2003, 352). From this it follows that every epoch seems to create its own positional goods. Following the erosion of external class boundaries the social connections of these goods are no longer as obvious and straightforward as before (cf. Hradil 1989, 122). As a result, it is very difficult to predict the direction and pathways of the spread of positional goods.

Thirdly, Bourdieu's understanding of class-based distinctions and the view that it is the working-class's lot to passively accommodate itself to those distinctions can be so interpreted that consumption culture has very little to do with moral value. Even though the positional goods that are visible at any given time are connected to social classes and even though they may trickle down the social ladder it does not necessarily mean that moral values trickle down, too. On the one hand, their moral superiority does not trickle down the social ladder along with their physical trickling down. On the other hand, the moral value of the commodities used by lower social classes does not, de facto, have to be lower than the value of the upper classes' status goods. Even though they carry no associations of social class they may still be first-class goods (Sayer 2003, 352).

The reduced ability of upper classes to decide upon the criteria of good taste is, fourthly, a consequence of the increased ambivalence of their position in relation to the lowest social classes – the peasants and working classes. Society has also had to hand over its collective educational mission and the production of publicity to the so-called new middle class, specifically to its 'mediacracy'. However, I will here pass over the role of this class in propagating new kinds of dispositions; suffice it to note that according to Bourdieu, it seems to be more preoccupied with providing guidance for the consumption of culture products and customs rather than with taste-training in general (see Bourdieu 1984). Instead, I turn my attention to how the relationship between the highest and lowest social groups has changed in the battle over good taste.

When the nobility in Europe's leading courts began to develop new ways of living and when their French members in particular began to make ever-finer taste distinctions, they took it upon themselves, perhaps unwittingly, to create a lasting set of taste standards. This, inevitably, led to internal competition (see Elias 1982, 91–201). In order to make an impression in court society it was necessary not just to conform to accepted tastes, to identify with the reference group, but also to set oneself apart, to depart in what was believed to be a positive direction. It also required making ever-more refined distinctions within the boundaries of good taste. While the pursuit of identification led to ritualistic conformity to etiquette, the refinement of taste distinctions in turn led to dandyism, the inordinate expression of one's own excellence. Together with ritualistic behaviour this has cast a negative shadow over adherence to good taste, over what is regarded as 'civilized' conduct.

As pointed out, the 'civilized' conduct of European elites has been above all a cultural demarcation from nature, both positively and negatively loaded. It has had both a sophisticated and a degenerated stamp. These cultural stamps have been contrasted with the ways of life of the peasants and the working classes, who have been considered to differ from nature only marginally. However, these two ways of life have not been regarded as equal. While the working-class's way of life dominated by the machine and characterized by rough leisure pursuits has been described in negative terms as brutal and overtly physical, the peasants' traditional way of life has received positive and idealizing descriptions that highlight its natural and genuine features (Ehn & Löfgren 1986, 40; see also Klinge 1972).

Over the past century then, cultural elites have begun to begrudge the working classes and peasantry their intense corporeality and presumed authenticity, as if these were their 'paradise lost'. As a consequence, the dispersion of styles has happened not only from the top down but also from the bottom up. Elites have begun to pick up style elements from ethnic subcultures and working classes and have incorporated them into their own circle of life (tango, rustic furniture etc.). Trickle down has been followed by 'spring up' (McCracken 1988, 95), which shows that the value of the commodities used by different social classes is not only class-dependent.

The springing up of style elements in the social hierarchy has caused a pandemonium of tastes in modernizing European societies, making it extremely difficult to predict the direction they will take. This does not of course, in itself, disprove the validity of Veblen's trickle-down mechanism but it is certainly harder to prove that it works in the area of food. Over time, the differences in food-content choices between different social strata have become less pronounced (Mennell 1991, 145–151; see also Bourdieu 1984). Besides, the confused mixture of styles, the tendency to elevate what used to be cheap and simple foods and on the other hand to depreciate old prestige foods has very much complicated the task of identifying which foods are perceived as true delicacies in our cultural circle, and which of them warrant being treated as status foods.

Besides, there is no empirical evidence that all foods that are regarded at any given time as delicacies trickle down from the upper classes. Although some positional goods have trickled down the social ladder and no doubt continue to do so, this is not true of all the commodities favoured and reserved by the elite. There are no doubt several reasons for this, but one clearly stands out. That is, trickle-down theory forgets that taste is always inherently subjective. Only some elite foods are accepted in lower social classes, and in turn only some of the foods that are their favourites are adopted by the upper social classes, and even then they will only be accepted as everyday foods.

Put simply then, *trickle-down theory confuses the location of commodities or styles in the social hierarchy with the meanings assigned to them by people occupying different positions in that hierarchy.* For instance, it is by no means certain that the middle classes want to imitate all upper-class styles or that people in the working class want to imitate all middle-class styles, as the trickle-down theory would have us believe. Wanting is dependent on the meanings given to those styles by people in different social positions. It is only those meanings that will decide whether or not those styles are desirable. This, however, is a question that even Bourdieu has not addressed; even he locates the classification struggle within the bourgeoisie (see also Gartman 1991, 438), assuming that whatever is higher up in the social hierarchy must be desirable lower down. This may be true of the new middle classes that possess cultural good will but not necessarily of the working class and peasantry. After all, it is precisely the negative determinants associated with upper-class life, its degeneration and artificiality that give rise to a sense of repulsion, if not outright amusement, in different population groups, even in the middle strata.

### 7.2.3.4 *New social anchorage for food styles*

When there is only one social hierarchy and when that hierarchy is clear, outwardly symbols and signs of style such as special delicacies can certainly trickle down, provided that they are valued on the lower rungs of the hierarchy. But what can be said about whole styles of consumption and food styles as part of them? Is the trickle-down mechanism applicable to these styles as well? The answer depends on how they are understood. If consumption styles are understood in the way that Bourdieu suggests, as deeply buried corporeal dispositions internalized by people occupying different positions in society, then the answer is no. Consumption and food styles cannot be passed on from one social group to another, even when one group or class in society wields considerable economic and symbolic power. This is because, firstly, consumption styles and taste also involve moral values that are not as homogeneous as the trickle-down process requires. Secondly, dispositions of action and cognitive structures are not transferred into vacuums, as Bourdieu himself points out, but into socially and culturally constituted spaces.

Newly assimilated dispositions are always confronted with existing earlier dispositions, which are not easy to root out because they have been buried as corporeal unconscious 'practical practices' (Bourdieu 1990, 65, 131). For this reason the elites' action dispositions cannot simply trickle down the walls of the social pyramid. On the contrary, trickling down will be slowed and resisted by earlier dispositions, such as the working-class's internalized cognitive and emotional dispositions that are liable to reproduce class structures, as Paul Willis has shown in his studies of English working-class boys and their difficulties of adjusting to school (Willis 1977).

The actual foundation of styles, the emotional and cognitive disposition to act in a unified way, does therefore not trickle in any direction because it is closely tied up, through education and personal life history, with the social positions to which people are attached. People's class position and consumption style or 'class sense' (Bourdieu 1980) reciprocally reproduce each other. This, however, requires that classes are homogeneous – which of course they are not and probably never have been. With the single exception of the nobility, location, race and religion have provided a stronger anchorage for social classes than class position. Styles, for their part, because of the connections just mentioned, have been heterogeneous even within the same class position (Thompson 1983).

If it is assumed that class position and consumption and food style reciprocally reproduce one another, this means we also have to accept the idea that society is heavily deterministic. Once individuals have internalized a class taste, an emotional and cognitive disposition, they are glued to that place in society to which they have happened to be socialized. At the same time, society inevitably becomes static, a machine that repeats itself ad infinitum (Miller 1989, 201–202). Bourdieu's theory of style or *habitus*, therefore, provides only limited tools for the analysis of social change. From this, then, it follows that the theory does not correspond very well with present-day reality, for the modern world is in a constant state of economic and social flux.

One might assume that the detachment from 'class sense' is manifested in two different ways. The first, of course, is that consumption and food styles are not as closely bound up with class position as was previously assumed.[6] One indication of this is that people do not react to the same class positions in a single, unified way. Local factors alone cause attitudes to vary. From this it follows that one very rarely sees a homogeneous 'class sense', for instance a working-class culture; we are more likely to see class cultures, in the plural. This, however, does not yet mean that variation in consumption and food styles within the same class position is greater than that seen between class positions. Styles and their underlying dispositions can still be class styles in a broad sense, even though there is internal variation. In other words, a homology between social status and *habitus* does not exist but rather *homologies* do.[7]

Another more radical form of detachment from class styles is where internalized dispositions are not deeply buried corporeally. In this instance it is possible to break with these styles at any time. This is, in fact, what Bourdieu seems to think himself, as he says that *habitus* is indeterminate and that it more or less completely reproduces itself (Bourdieu 1990, 77). This, of course, opens up the possibility that *habitus* not only restricts the choices available to individuals but also serves as a tool that allows for variation with regard to individual strategic-consumption styles and tastes.

When the relationship between styles and social status is so understood that individuals occupying the same social status can develop different dispositions and that those dispositions are not routine-like deeply buried behavioural dispositions, it is no longer necessary to look upon the cycle of reproduction between social status and consumption style as predetermined and closed. This means it is natural to think that consumption styles are not strictly class-based. A polysemia of consumption and food styles prevails even among people who occupy the same social-status positions, both historically and contemporaneously – which is precisely why there is little point disputing matters of taste.

However, we must beware of overextending our critique of the thinking that ties social classes together with consumption and food style (e.g. Featherstone 1991, 95, 110). We clearly do not live in a mass society that is individualized through and through and styles have not become completely detached from their class foundations, as has been made clear by Bourdieu and many others in their investigations of cultural products (Bourdieu 1984; Bourdieu 1986; Becker & Nowak 1981; Rahkonen & Purhonen 2004; Räsänen 2005). Likewise, there is no convincing empirical evidence of people toying with their consumption and food styles. If this does happen outside the television screen or carnivals or popular restaurants, it mainly concerns outward elements of food style rather than prestige foods.

Consumption and food styles may, on the other hand, be fragmentary and disjointed. The heterogeneity of styles is due to the fact that they are at least as sensitive to variations in social situations as they are to class background. In this case style requirements are adapted to the specific situation and physical scene. The taste and aesthetic qualities expected of a hurried lunch at a fast-food place are completely different from those at a nice white table-cloth establishment at dinner time (e.g. Warde 1997). Nonetheless, even the fast-food place furthers the 'function of taste' (Bourdieu), whether the purpose is simply to replenish the human machine or to kill time.

Good taste is not, however, only bound up with the situation, social background and personal history, but also with the dining company. The most important aspect of food choice, in this case, is that it hits the right style register, that it fits the situation (time and place) and the presumed eating habits of the people with whom one is sharing a meal (see e.g. Prättälä 1989, 29–30, 36–37; Schulze 1992, 291–330; Warde & Martens 2000, 69–91, 204–207). When there are only men or only women around the table, food choices may be different than when one is eating alone or sharing a meal with a loved one or with one's teenage son or daughter. In fact it is quite possible that these kinds of factors are more decisive nowadays than social class.

Despite their possible fragmentation, therefore, food styles are still socially anchored but in a more complex manner than Bourdieu fashions for us. This anchorage is further complicated by the application of prevailing gustemes to food choices. When food is regarded simply as a medium to achieve some goal, which is what athletes or health enthusiasts (or people on a diet) are inclined to do, then the choice of content is more important than style. For instance, the athlete who is on a strict fitness regime will be interested in the food gusteme strong/light. His or her food choices will be in the former category to ensure adequate protein intake for muscle development. However, not just any high-protein food will do; there are also some style requirements. By contrast, for people whose way of life gives absolute priority to health or sacredness, the main choice criterion is the physical and symbolic lightness of food (see Prättälä 1989, 58) – but again, not just anything will do. In other words, there is no single class-based mechanism that steers tastes in today's fragmented and pluralistic society.

Secondly, historical research on taste has two opposite but mutually complementary ways of understanding the change of taste. The first covers the notion presented earlier about the *constant refinement of taste*. This position, already advanced by Baron de Montesquieu (Meyer 2000, 38–39), is represented by Bourdieu's view of taste as a hierarchical class-based compulsion to distinguish oneself from others in the upper classes, while the working class takes a conformist attitude to taste. Another conception of taste is connected with *authenticity*. This position is represented among others by Rousseau. For him, 'snobbery', the development of taste towards ever-finer distinctions, is a reflection of the hierarchical nature of society, of the fact that it is the elite who get to dictate what is 'good' taste and what is not. When the elite criteria are in place, people give up looking for what pleases them and turn their attention instead to finding how they can set themselves apart from others. Rousseau considers this an alienated principle of taste formation (Meyer 2000, 44). As far as he is concerned, all people are equally competent taste judges. When good taste is by nature a sociological phenomenon the preferences of the majority represent good taste.

When these two understandings of food styles are coupled with food style as a collective or individual choice criterion, we get four different combinations. Style appears, on the one hand, as an individual tendency to err on the side of caution and choose what is familiar, i.e. conventional food, and to avoid anything alien and any strong flavours. The opposite style is characterized by an *individual pursuit of variety* and a *search for new taste experiences.* According to Ann-Mari Sellerberg (1978), higher educated women in their early thirties are more inclined than others to try something new, whereas less educated men over 50 and living in rural areas are more likely to go for familiar tastes and to look upon food primarily as a source of body energy.

On the other hand, taste can also be understood as a *collective disposition* to combine food ingredients in the 'right' authentic way (cf. the Chinese ying/yang principle of combining sweet and sour; see e.g. Hallenberg 2004, 24–28). The idea is to engage in collective fine-tuning of styles and to mark oneself apart from other social groups. The former strategy can be seen as a *paying homage to tradition* and the *good taste it represents* as opposed to *experimentation that breaks with tradition* (cf. classical French cooking à la Careme & Escoffier as opposed to *la nouvelle cuisine* that started in the late 1960s; Rao, Monin & Durand 2003, 799–803; see also Ilmonen 1990, 44).

Figure 7.2 presents a summary illustration of these simplified dimensions of taste (cf. Douglas 1996, 45).

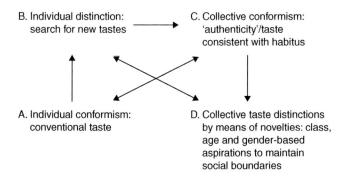

*Figure 7.2* Style as a two-dimensional social mechanism of choice

In this figure the diagonals drawn between A and C and between B and D can be regarded as socially asymmetric in relation to each other. People who conform to authentic taste do not usually approve of those who are drawn towards the diagonal of distinction and experimentation. They tend to reject all and any experimentation with food, both at the individual and collective levels. The more adventurous, on the other hand, may also choose the foods that are favoured by conformists. For them, a conformist choice may in itself be a kind of experiment. In principle, however, the two diagonals are each other's opposites, although the positions that individuals and collective groups take up on these diagonals vary depending on the situation and dining company. Even conformists who travel to the Greek islands no longer spend their entire holiday eating meatballs and mash as they did in the 1970s (although there no doubt still are some who do). Instead, they might be tempted to venture into the world of tourist menus, whereas the adventurous experimentalist will in the same situation try any of the 'genuine' local dishes that are on offer at the tourist resort. However, these choices will not affect the conformists' and the experimentalists' basic dispositions when they return home. In making their food choices they will receive style guidance from the *gustemes of distinction (towards something new) and authenticity (learned)*.

Gustemes do not, however, resolve the inherent conflict between the individual and collective nature of taste. Therefore, Gronow suggests that we connect good taste with fashion instead; that could help establish a firmer foundation for our analysis. Fashion does not require adherence to the same kind of principle of good or legitimate taste as style does (Gronow 1997, 91). There would also be the added benefit that fashion is a more inclusive principle of selection than style. The latter only covers the objects of consumption and the way they are combined, whereas the former 'characterizes the whole social pattern of distinction and adaptation' (ibid., 99). Indeed, Gronow's solution can help to overcome the contradiction inherent in taste between the individual and the collective.

But his solution is not without its flaws. As Simmel points out, fashion is merely the product of social and formal psychological needs. There are no grounds whatsoever for its manifestations (Simmel 1997 [1900]). According to Simmel, *fashion has nothing at all to do with objects of consumption*, but it only serves the consumer and the consumer's needs for social distinctions and conformities. In this regard it is no more inclusive than style, but is a distinct mechanism of selection.

Secondly, fashion people, or in Simmel's words 'fashion clowns', are not in fact in the frontline of distinction or pioneers of new fashion at all; it just seems that they are marching at the front of the fashion community but in reality they are being led. Even they do not make true distinctions based on fashion – they simply adapt to its requirements.

Thirdly, not everyone follows fashions, yet they may still make choices based on their style – whatever that is. Besides, some people may go against fashion as a matter of principle, go out of their way to avoid anything and everything that is fashionable, and in this sense break away from the principles of distinction and identification included in fashion, choosing instead to follow their own style as 'critical' consumers. Indeed, we should not yet discard style as an analytical tool for the investigation of consumption and social action.

### 7.2.4 Fashion and choice of food

Fashion is the last but by no means the least of the social mechanisms that implement consumption choices. It has its origin in the same historical process as way of life and style, of which it initially was an integral part. Fashion started in European court societies, most notably in the French court in the sixteenth and seventeenth centuries. It was there that the idea first came up that it was shameful to wear outdated clothes that had gone out of style (Wilson 1985, 20). However, this thinking was still confined to court dress and continued to remain so until the French Revolution. One of the reasons for this was that in many places dress was restricted by legal means, the purpose of which was to preserve distinctions in rank and other social distinctions reflected in dress. These were beginning to break down with the rise of the power-hungry bourgeoisie (ibid., 24).

#### *7.2.4.1 Fashion and time*

The Industrial Revolution dispensed with the legal regulation of what people were allowed to wear and, consequently, fashion was 'democratized' in the nineteenth century. Women were particularly instrumental in disseminating the idea throughout the population. In the European metropoles of the day they adopted new styles of dress that began to obscure the connection between fashion and social class. However, that connection was not completely severed, for in the early twentieth century Simmel still wrote that fashions are always class fashions. But this view was already being contested. As Durkheim's great rival Gabriel Tarde had already pointed out, fashion was anchored to *time* (Tarde 1890 according to Sellerberg 1987, 111; see also Simmel 1997 [1900]).

The fading of the connection between fashion and social class, on the one hand, and the attachment of fashion to time, on the other, was largely due to the way that fashion worked, to its appearance in society as *novelty*. The novelty of fashion is independent of the technical/ functional use value; it is novelty for its own sake. The fascination of fashion lies in the sense of nowness it creates. A fashion item is a *sign of here and nowness*. However, no item can retain its novelty value forever – as soon as it begins to spread more widely its novelty value will start to wear off. It is at this point that the next 'novelty' enters the scene, picking up the thread of fashion. In the aphoristic words of Walter Benjamin, fashion is a feminine usher that mocks death. At the very moment that death closes in to strike, fashion moves on to some other place (Benjamin 2003 [1939]). Indeed, there is nothing curious about the understanding of fashion as the eternal return of novelty (Simmel 1997 [1900]; Benjamin 2003 [1939]).

But death never completely misses his mark. In its relentless pursuit it wipes the slate clean of old fashion. If it didn't, there would not be enough room for new fashion. As old fashion withers away, so new fashion emerges to take its place. This, however, is never a clean-cut changeover as the withering of the old and emergence of the new are overlapping processes. The departure of the old and appearance of the new are therefore visible at one and the same time. This simultaneity draws the focus of the consciousness that follows fashion to the present time, which at once implies an emphasis on variety. This has its most intense manifestations in the middle strata of society (Simmel 1997 [1900]; Gronow 1997, 90).

Although fashions keep following one another in relentless succession, as if on a conveyor belt, the break between old and new must nonetheless be clear. The new fashion must make it clear that the old fashion is ragged and out-dated. At the same time, it must be able to prove and justify its own here and nowness. New fashion does that by asserting that it reflects the current spirit of our times, current social, economic, political and aesthetic trends. This is indeed how new fashion needs to be seen: *it is an attempt to give shape to the spirit of our time*. This requires a tightrope performance. If the fashion designer is too cautious in his or her interpretation of the spirit of the time, then it will be impossible to seriously challenge the old fashion. If, on the other hand, the designer is too bold in his or her interpretations of current trends, then the new fashion runs the risk of being perceived as too daring or as causing offence (Blumer 1969, 279; Sellerberg 1987, 83, 101–108, 156).

However, attachment to time will not alone allow fashion to keep up its perpetual movement. It must also have a social foundation in order to avoid the trap by death. So what is it that can support and sustain fashion in society? Simmel offers an answer that still seems applicable today. He says that fashion is a *compromise* between two human tendencies, i.e. separation from the social group or individuation, on the one hand, and assimilation with the group, on the other (Simmel 1997 [1900]).

However, this compromise would be impossible if it concerned the contents of fashion. The dualism can only be resolved at the *level of form*. This leads Simmel to conclude that fashion is merely a form that is arbitrarily materialized through different contents (Simmel 1997 [1900]). Fashion does this primarily over the dimension 'time' by declaring that the most recent is always the best. Every social group has to adapt to this condition, which is laid down by fashion itself. Therefore, the attempts by elite groups to distinguish themselves from other groups also take place within fashion's temporal framework, i.e. in relation to earlier fashions. This has its impacts on the shape assumed by fashion but it is not the ultimate cause of the variation in fashion. Consumers in different social positions follow fashion 'only' because it is fashion – not because it is valued by the elite class, as Herbert Blumer points out (Blumer 1969, 280; Noro 1991, 72). From this it follows that even those who on the surface appear to be leaders of fashion are, in fact, led by fashion (Simmel 1997 [1900]).

The attachment of fashion to time rather than social class makes it a special form of time-consciousness. This point is emphasized among others by Benjamin, who says that the more flowing the motion of time, the more fashion-oriented it is (Benjamin 2003 [1939]; see also Noro 1991, 87). One could point out, however, that Benjamin has got the relationship between time and fashion the wrong way round; surely we need to say that the more fashion-conscious the time, the more flowing its motion? In other words, the more closely the waves of fashion follow one another, the more quickly time passes. Fashion would thus be not just the 'child of modernity', as Arto Noro says, but also the engine driving its quickening pulse (Noro 1991, 79). This would mean that as the pace of fashion accelerates, so the duration of the present time grows shorter.

### 7.2.4.2 *The lure of fashion: communicating contraries*

'Novelty' is a property that is independent of the commodity's use value or the weight of opinion and that is anchored to the latest stage of our experiential existence (Benjamin 2003 [1939]). It is this that gives fashion its extraordinary lure. However, the cycles of fashion are so short that we must beware of getting overly excited. It is good to keep a distance to fashion, to take a detached attitude and consider it as just one possible course of action. This will help to ensure that fashion does not gain a monopoly on guiding our consumption choices.

Imitation and distinction are not the only contraries that fashion is capable of bridging. Sellerberg has discovered in her analyses of fashion that it also helps to connect involvement and indifference, following and breaking rules, the practical and impractical and authenticity and inauthenticity (Sellerberg 1987, 32–54). We could go on, because historically fashion has also been regarded as an attempt to reconcile between natural and unnatural and between tastefulness and tastelessness (Wilson 1985, 231–244).

The latter two contraries have held a special place in the history of fashion because they have been part of the political vocabulary dealing with fashion. In the wake of new mass fashions in particular, fashion has come under attack for being unnatural and tasteless. These attacks have not been limited to verbal abuse but they have been backed by organized social movements. In the late nineteenth century the UK saw the establishment of the Rational Dress Society and later even the Men's Dress Reform Party (Wilson 1985, 213, 218). These anti-fashion movements gained a strong following among socialists by the turn of the previous century, which subsequently was reflected in the affection shown by communist parties, in particular, for uniforms. The uniform, of course, is a closed code that is opposed to any and all change – the antithesis par excellence of the whims and vagaries of fashion.

The contraries of tasteful/tasteless and unnatural/natural are also important in the sense that both of them open up one further perspective on fashion which is crucial to understanding how fashion works and particularly how it ties in with food. Fashion is not just a static bridge between the contraries mentioned, or a 'third', as Noro suggests (Noro 1991, 89). As a compromise, fashion is also a constant balancing act between these dualisms. This presents a constant and at once an unresolvable threat to fashion. This is because the terms on either side of the dualisms are not equal. Unnatural and tasteless are to be shunned and avoided, whereas natural and tasteful are desirable options. In reconciling these two sides, items pushing to become fashion constantly run the risk of slipping over onto the negative side of the dualism and therefore losing all chances of becoming the next big thing in fashion.

Yet this is precisely where the fascination of fashion lies. It flirts all the time with the negative side of dualisms and aims to hijack elements and bring them over onto the positive side. This kind of flirtation takes on a special charm when fashion approximates spheres of life that are regulated by taboos, especially sexuality and gender identity, as well as manifestations of the sacred that are maintained by rituals, especially religious and national symbols. Indeed, the fashionable body in particular has been accused of being unnatural (see Christensen and Lykke 1986, 14–15; Christensen 1986, 69; Knudsen 1986, 54; Povlsen 1986, 125). Bringing erotically charged areas of the body and religious themes into the realm of fashion has, in turn, been denounced as being indecent and in violation of good taste. This has not, however, suppressed any nascent fashion trends, except in cases where legal bans have been put in place. Otherwise it may in fact have contributed to furthering the spread of fashion and turned fashion items into permanent fetishes, as we have seen in the case of suspender belts and women's and men's underwear.

So, flirting with what is defined as tasteless and unnatural involves certain risks, but it may also blow the bank, improve the prospects of something or some item becoming fashionable because it makes fashion exciting and by the same token interesting. Indeed, in this sense fashion is not perhaps entirely indifferent with respect to contents but it *has an inherent tendency to drift towards the very edge of good taste and the unnatural*. As a result of this movement, fashion acts to transfer elements of the tasteless and the unnatural over to the other side, into the realm of good taste and natural.

### 7.2.4.3 Food fashions

When food choices are steered by the mechanism of fashion, the only thing that is constant is change. This applies particularly to choices of food content. As a result of the alternation between distinction and identification, both food ingredients and dishes come successively into fashion and are then forgotten again. Pizzas, pastas and hamburgers have given way in quick succession to Turkish kebabs and TexMex and then to Japanese food, and most recently to fusion or crossover cuisine.

It is clear from the pace at which new foods and cooking styles are adopted that in food choices at least, fashion reaches its limits very quickly. The shifts and changes it brings about cannot be very dramatic because like language, food is a major determinant of social identity. Foods and eating habits that are central to the reproduction of that identity are therefore protected by rituals and traditions. They turn eating into a domain that is highly resistant to change. Food is a much more closed circle of life than, say, clothing and body shaping, the basic terrain of fashion. Traditions and conventions, style and routines also have a significant role in the domain of food, which further curtails the scope of fashion.

Nevertheless, fashion today has perhaps a greater impact on food choices than ever before. This is because the avenues that fashion takes are so highly unpredictable. Food fashions not only give public exposure to new ingredients and new dishes only to discard them at the next opportunity. Fashion is not just a publicity strategy. It is also cleverly concealed in existing accepted gustemes. These days it is fashionable to eat foods that are officially certified as healthy and practical (olive oil, green salads). However, these definitions are not necessarily grounded in nutrition science as they are often external aesthetic elements that have been added on afterwards. For example, wholegrain seeds sprinkled on top of a loaf of bread may give the impression that it is extra healthy, even though the bread itself is packed with additives and preservatives. Likewise, tomatoes wilt and wither away for months on end, while apples refuse to wilt at all even after weeks at room temperature (Sellerberg 1987, 83).

To sum up my account of the impacts of fashion on food choices, I would say that fashion has seriously called into question traditional food choices and set them in motion. It emphasizes variety at the expense of conventional choices. Its trump cards are the ability to push to the very edge of bad taste and the unnatural as well as the possibility to make distinctions vis-à-vis others and to identify with others. Even more important than that is the relationship of (food) fashion to time. Fashion, if anything, provides a means to keep up with the fast pace of everyday life, to swim along in its swift current. Indeed, the big question for today's Hamlets is, to follow (food) fashions or not to follow?

If the answer is in the affirmative, one must beware of not developing too strong a liking for the foods and dishes to which fashion happens to give prominence, since fashion is first and foremost a mere form. All that remains unchanged as fashion hurries along is the notion of what it means to be 'in fashion'. The alternative is to get left behind, voluntarily or otherwise. For this reason it is justified to argue that fashion not only implements existing gustemes but it also produces new ways of thinking. *To be and not to be in fashion* are nowadays important gustemes of food choice and must therefore be added to Figure 7.1 (page 145).

Just as with gustemes of style, they are not anchored to either the every-day or special occasions, but are independent of them.

## 7.3 Mechanisms of food choice and the selection event

Tradition, convention, routine, style and fashion are the most impor-tant mechanisms involved in the choice of food and any other con-sumption item. In modern society these mechanisms are all at work simultaneously. For this reason it is necessary to explore how they are connected to one another and to the final stage of the process of con-sumption choice, i.e. the actual selection event.

Erik Allardt concludes from his studies on the relationships between the different mechanisms of consumption choice that at the level of the indi-vidual, those mechanisms are mutually exclusive. When the emphasis in making the choice is on continuity the choice is ultimately informed by way of life. When the choice is made on the spur of the moment we need to point our finger at fashion. Finally, when the purchase is weighed in terms of whether or not it made good sense relative to choices already made or to the financial resources available, it turns out that the con-sumption choice is based on rational reflection (Allardt 1986, 7).

Allardt has built his position on three variables. The contrast between reflection and way of life is based on the level of consciousness. While reflection is always a conscious process, way of life is automatic, uncon-scious. The contrast between reflection and fashion, then, is manifested in the degree of rationality; and the contrast between fashion and way of life is temporal. Way of life is constant, fashion is variable (Allardt 1986, 7). These contrasts and distinctions are all very clever, but on closer examination they seem to lack rigorous justification.

First of all, way of life and the other mechanisms of consumption choice mentioned are *phenomena that occur at different levels of analysis.* Way of life reflects cultural categories, but as we have seen, it does not yet in itself steer consumption choices; that requires the choice mecha-nisms just mentioned. In other words, people who lead an athletic way of life do not choose their golf clubs or trainers or other sports' gear based on their way of life but for reasons of style or fashion and the price of this equipment.

Secondly, rational reflection does not occur at the same level of analysis as the phenomena that in this book are called mechanisms of consumption choice. The latter give material shape to cultural catego-ries; the ways of thinking that lie behind production and consumption. They serve as mediators between those categories and the selection event. *Reflection*, on the other hand, is part of the actual selection *event*. It takes account of the price of the desired goods, special offers and the subjective use-value promise. Reflection is also applied in the style or fashion framework. When fashion is followed, that is not done blindly and irrespective of the economic conditions. Since fashion lies outside the individual, it is possible for us all to keep a distance from fashion, as Simmel has pointed out (Simmel 1997 [1900]), and to use fashion strategically for social games (distinction) or for public appearances.

Thirdly, empirical reality has shown that neither way of life, reflection and fashion nor tradition/convention, routine, style and fashion are mutually exclusive lines of action – they overlap and intertwine. Tradition, convention and routine are admittedly closed self-repeating patterns of behaviour that confront fashion and that are said to be replaced by fashion (Blumer 1969, 289), but on the other hand, fashion has done a lot to expose and revive old traditions. It is also possible that this or that style will come into fashion. The relationship between cultural fixations and style is equally complex. There may be several different kinds of styles within one and the same fixation, and vice versa: people who share similar inclinations of style may have adopted very different kinds of gustemes. I prefer mutton kidneys, you prefer paradise salad.

It is this interweaving of style, routine, tradition/convention and fashion that makes it possible to move so easily from one mechanism of choice to another according to current wants and desires. Since they are parallel to one another, no one of those mechanisms will gain precedence over others. However, I do not want to deny that it is probably easier to abandon some of these mechanisms than others. No doubt routines and conventions keep a closer rein on people than tradition, fashion and style. While the former are codes of conduct with the power of coercion, the latter are nowadays relatively weak codes with no such powers.

Fourthly, even though new traditions are continuing to emerge all the time, styles and fashion have gained ever-greater prominence in the process of consumption choice. Styles and fashion are weak codes and as such allow for the openness and randomness that the capitalist markets 'need' in order to expand and to keep their production machinery running. At the macro level, therefore, they are beneficial to capitalist markets but at the same time they contribute to the 'creative destruction' that is transforming them. If the spirit of the times is misinterpreted, decisions may be taken to start up the production of fashion items for which there is no demand, which will then jeopardize the continuity of the business concerned.

Tradition, convention and routines, then, are closed codes and as such are liable to deter the expansion of capitalist markets and to create bonds with commodities, *brand and product loyalties* that are not easy to shift. Indeed, private companies have no reason to even try to do that if they have succeeded in creating such strong bonds. It is in their interest to keep their customers and to prevent rivals from coming in-between their products and their customers. For this reason their sales efforts are primarily focused on traditions and widely accepted conventions as well as on items and products reflecting those traditions and conventions. In other words, at the micro level of the economy there are countertendencies that prevent fashion and style from achieving hegemonic status among the mechanisms of consumption choice. At the same time, these tendencies cause tensions between the macro and micro level of national economies.

Finally, the social mechanisms of consumption choice are also *anchored to time in different ways*. Tradition, convention and routine are *diachronic* social mechanisms that favour continuity. They are long-standing and highly resistant to change. For these reasons they contribute to greater predictability in society and in that sense maintain order in social life. Style and above all fashion, on the other hand, are *synchronic* social mechanisms. They anchor people to the present time. They engender simultaneous activity among consumers and in that sense create social order.

However, the ability of tradition, convention, routine, style and fashion to create order in social reality does not provide a final solution to the question of consumption choice. Based on the style prevailing in a given group it may be possible to speculate what will certainly be excluded from the range of consumption choices, to say which ingredients and meals are considered incompatible with that particular style. Accordingly, based on what is known about cuisine fashions, it might be possible to deduce what will probably not be included in the food basket. In other words, it is fairly easy to tell what will be excluded from the range of choice (cf. Douglas 1996, 45). It is much harder, on the other hand, to predict what specific concrete choices the various social mechanisms will lead to. Like cultural habits of thinking, they only provide a *general framework for choices*; they do not determine choices. The ultimate choices are made *individually* and they are only put into effect in the actual *choice situation* in the markets, depending on the current supply (prices, special offers, product display, peripheral products) and the actions they elicit.

Very crudely, it may be said that in the ultimate choice situation there are three mutually independent factors at play. The first is the interpretation of the situation and the subjective use-value promise (i.e. persuading oneself that the purchase is 'necessary'); the second the resources available; and the third the current supply available. The mechanisms of consumption choice belong to the first of these categories. Together, they help form an emotional and cognitive understanding of the situation and above all narrow down the range of choices within the supply available. Once it is clear to the consumer what choice mechanism to apply in each situation, he will already have formed a basic analytical understanding of the situation.

As regards the resource factors related to consumption choices, the most important are *information, time and money*. Time is one of the most valuable resources in today's society. Even though there is also recurring cyclical movement of time, the passage of time in modern society is predominantly linear, and every decision on what action to take precludes other lines of action. There is no going back – every decision taken will have to stand. This infuses action with time-bound rationality. It is good to weigh and contemplate one's approaches and strategies in advance, particularly when time is scarce. And consumers seem to do just that. They allocate their time according to how much free time they have and how much of that time they want to spend on consumption.

Given that people can allocate different amounts of time to shopping during the week and over weekends, there is also much variation over time in terms of the mechanisms of consumption choice within which they operate. For instance, it seems that during weekdays consumers are content to make do with a smaller choice of foods than during weekends. This further narrows the range of choices from which the final selection is made.

We must also not ignore the role of money in the final selection process. As we have seen earlier in our discussion of the methods of consumption research, financial considerations figure prominently in making the final choice. However, the connections of money to food choices are more complicated than those of time because in this case we have to take account of at least two simultaneous factors: disposable income and prices. With respect to income, the following generalization can be suggested: the higher level of disposable income, the greater the opportunities to sound out different mechanisms of consumption choice and the different preferences they suggest. However, these opportunities are not necessarily exploited, since part of that income is set aside for special purposes and traditions, conventions and routines tend to uphold continuity in consumption choices. For this reason it is possible to find very similar patterns of food consumption, for instance, across different income brackets.

An examination of the connections between prices and food choices, then, throws up a whole web of questions that has received extensive treatment in the economics of consumption. There is little point revisiting its solutions or indeed its underlying assumptions about consumer rationality. These solutions and assumptions are highly idealized and fail to take account of such factors as how little consumers really know about goods and their prices. Research has shown that the average consumer knows the prices of no more than 5–8 staple foodstuffs (cf. Jonsson 1979, 130–131). In countries that have joined the euro, consumer price awareness has further declined since the introduction of the new currency.[8] From this it follows that instead of price competition, retail trade has been inclined to use special offers. That does not necessarily mean reduced prices but different ways of setting and quoting prices.

Time and price are not, of course, the only situational factors that channel the final consumption choice. Another significant factor is what consumers know about goods. In this respect the consumer is confronted with two main types of problems. Firstly, as the range of products available in the market has continued to expand, so the amount of both product information and marketing information about the merchandise has multiplied. So overwhelming is that flood of information now that even the experts can't keep track, never mind the consumers (Varjonen 2001, 62). The more technical the product, the harder it is to find the information that is relevant to making the purchase. This means that people are now making their decisions to purchase based on images created by marketing and subjective use-value promises formed on that basis. Secondly, as even experts are uncertain about the effectiveness of functional foods or the true impacts of bird flu, for example, consumers are having to take ever-greater risks in making their choices. That has the effect of deterring decisions to purchase or persuading consumers to avoid risky products if at all possible.

The three factors mentioned have the greatest effect on the consumer's choice of outlet. But even inside the shop there are still a number of factors that influence the final choice or that may turn a decision already made. These include the way that goods are displayed in the shop, the size of the shopping basket, the general layout of the shop, lighting and the muzak. Despite these factors that complicate the consumer's choice, there is one general principle that warrants separate mention: during the week when consumers are working and have less time at their disposal they buy from the corner shop those foodstuffs and foods that are a) on offer, b) according to some choice mechanism regarded as more valuable than others, and c) considered to form part of an everyday meal. During weekends, on the other hand, consumers spend more time and money buying food at the supermarket. This is particularly true ahead of a public holiday, which calls for a special feast.

## 7.4   Consumption choice – where structure and action meet

My path has been winding but I have finally arrived at the end-point of my description of consumption choice. What I have wanted to show is that the process of consumption choice proceeds through a number of successive stages, each of which narrows the scope of choices available. Each of those stages works according to the *principle of exclusion*. (*See Figure 7.3*) However, it is impossible to infer from these stages how the selection process will unfold from there on. In other words, the selection process *does not follow a determined path* as there is always scope for randomness (e.g. impulse purchases) at the next step of the process. However, the scope for individual spontaneity becomes more constrained after each stage. Thus the whole process moves progressively towards limiting randomness within the broader framework of order.

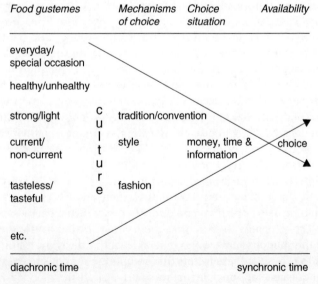

*Figure 7.3*   The process of consumption choice

The random element is explained by the fact that at each stage of the selection process the 'guidelines' of the previous stages are variably interpreted. To revert to the food example, new ingredients and new dishes are brought under the umbrella of existing gustemes by new styles, habits and fashions, which at the same time remove old ones. Therefore within the gusteme of healthy and unhealthy, for instance, ingredients and dishes have at different times been moved around from one side of the fence to the other; good examples include sugar, eggs and animal fat, which not so long ago were still regarded as healthy eating (cf. Hirdman 1983). Temporal and economic resources, then, determine how the choice mechanisms are followed in each situation, for instance, whether grilled fished is served at a barbeque party with an expensive white wine or just plain mineral water. The final choice will, of course, also depend in part on what is available in the shops.

As the process of consumption choice unfolds from stage to stage, the element of randomness means there is a greater likelihood that the contents rather than the form of choices will change. The resistance of form to the ravages of time, in turn, injects rigidity into the selection process. The stability of choices concerning the form of food, for example, is based precisely on the existence of parallel interpretations of gustemes and on the principle of exclusion. The former guarantees that the gusteme does not become cemented into a dogma and break down as soon as it is confronted with a deviant interpretation. Therefore, at least some degree of freedom in the interpretation of gustemes must exist. In fact, it is reasonable to assume that the wider the possible range of interpretations, the more elastic and the more resilient the gusteme. On the other hand, there are also some dangers involved in this. If just any interpretation goes, the gusteme will risk losing its significance as a thought-form. This means that the viability of the gusteme is only guaranteed if it is positioned in-between the extremes of a very narrow-minded and a very liberal interpretation.

The principle of exclusion, then, guarantees the continuity of the selection process. The way this principle works out is that the current stage (e.g. style), which is more restrained and restricted than the previous one, is incorporated as part of the earlier stage (the gusteme tasteless/tasteful and way of life) or placed within the boundaries of that stage.[9] In other words, provided that this is possible, the new stage of selection is incorporated in the framework constituted by the previous stage. This serves to maintain the continuity between the cognitive and normative framework and action. At the same time, the cultural classification that lies behind the choice is also reproduced.

Gustemes are not ageless, however. Social development is interspersed with ruptures and turning points that give rise to conflicts between the social organization of society and cultural ways of thinking. When the social organization changes decisively as a result of either internal conflicts (e.g. revolution) or external factors (occupation, economic integration), changes can be expected in thought-forms, including gustemes. However, these changes are not inevitable, except where the new social and material situation differs so profoundly from the old one that it no longer fits with the existing cultural frame of reference. New gustemes emerge in their place or the new seats of power try actively to create them. For example, the October Revolution in Russia, the Cultural Revolution in China and North Vietnam's war against South Vietnam all aimed to produce new gustemes that differed from old ones. They turned scarcity into a virtue, regarded temperance as praiseworthy and denounced pleasures as vices (Goody 1984, 149–150; Gronow 1997).

The cultural gustemes created by social ruptures are not all new, however. On the contrary, they are built into the situation preceding the rupture, with the group pushing for social change adopting cultural codes that run counter to existing thought-forms. In other words, change does not only run from the social organization in society towards cultural thought-forms, but also in the opposite direction.

Cultural heterogeneity and the struggle for cultural hegemony are the fundamental triggers of social change. If social integration is weak and social groups are antagonistic towards one another, change will not happen unless there exist competing ways of thinking (Archer 1988, 107, 145). Only this will provide social groups with the cognitive and emotional tools they need to change their situation and to circumscribe their social identity. There is no doubt that gustemes are important in the latter respect. Competing social groups define their mutual relationship through the medium of food, too.

Gustemes, thus understood, constitute an independent layer in social reality. However, they are not independent of ecology, the economy or the prevailing social organization in society (e.g. relationships between men and women), which express both gustemes and other cultural codes that impact consumption choices. Ecological, economic and social changes cannot but be reflected in cultural codes and styles, particularly if they are dramatic enough. On the other hand, our ecological environment, the way our economy works and the social organization of society and its erosion (e.g. because of long-term unemployment) are not independent of cultural codes or from the basic way of life (hunter–gatherer, industrial, commercial). Living environments are shaped according to the meanings they are given and according to what people want to get out of them within their primary way of life. Production, in turn, is allocated on the basis of what in each cultural circle is regarded as valuable at any given time, for instance, as traditionally appreciated food. This means that not even whales, those majestic distant relatives of ours, are left in peace, despite the almost unanimous condemnation of the international community.

# 8
# Consumption As Ideological Discourse

Consumption so far has been understood in the relatively narrow sense of purchasing goods in the market. However, the event of buying actually forms only a small part of the wider process of consumption, as was discussed earlier in connection with the various dimensions of commodity. Consumption is first and foremost about moving goods into the category of commodity, about their actual use. When consumption is approached from this vantage point the mechanisms mediating consumption choices and advertising also appear in a different light. They serve as messages to others and as ways of steering the use of consumption items. How else could we know what is in fashion, for instance, if not by observing consumers' everyday life and the media?

Consumption thus finds expression in discursive forms that shape consumer preferences. We talk about consumption, frown upon consumption, adore consumption or try to convince others how little consumption means to us (Wilska 2002). In this chapter, however, I will not be examining the various discursive forms via which consumption has been approached historically. Instead I shall focus on one, perhaps the most significant discourse that aims to influence consumption. It is my intention to examine how marketing and consumption in themselves, as discourses, maintain hierarchical social divisions. They serve not only to guide our consumption decisions but also to legitimize social relations that are created through consumption and to produce discursively 'appropriate' styles of consumption.

As we have seen, consumption, on the one hand, reflects and in fact also reproduces social inequality (cf. positional commodities). On the other hand, it also contributes to social integration (cf. fashion, tradition). The question is – how can it do both at one and the same time: *how can consumption simultaneously maintain both social coherence and social inequality?* To shed light on this question I will discuss below the associations of consumption with the *maintenance of the gender division.* The reasons for this choice of focus should be obvious.

Firstly, men and women differ markedly in both their consumption inclinations (e.g. taste) and real consumption (see e.g. Rahkonen & Purhonen 2004, 166–179). Secondly, the gender division is one of those systems of distinction in society that places people in an asymmetric hierarchical relationship with one another. Unlike horizontal social relations, they are of great sociological interest in that they present a fundamental problem to those groups who have risen to a more favourable position than others: how do they make sure they can retain that position in the future?

Historically, the privileged groups of society have solved this problem by asserting their control over the tools of social governance; the economy as well as the political and legal system. In this way they have been able to protect and perpetuate their privileged position in society (see Giddens 1984, 150). The gender relationship is no exception. At least in Europe, male control over governance regimes has made it possible for men to defend a whole range of privileges (see e.g. Abbot & Wallace 1990, 16–93, 121–150, 184–210; Dean 1999, 23, 29–33).

However, it is not possible by social governance alone to safeguard the continuity of asymmetric social relations. This is because social governance does not guarantee that the underprivileged groups will accept or publicly acknowledge the legitimacy of the demands of the privileged group. In particular, if the group that is subjected to governance is relatively large, if it recognizes the prevailing injustice and if it is in the position to mount a unified response, then it will in all probability try to redress the situation. The privileged group, therefore, will have to resort to one or the other or both of the strategies that are open to it for protecting its position. First of all it has to try and 'reduce' the number of people governed by sowing seeds of suspicion and fanning the conflicts brewing in their midst.

If these 'divide and rule' strategies don't work, then the people in control of the instruments of governance must, secondly, try to make the existing hierarchy appear natural and *legitimate.* This is easiest to achieve by acting in a way that provides justification for the legitimacy of their actions. This may help to affect *voluntary acceptance* on the part of the governees of the justification offered for the hierarchical relationship. It is here that *ideological effect* enters the picture (cf. Thompson 1983, 222). I refer to ideological effect here in a politically neutral sense.

In other words, no judgement or valuation is implied of the content of the governance ideology (cf. Eco 1971, 273).

It is easiest to examine the ideological effect when the focus is restricted to just two groups, as in the case of the gender division. However, their existence does not in itself suffice to describe the ideological effect. There are two further requirements. The groups concerned must also have *different ways of making sense of social reality*. Their sensemaking must produce understandings that in some respect are mutually antithetical. Furthermore, one or the other group must be able to *establish its own sensemaking and framing of reality as predominant* (see Archer 1988).[1] This can be achieved via two routes.

Firstly, steps can be taken to make the *interface* of hierarchical social relations porous so that it becomes invisible to the outside and relatively easy for the subjects of governance to overcome, for instance, by means of education. This strategy requires that the subjects of governance believe that they have real prospects for upward social mobility (Giddens 1984, 304–310). Only then will it be possible for social mobility to achieve significant levels and release some of the pressures coming from below.

The possibility of upward social mobility and individual social climbing serves to maintain and reassert existing hierarchical divisions, without any real need for social engineering. At the same time, the objective existence of those phenomena contributes to sustain the prevailing divisions in the future. They can also be consciously used for cultivating a *civic religion* whose message is that anyone can redeem a place on the sunny side so long as they try hard enough.

The situation is very different a) when hierarchical divisions are so deeply engrained that they are difficult or impossible to overcome and b) when the underprivileged groups realize this. This has happened especially in situations where social divisions coincide with external visible characteristics, such as skin colour, religion and gender. In this instance, the governing classes will become concerned about the prospect that the underprivileged groups might begin collectively to voice their dissatisfaction and call for social change. How can the privileged groups stop this from happening if they cannot resort to naked violence?

The *gender division* provides interesting and useful elements that can help shed light on this complex problem. The problem, of course, is so fundamental to all communities that the use of overt violence would have disastrous consequences for both parties. If men used brute force to defend their privileges it would be tantamount to a declaration of war against the female gender. That, in turn, would run counter to male interests even in the short term, never mind the longer term implications of such an imaginary war that would undermine social order more generally.

Studies on the maintenance of the gender division by feminist women researchers, in particular, have often referred to the family and school system and to the techniques of governance applied through various bodies of government. The thinking behind these studies has been that these social institutions are, among many other things, channels of ideological influence that favour men (e.g. Barrett 1988; Althusser 1976; Abbott & Wallace 1990). The discussion here is also grounded in the ideological perspective. However, since the gender division is always also cultural, it is necessary to examine the relationship of culture and ideology in the formation of the gender system. This analysis is couched in the framework of consumption.

## 8.1   Ideology and everyday practices

The basic condition for ideological persuasion is that *ideology is not recognized as ideology*. Indeed, the dominant ideology is usually hidden away in areas of historical activity where one least expects to find it. In feudal society, for example, ideology is hidden in the area of religion and the 'sacred' more generally. In this instance man is ordinarily represented as a mere medium for cosmological forces, as a 'victim of fate' who must be content with his lot (Lovejoy 1960). In modern capitalism, ideology is connected with consumption, which presents itself as an ideal scene for individual choice and freedom in keeping with neo-liberal thinking (see du Gay & Pryke 2002). This, however, is a rather obscure statement, for it turns consumption wholesale into ideology. That is hard to accept. After all, buying a pork pie or sitting in an armchair do not yet, in themselves, make these actions ideological. They can only become ideological through the meanings that are given to them.

To test this idea we must be able to identify the distinctive features of ideology and the way it works within consumption. This is not a simple task. Even though there is an abundance of social science research on the subject there is still no consensus among researchers other than on the purpose of ideology. This shared understanding says that the purpose of ideology is to *reproduce and legitimize existing hierarchical divisions*. For ideology to fulfil this purpose it must be a *collective frame of thinking* that has a strong following in society (cf. Durkheim 1951 [1897]).

Critics of this view of ideology have been keen to point out that the ability of ideology to wield an influence is based not just on the ideas and arguments it contains or on its discursive form in general. Its influence also has to do with how ideology pervades the ways in which the parties to different hierarchical divisions act in the everyday. According to this view, ideology reflects the parties' *lived* relationship to the conditions of their existence (Althusser 1976; Giddens 1979; Williams 1977, 110).

This idea of a 'lived' relationship to reality sounds rather vague and woolly, but we can elaborate. The notion refers, on the one hand, to *daily routines* and to the organization of those routines into coherent ways of acting. On the other hand, it is related to stylistic *bodily dispositions*, gestures, movements and other characteristics of activity. These provide the foundation for *social identities* that are understood as 'normal' (Chaney 2002, 93). It is precisely when it is hidden beneath the veil of normal identities that ideology can present itself as a matter of course and so deny its own existence. In other words, when it is masked as normal and expected, ideology camouflages itself as a thought-form; this is the only way it can survive and work. It sinks into 'practical consciousness' (Giddens) and transforms into a flow of actions whose ideational sources can no longer be normally stated, let alone criticized.

Not all everyday practices and bodily dispositions, of course, contain ideological patterns of thinking. So what is it that sets these practices apart from those that are ideologically loaded? In the search for an answer we need to follow the above characterization of ideology. For everyday practices and bodily dispositions to carry and convey an ideological message in society they must be shaped in accordance with the collective identity and be perceived as normal.

These kinds of everyday routines and bodily dispositions, we find, occur in virtually all major scenes of social activity. One of them, however, seems to have gained greater weight and significance than others in the past few decades. That one scene is consumption. We are all completely dependent on consumption. Without the use of commodities our everyday life would quite simply grind to a halt (see next chapter). Commodities are a necessary condition for modern life.

Furthermore, despite the apparent freedom of choice and individualism, consumption is largely a collectively organized activity. It is guided by the choice mechanisms discussed above, such as fashion and style, which convert consumption into a 'lived relationship' to reality. This is no doubt a necessary, albeit not a sufficient condition for consumption to become today's main battlefield for the justification of hierarchy, as Benjamin has shown (Benjamin 2003 [1939]).

Another reason why some everyday routines and bodily dispositions are better suited than others as justifications for hierarchies is their ability to *conceal their ideological message.* In order to perform this conjuring trick, consumption must first of all get across the message that *the interests of the privileged group are universal,* that they apply to all and sundry. Secondly, they must *deny the contrasts and contradictions implied by hierarchical divisions.* Thirdly, they must represent *hierarchical divisions as taken-for-granted,* as 'natural' (Giddens 1979). Consumption must make all these modifications before it can discursively justify the hierarchical divisions of modern society. To find out whether consumption can do this, I turn my attention now to the stylistic side of consumption. Even though style has become increasingly complex in the way it works it is still the mechanism that is most clearly and closely associated with hierarchical divisions, and in that sense it is in the position to communicate ideological messages as thought-forms and as lived practice more effectively than any other mechanism.

## 8.2 Consumption as mediator of ideological meanings?

If the above analysis of the workings of ideology is accepted, the next step is to see how consumption manages with the 'tasks' it is set by ideology. We begin by observing the fact, known from anthropology, that consumption items are in themselves bearers of cultural meanings. They do this in two ways. Firstly, all goods carry meanings in the sense that they are distinguished from other similar brands from as early on in the production process as possible. Secondly, users of different goods unwittingly contribute to this distinction process by associating them with their own social background. Thirdly, it is precisely the ability of goods to get consumers to act in 'their own distinctive ways' that conceals messages. Umberto Eco makes the point that women's clothing has subjected women to a constant condition of exposure: it forces women to behave in a certain way and in this sense serves as a semiotic means of communication (Eco 1987). This statement could well be generalized to all consumption. It has made consumption one of the key areas of study in the field of semiotics, even though it is only in exceptional cases that clothes are a collectively intelligible language (see McCracken 1988).

Consumption items (and in this sense the economy in itself) thus play a central role in materializing and expressing semantic systems in modern society. Here, the relationship between commodities and signification is settled into a regular pattern (Sahlins 1976, 212–213; Clastres 1989). This is based on the fact that in the modern world goods are primarily produced for the market. There, they are confronted with the fundamental question of whether or not they will be exchanged for money. To make sure that exchange does take place, the production machinery is geared to making goods that have already-existing cultural acceptance. Furthermore, novelties are designed in such a way that they pass through a cultural filter to make sure they are suited to current everyday practices. This, too, has contributed to increasing the significance of the commodity's symbolic aspect with the continued expansion of commodified consumption (see Chapter 3). This, in turn, has multiplied opportunities to attach ideological meanings to goods.

The existence of opportunities, however, does not necessarily mean they will be exploited. They must first of all be recognized. Whether that happens, whether goods are used for ideological purposes, depends on how the good is perceived. To consider this issue it is useful to return to the symbolic aspect of the commodity. I shall do this by using Roman Jacobson's distinction between the code and message of communication. *Code* refers to the *form of the communication*, *message* in turn to its *content*. This distinction implies four possible relationships between code and message. In the first case, the *message refers to itself* (message/ message). An example is provided by a newspaper report on someone's speech. In the second instance, the *code relates to itself* (code/code). This case is illustrated by a proper name (e.g. Elvis): the code refers only to the person to whom the name is associated. In the third case, the *message is related to the code* (message/code). An example is provided by a metonymy, where a person is called a 'pig' or a 'tiger', for example. The fourth and last combination is where the *code relates to the message* (code/message) (figure 8.1). Here, an example is the use of the pronoun 'I' in a sentence. It refers to the speaker, but since it is the speaker who is using the 'I', the expression is ultimately associated with the phrase, with conventional language use (Barthes 1967, 22).

The symbolic aspect of goods is mainly associated with the trademark. In Jacobson's and Barthes's classification it represents the second case. In a branded product, the code relates to itself. In other words, *a brand refers to nothing other than itself*, and it cannot be understood

| code/ message | code | message |
|---|---|---|
| code | trademark: Lalique | use of the pronoun 'I' in marketing communication: I use Fairy liquid |
| message | metonym: Adidas logo three stripes | excerpt from someone's statement: Claudia Cardinale uses Rexona |

*Figure 8.1*  Code and message

symbolically other than from that vantage point. Brands, therefore, are closed symbolic spaces, and as such they cannot be used for purposes of ideological signification. Indeed, brands primarily have an *economic function*. They produce the good at a symbolic level and through this symbolism aim to create an artificial *monopoly status* amongst other similar products (see e.g. Slater 2002, 66).

A monopoly brand and brand advertising are also attempts to interpret our desires and to point them towards an object. Advertisements do not, however, always succeed in doing this. Despite all the marketing research designed to support advertising, commercials very rarely increase the sales of a brand. Much of advertising is completely wasted. Ironically, though, even advertising that has very little impact does serve to increase consumption overall. Although consumers take a dubious attitude to advertising, research suggests that they place greater trust in products that are advertised than in those that are not (Ilmonen 1984, 59–66).

For branded products to serve ideological purposes, marketing must get them out of their smug isolation and try to get them to 'talk' of other things than just themselves. They must be made to refer to the outside reality. Marketing applies two different strategies to do this. First, a positive charge is connected to a branded product by highlighting its specificity. For instance, butter is advertised as a 'natural' product. Then, the marketing machinery proceeds to compare the branded product with other similar products. Based on this comparison, distinctions are made in favour of the advertised product (cf. Bourdieu 1986, 96).

The greater the success that the new commodity has in translating its manufacturer's name into a symbolic language and selling it to the public, the easier it is to make accurate advance classifications and to legitimize those classifications (Bourdieu 1986, 112). Barthes describes this process by the concept of *logo technique* (Barthes 1967, 39). This concept refers to the creation of a brand logo (the Adidas three stripes or the Nike swoosh), which then provides the focal point for the development of the symbolism of the commodity.

The key importance of the logo in the modern market economy is well illustrated by the urgency with which work is always started to create a new logo after company mergers, despite the huge costs of the operation. The reason for this is that public awareness of the company is largely based on its logo. The logo is used to launch new products in the markets. In other words, once the manufacturer has established the specificity of its product through the use of the company logo, the logo technique will be applied to marketing (cf. Bourdieu 1986, 111). It is no longer necessary to use the brand name, just the company logo will do. Nike's swoosh speaks for itself when it is associated with a famous golfer or basketball player. The purpose is to strengthen perceptions of the high quality and specificity of the brand compared to other corresponding products. Nike is no exception. A similar technique has been used in visual communications by many other trainer manufacturers and airlines and shipping companies.

However, the logo technique serves not only to promote sales. It also serves as a source and symbol of group identity. The Nike logo, for example, is so revered that company employees in the United States have had themselves tattooed with the swoosh. This no doubt reflects their commitment to the company. At the same time, Nike also appeals to consumers. Its logo technique emphasizes the role of sports as a form of collectivity. According to Nike adverts, what matters most is the sense of *camaraderie* in the sporting community (Goldman & Papson 1998, 37). It is precisely by virtue of its abstract logo (Coca Cola's is another example) that Nike has been able to position itself *beyond racial, gender, class and age boundaries.*

By signing up sports' stars from different ethnic backgrounds, Nike can get across the message that sport is all about individual performance and the will to win, regardless of race (ibid., 157). Indeed, this is exactly what it wants to highlight in its advertising, not the actual footwear. Nike's aim is to divert the attention away from racial and political conflicts and to turn the focus to the skills that depend on its brand. Nike is associated with a professional sports' performance that is independent of external social characteristics; it represents pure excellence and togetherness. Nike's marketing urges people to brush aside social inequalities. In this respect it fulfils the first function of ideology, which applies more generally to products that are aimed at conquering global markets (soft drinks, mobile phones etc.). However, not all marketing works in this way.

The power of the brand to control, through its symbolism, the respective field of commodities is not, however, based on the trademark itself. The brand works on the strength of the field constituted by the category of goods (the everyday system) in which it is located and on its ability to take advantage of the 'symbolic energy' (Bourdieu) produced by that field ('athletics', 'football', 'smells') (Bourdieu 1986, 17–19). In this respect Nike works in the exact same way as all other sports' brands. When Nike has gained access to the 'symbolic energy' of the field of sports' goods, the international community that so loves individual competition and sports, it can sell just about anything with its swoosh logo, even products that the company doesn't itself manufacture under that name. This, of course, applies to other brands as well, not just Nike.

Through their interaction with logo techniques and the symbolic meanings given to them by consumers, brands thus become 'islands of meanings'. As a consequence, the closed semiotic space residing within individual goods transforms in consumption into 'collective communication'. As communication, consumption can obviously disseminate thought-forms and ideological meanings, but only on condition that its messages are not too ambiguous. Insofar as consumption has ideological functions at this level, those functions will be fed back to the supply side and to consumers.

We must not, however, draw too far-reaching conclusions from this understanding of consumption as communication, as semiotic consumption research is inclined to do. *Consumption does not constitute any clear uniformly intelligible language.* This is confirmed by the small-scale experiments devised by Grant McCracken, who has studied the communicative powers of clothing, the example par excellence of semiotic consumption research (Barthes 1983). Different clothing items can be more freely combined than components of language (McCracken 1988, 64). It is only when there is an established dress code, as in the case of national costumes and uniforms, for instance, that clothing works like language. It allows for no variation, which means it is relatively easy to 'read' (providing one knows how the army, for instance, communicates its hierarchy). But as soon as clothing problems are resolved creatively there are bound to be problems of interpretation. This is because in this instance no learned clues are available on the person's style. An alternative rule is that inferences are drawn from the person's cloth-ing based on the single most conspicuous clothing item. But as soon as clothing is contradictory and in that sense 'tasteless', the interpreters are lost. They will not be able to understand the message communicated by the clothing (ibid., 65–66), if indeed there is such a message.

Contrary to what Barthes would have us believe, it is clear from McCracken's experiments that clothing allows for only very limited deliberate communication of messages. Its code system provides us with no rules on how to combine different clothing items ('words') into a coherent chain so that the intended communication effect is created. It is impossible, therefore, to produce different variable messages using the clothing code system in the same way as it is using the code sys-tem of language. This applies to consumption more generally. This does not, however, mean that consumption cannot be used to communicate *something*, that such as place, time and nature of occasion. However, messages can only be communicated when they have been prepared in advance. This means that codes are not language-like tools with which to create messages but instead a collection of messages that cannot be modified without this severely affecting their power of communication (McCracken 1988, 66–67; Chaney 2002, 98).

## 8.3    Commodity fetishism and consumption as a means of classification

It is only once consumption has been cemented, by means of logo tech-niques, as permanent message–code structures that it becomes a semi-otic system which supports hierarchical social divisions. Hierarchical classification based on consumption happens via two routes. Firstly, social status is demonstrated by means of *self-classification*. In this proc-ess consumers use different commodities (say a car marque or a clothes brand) and their taste to identify themselves as a member of some social group or class, for instance as women, mothers, middle class or *nouveau riche* (Zukin & Maguire 2004, 184–185). Secondly, classification takes place from the outside as a result of being *ascribed to a particular social group*. In this case the collective and stereotypical characteristics of that social group are superimposed on the individual's characteristics on grounds that that individual uses goods that have a given advance social classification (e.g. golf equipment). In this case, the given clas-sification transforms into what Bourdieu calls 'classifying practices' (Bourdieu 1986, 299). Because of the dual movement of this classifica-tion we may talk about its inductive and deductive aspect.[2]

When goods are used as tools of self-classification and for external classification they serve the purposes of social distinction and identification. They become part of social representations, one stage of the process of signification that defines social identity (cf. Turner 1987, 206–207). When goods are integrated as part of that identity people's relationships to one another become mediated by goods. Georg Lukács has described this phenomenon by using the concept of *commodity fetishism* (Lukács 1971).

However, commodity fetishism is a far more complex phenomenon than Lukács suggests. It involves a dual reification of social relations. As Theodor W. Adorno points out, commodity fetishism means, firstly, that *commodities make social relations between people invisible,* hiding from view the underlying (workplace) relationships. When we slip on a pair of Nike trainers we are usually ignorant of the slave-like working conditions of Nike's assembly-line women in Indonesia, who are slogging away to satisfy their American mother company's unquenchable thirst for profits (see Klein 2000). However, Nike's logo techniques are understandably silent about the global relationship between these wretched working conditions and the profit expectations invested in Nike. It has even been suggested that the crafting of the meanings of commodities is a deliberate strategy to hide the structural features of the international economy (cf. Rose 1978, 136, 139). Consumers cannot see them because they are hidden behind the brand and the markets.

The concept of commodity fetishism also refers, secondly, to the situation where *social relations mediated by commodities appear as transparent and therefore as easy to recognize.* This is explained by the fact that the meaning crystallized in commodities through consumption helps to express social status and to make it immediately known. As a consequence, social divisions between people that would otherwise be invisible in urban conditions are crystallized as relationships between the meanings of commodities. This has led to the emergence of totemic groups whose relations are reduced to those between the commodities they carry.[3]

The view outlined above entails that the meanings of branded products and people's social relations are filled with the form of commodities. This, however, is an exaggeration that stems largely from the follies of French structuralist thinking (see e.g. Lévi-Strauss 1962). At least the conspicuous consumption mentioned by Veblen (1994) certainly does nothing to obscure the vertical differences seen between social groups; quite the contrary. This was also a prominent feature of the much maligned 'yuppie culture'. Likewise, it is very clearly in evidence in the consumption habits of those people today who have made a fortune on options. But this thinking is just one side of the story of commodity fetishism.

The other side of the story suggests that commodity fetishism not only lays bare the hierarchical relationships between people but is *capable of creating entirely new social groups*. One example is provided by new groups of football-club supporters, who no longer have any contact with the social base from which the clubs themselves grew up but only with the symbolism they represent. *New tribes* are thus created (Maffesoli 1995). These are largely imaginary communities whose boundaries therefore tend to be rather fluid. In order to solidify those boundaries, then, it is necessary to have various fan products and shared activities, one manifestation of which is crowd violence. This, however, has little to do with the social background of these clubs' supporters and their related ambitions. Instead, crowd violence has to do with the fact that football clubs do not stand in a hierarchical relationship to one another, regardless of league tables. One way to create grounds for such a hierarchy is through violence in the stands, confrontations to decide 'who's who'. This, however, does not provide an exhaustive explanation of crowd violence.

The latter perspective on commodity fetishism deserves further attention in that it may have the kinds of effects assumed by Adorno. New tribes are formed by virtue of symbolic commodities (e.g. football scarves and shirts) and totems (e.g. football stars) that are important to people. It is a different matter to what extent the symbols of football clubs and images of pop stars, for instance, are developed with the specific intent of distancing people from social reality, though this is probably not a major motive. Instead, what football clubs and the record industry and others are trying to do is reinforce their supporters' and fans' ties to the club or their pop icon and so make it easier to sell them. This, of course, requires the approval of consumers, which may involve an element of self-irony (e.g. Miller 1987). Not everyone who wears the Arsenal scarf takes their club dead seriously.

In other words, consumers are not a faceless mass who blindly follow the marketing pied pipers. If we work from Adorno's assumption that society's privileged groups aim specifically and consciously to persuade others, among other things, by transforming social relations into goods-mediated relations, then we ignore two facts. The first is that the primary purpose of logo techniques is *to promote sales*, not to shape social consciousness, although in the long term they no doubt do that as well. The second point is that *society's privileged groups are themselves influenced by those techniques.* Whether they want it or not, they contribute just as much as others to the process of locating goods in social space. The end result is not necessarily to the liking of the market captains but they have no option but to take it into account.

All parties to hierarchical divisions, including that between men and women, are to some extent unintentionally involved in the chain of events where consumption is at least temporarily cemented as discourse and where it is maintained as discourse. At the same time, they also reproduce their mutual hierarchical relations as goods-mediated relations. If this really happens, their only alternative is to *try and reclassify themselves* (cf. Klein 2000), to build up a new kind of social identity. In this process, according to Bourdieu, the 'class struggle' becomes a 'classification struggle' (Bourdieu 1986, 166–167, 297–300; see also Nietzsche 2006).

For this reclassification to make sense to underprivileged groups it should lead them in a more positive direction. This, however, is not automatically the case. In order to emerge victorious from the 'classification struggle', those in a weaker position must make the right choice between two strategy options. As discussed earlier, they can a) try to *improve their position on the dimensions of the dominant values in society,* i.e. conform to current existing tastes. This was the avenue taken by the American civil rights movement when it adopted the slogan 'black is beautiful' and when it chose to celebrate its African roots in music, clothing and food (Eyerman & Jamison 1991, 120–124). The feminist movement has chosen to pursue this same route in seeking to redefine femininity as 'liberated from the male gaze'.

If the former strategy fails on account of public opposition, the disadvantaged can still try to b) *positively redefine the attributes associated with themselves,* in other words, to create their own rules, to create new value categories. Since under conditions of dual-commodity fetishism these categories are most clearly manifested in consumption, the most natural reaction for these groups would be to enhance the value of the consumption items with which they are most closely associated (food, drink, dress, car marques). The contest over their value would thereby be not so much an economic as a moral and aesthetic issue. It all boils down to what the community regards as morally valuable at each moment in time (Sahlins 1976, 214).

The dispute over what is precious and valuable is often harnessed for marketing purposes. In the manufacture and marketing of goods this is seen in the inclusion of the distinctive characteristics of less valued microcultures.[4] Those features are translated into marketing language and put to use in advertising. Che Guevara, the icon of the Cuban revolution, is sanitized and made politically harmless by using his picture to sell t-shirts and other consumer items. In Hollywood this trend is seen in the film genre specifically aimed at the Afro-American population (e.g. the Shaft films), which has now become known as *blaxploitation*. Similarly, 'softer' versions have been produced of traditionally male alcoholic drinks (whiskey, vodka) to increase sales to women customers (Heinonen 2003).

It is highly unlikely that people who occupy lower positions in hierarchical divisions will have any success in either of these classification struggles. This is at least what Bourdieu seems to think. For him, the people with the greatest competences in these struggles are those who have the most cultural capital, i.e. usually men who are higher up in social hierarchies. For Bourdieu, these people have the best taste and they are also the best capable of giving taste the most innovative applications in their own consumption styles or in those they have recommended to others (cf. male designers) (Bourdieu 1986, 72, 90; Frank 1997). However, this does not mean to say that the position they represent always has the upper hand. First of all, the legitimacy of that position is constantly challenged and called into question by understating its value or by highlighting the importance of its antithesis.

Secondly, the validity of Bourdieu's argument is culturally limited to France. In the Nordic countries at least, women have an abundance of cultural capital that they can apply in 'classification struggles' (see Rahkonen & Purhonen 2004, 177). Thirdly, the classification struggle concerns commodities but only very rarely their moral value. Therefore the classification of ego by means of products, and particularly the attempt to enhance one's own moral value by reclassifying those products, is doomed to failure. The struggle becomes meaningless (Sayer 2003, 352). In the proper sense of the word there is no 'classification struggle'. The hierarchical relationships between products are accepted as they stand. The only option remaining for the disadvantaged groups is to hold tight and hope for a lottery win so that they could go out and buy products that are already branded as 'high class'.

## 8.4   Structural differences between men's and women's consumption

It is very rare that an ideological form of thought or action embedded in consumption has the force to fade, let alone change hierarchical divisions in modern society. It is more likely that instead, social relations will be transformed in consumption into goods-mediated relations, for it is rarely that those relations can be hidden. Nor is that always even necessary. In order to achieve an ideological effect, for instance to reproduce the gender system, it may suffice simply to make these divisions appear normal in the eyes of the weaker group, i.e. women.

The existence of a hierarchical gender division is a more or less universal phenomenon. However, each form of society produces and reproduces the gender division as well as the hierarchy inherent in that division in its own distinctive way. It carries over not only into the division of labour but also into the field of culture. Women themselves act in certain ways to create an identity that is compatible with their own feminine style (self-definition). In part, however, the female identity develops independently of women, as a result of men assigning stereotypical attributes to women, which women then pick up and put into practice (external definition). In other words, the feminine microculture is both specific in its femininity and at the same time a reflection of mainstream culture internalized through the male gaze.

Studies on the ways in which the category of femininity is produced and maintained have pointed, among other things, at the social division of labour, the education system and the state, but also at the traditional household system and the family ideology (Barrett 1988, 48). Unlike anthropologists, sociologists have paid only scant attention to the role of consumption habits and consumption items as determinants of feminine taste and related dispositions. However, this is clearly something we have to look at more closely if we are to properly understand the determinants of femininity and the ways in which its form is reproduced.

The research evidence available is quite limited but even a cursory examination of consumption research lends convincing support to this argument. The construction of the social categories of masculinity and femininity start very early on in childhood, indeed virtually from birth. The clothes that are chosen for boys are often light blue, for girls pink. This cannot but have an effect on clothing preferences at a later age. The same is no doubt true for gendered toy choices, which become more and more differentiated with advancing age: boys will typically have their cars and war toys, girls their dolls and miniature houseware sets, which further contribute to their socialization to housekeeping (Ilmonen & Pantzar 1989).

Clothing becomes an increasingly important marker of gender identity in late childhood. At this stage boys are not yet particularly interested in clothes, so long as they don't have to wear anything that is too conspicuously different from prevailing trends, and so long as they are sufficiently ungirly. Girls, on the other hand, are more aware and more appreciative of style from a younger age, more conscious of the impressions they create by the clothes they wear (Autio, Marjamäki & Peura-Kapanen 1985, 16; see also Heinonen 2003).

It is only at around age 14–15 that boys' and girls' consumption patterns begin to diverge. At that point girls begin to spend more and more on clothes, shoes, travel, books and beauty and health care. Boys, on the other hand, spend more on electronics and sports' equipment and clothing (Autio, Marjamäki & Peura-Kapanen 1985, 16–18). Age 14–15 also signifies a watershed in the sense that boys' consumption spending now exceeds the amount of money spent by girls (Siurala 1987, 81). This situation remains the same throughout the years of youth and continues into adulthood. Part of the reason for this is that boys' leisure activities are more expensive than girls' (Autio, Marjamäki & Peura-Kapanen 1985, 19–32). Another reason is that from teenage years onwards, boys spend more and more of their money on their own needs and interests, whereas girls at this point are beginning on the path of socialization to family-oriented consumption.

Why, then, is it not until around age 15 that these structural differences in consumption begin to surface? There are probably at least three types of reasons. Firstly, finances enter the equation in the sense that it is at around this age that youngsters begin to earn their own money and to decide how they want to spend it. Secondly, the reasons are also evolutionary in the sense that this is the age when boys and girls are in the middle of puberty and starting out in search of their social identity. Thirdly, they are cultural in the sense that this is the point where girls and boys begin to develop their self-image in line with existing gender stereotypes. From this it follows that the differences continue to persist in the future. Men spend more of their income than women on cigarettes, alcohol, eating out and on transport than women, who in turn spend more of their money on clothes and beauty and health care.

These gender differences in consumption are far from ancient; in fact they have only become possible with the development of modern society. A good example is provided by the marked gender differences in spending on health and beauty care. There are no doubt several reasons why women spend so much more on health and beauty products than men, but one explanation seems more convincing than others: this is the attitude to one's own body and the accumulation of dirt on the body.

As Mary Douglas has observed in her anthropological studies, where there is dirt, there is a system (1966, 36). The system, according to the middle-class ideals of modern Western society, dictates that it is the role of women to keep the home as tidy as possible and to make sure that all the family have clean clothes to wear. Women are particularly keen to apply this norm to themselves, to their clothes and their body. The outcome is a disposition that is not without its moral dimensions. A woman who looks dirty and unkempt is easily branded a person of dubious morals.

For men, the situation has always been different. As they moved out-side the home to work in industrial and other jobs, the dirt and smells they picked up became a distinctly masculine characteristic: the linger-ing smell of sweat and the eternal dirt and grime that covered their hands became a permanent feature (Arvastson 1987, 83). It was just not 'right' to remove them, let alone adorn oneself with scents: that would have severely undermined the modern male identity, if not been considered an outright insult that almost certainly would have meant being labelled a homophile. In this situation it is only natural that the consumption of skin-care, cosmetic and health-care products has been greater among women than men, even though this gap has narrowed somewhat with the introduction of separate 'male' and 'female' scents and tastes (e.g. aftershaves and colognes, deodorants for men).

However, the idea that perfumes on men are 'feminine' is a rela-tively new one. In the late eighteenth century the consumption of per-fumes among upper-class men and women was still equally common, even though it was regarded as frivolous. Indeed, the use of perfumes decreased sharply in the nineteenth century. The situation changed yet again with onset of the First World War, when the European perfume industry started in earnest. In those days scents were all about senti-mentality and nostalgia. The new way of thinking created a difference between men and women. It was now 'permissible' for women – and in courts 'compulsory' – to wear perfumes and to waft strong scents around. Men – if they wanted to be real 'men' – were not granted such licence in industrial society (Classen, Howes & Synnott 1994, 83–84, 88, 100–101). However, by the latter half of the twentieth century the smells of sweat and physical labour were no longer accepted. Men were now expected to be clean and odourless (ibid., 185).

However, patterns of health- and beauty-care consumption are chang-ing yet again, with boys now spending more of their money on cosmet-ics than earlier. One possible explanation for this trend of 'feminization' could lie in the growth of ambivalence surrounding male role models, driven especially by the world of pop and rock. Secondly, young men have also started to promote themselves in the marriage and labour market. To this end they, too, have begun to place ever greater premium on their outer appearance and started to accumulate what Bourdieu (1984, 206; see also Ewen 2000, 45) calls 'beauty capital'. In this drive for self-promotion, looks are ever-more important, so much so that they call not just for hair gels but other cosmetic products as well. Thirdly, men have also changed their attitude to their own body and its excretions: the earlier attitude of acceptance has been progressively undermined by the new ideas of hygiene and health. Men are now duty-bound to look after their own health and to demonstrate that in public (Shove 2003, 108). Today it is not just unkempt-looking women, but also unkempt-looking men who are branded as outcasts or even as alcoholics.

## 8.5   Consumption and hierarchical divisions

The structural differences seen between women's and men's consumption provide only a crude indication of the ways in which consumption is used both for the creation and reproduction of social gender. The gender differences in the consumption of sanitary and cosmetic products, then, probably serve to illustrate just how firmly consumption is rooted in old cultural thought-forms. The examples discussed above tell us nothing about how consumption *manifests and naturalizes the asymmetries* of the categories of masculinity and femininity. In order to come to grips with this, we must move on to look at the qualitative differences between women's and men's consumption. We do this by concentrating on women's and men's clothing, particularly the materials, design and colours of their clothes.

All these aspects are largely determined by social identity. Let us take a few examples. Firstly, material: rich and lustrous fabrics, silk in particular, are predominantly indicative of a feminine style, although men too have begun increasingly to use clothes made of silk, such as shirts and socks. A women's skin is 'soft like silk' and represents the opposite to rough wool, which in our culture is regarded very much as a male material (cf. Sahlins 1976, 182). Secondly, design: right-handed buttons and simple and straight cuts are typical of male dress preferences. Women, on the other hand, tend to favour more curly and frilled designs, with left-handed buttons. Thirdly, colours: with the exception of their sometimes extraordinarily colourful sportswear, men usually dress in monotonous blues and greys and blacks. Women, by contrast, are much more adventurous in their colour choices, although they do tend more often to go for reds and softer pastel shades – depending to some extent on current fashion.

These examples are of course first and foremost indicative of style choices but they nonetheless speak volumes. Above all, they convey the message that men are 'sensible' and 'rational' in the way they dress. This contributes to reinforce the social status of the individual concerned, particularly at the highest levels of the work organization. The dark colours and simple cuts of men's suits aim to express 'ability, discipline, and reliability', qualities that are routinely associated with managerial positions and occupational roles (McCracken 1988, 99). Women's dress styles, on the other hand, are readily described as 'irrational', if not 'enigmatic' and 'whimsical' – all qualities that you definitely do not want to see in managerial positions because they imply low predictability. On the other hand, they are very desirable qualities indeed when one is looking for a sexual playmate. By the late nineteenth and early twentieth century, magazines aimed at women reviewed etiquette manuals that underlined the qualities just described. They also urged moderation in dress, for that was considered the most important manifestation of the ideal of femininity (Delhaye 2002.

Studies of career women have drawn attention to their experiences of ambivalence in male-dominated organizational cultures. On the one hand, they still want to express themselves and their femininity. On the other hand, they feel that in order to be taken seriously they are under great pressure to dress in a way that is acceptable to men, to be 'businesslike'. A compromise of sorts is a woman's jacket suit, which conforms to the male dress code but still allows for the expression of sexuality and playfulness (Zukin & Maguire 2004, 182).[5]

It is not hard to deduce from the descriptions above which gender has had the upper hand in determining the meanings carried by different styles. Silk and all other materials that glitter are connected by the male gaze to femininity and sexuality. Their opposite, i.e. wool, is a distinctly non-sexual material. It is hardly surprising then that women's woollen underwear continues to remain a source of embarrassed amusement for men: after all, it covers the most sexually charged part of the female body and in that sense contributes to desexualize it and threaten male potency.

The same male gaze is repeated in advertisements for men's and women's clothes, which are standardized, simplified and at the same time slightly exaggerating presentations of gender. Unless humour is used to confuse gender stereotypes, clothes advertisements typically represent women either as sexual objects or as vulnerable individuals who need protection. Or as Thomas C. Hood says, women in advertisements are on display. Men, on the other hand, are always going somewhere (Chadwick 1988, 7).

It is no coincidence that the male gaze determines the gendered features of our clothing and the way we look in general. Instead of clothes, this discussion could just as well have dealt with hairstyles. Virtually all features of masculine and feminine style are at variance with each other. Consumption of products that are thought to be feminine is ordinarily restricted to women only. Men are not allowed to use them without risking being labelled 'feminine'. This rule can only be waived in exceptional circumstances. For example, there are some special occasions where it acceptable for men to wear shiny and frilled clothes (such as theatre performances, in a music band). By contrast, many of those goods that are classified as male (long trousers, razors) are nowadays used by women as well, or at least new models have been developed that do not evoke condemnation or disapproval (Sahlins 1976, 190–191).

Men, however, have not been content just to watch from the side-lines as women have started to use commodities that are in the male domain. This has been actively discouraged through the imposition of strong moral codes or even laws. Where these have failed to uphold gender consumption differences (cf. the burkha), even finer distinctions have been applied to keep those differences alive, for instance, by putting pockets or rivets in trousers. This has helped to maintain gender differences in consumption styles, even though the ways of making these distinctions are in a constant state of flux. That, in turn, is explained by the very fact that the gender relationship and the corresponding consumption patterns are asymmetrical. This is also the reason why gender barriers in consumption may only be broken in exceptional circumstances (at carnivals, fancy dress parties, drag shows) without causing moral disapproval, and why it is usually women who overstep those barriers. From this it follows that women's consumption is subjected to moral censure more often than men's – and it is worth noting that it is not just men who are behind this censuring.

The second message conveyed by the examples of the design, colour and materials of clothes is that there are always outward immediately apparent differences between male and female modes of dress. The cultural meanings of femininity and masculinity that are materialized in commodities coincide with the differences in female and male ways of dressing. This correspondence is not just haphazard – it is always determined by cultural meanings. Meanings steer observations, the way that differences are perceived (see Juntunen 1986, 75).

This steering is not a conscious process, however. Instead, meanings are masked as part of the observation and give the observation its shape. In cultural anthropology this way of grasping the world is called 'savage thought' (Lévi-Strauss 1962). In savage thought, typically, *the observation and its interpretation are inextricably intertwined*, with the interpretation leading the way: the observation is always preceded by an interpretation which already labels the observation as something (Gadamer 2004, 219). It is precisely because of this intertwining of observation and interpretation that the categories of male and female taste that we see in consumption are considered normal in everyday thinking. And it is as such that they are reproduced. Therefore, it is typical not just of eighteenth-century thinking to say that men and women have consumption patterns that come 'naturally' to them; this view is still prevalent today. For instance, a woman represents skirts, a man trousers. This is one reason why it is so difficult for us in Western culture to know what to make of Arab dress (or the Scottish kilt). Long, skirt-like gowns, as far as Western male thinking is concerned, is an anomaly.

Finally, let me repeat that in this chapter I have described the main distinctive features and determinants of ideology. I have said nothing about its contents. I have suggested that the purpose of ideology is to naturalize prevailing social relations by hiding itself in some important area of social activity. Consumption is one such area. It can reproduce unnoticed, social relations both discursively and functionally. It does this on the strength of logo techniques, the mediatedness of social relations and style factors. This applies equally to the ethnic, age and gender systems and to some extent to the class systems, depending in part on the country concerned.

# 9
# Consumption As Use: Our Relationship to Commodities

If consumption mechanisms and discourses about consumption also influence our use of goods, they can shed only limited light on the basics of those everyday uses. In this final chapter I intend to look more closely at consumption as use, giving special focus to the co-existence of consumer and commodity, which lies at the very heart of the event of use. My aim is to create a general framework for the everyday use of commodities, a 'theory of use', if you like, and at the same time demonstrate that commodities are central to the functioning of our social networks.

## 9.1  Consumption and our relationship to objects

In his epic tale *The Lord of the Rings* (1954–1955), J.R.R. Tolkien creates the most wonderful setting for his treatment of the eternal theme of good versus evil. The battle focuses on the ownership of a special magic ring, which is the subject of much envy and strife because it affords its keeper great powers. The ring can make its bearer invisible, for example, but at a cost: he or she will become its slave. This is an ancient and widely spread belief, which has it that ownership and, in fact, even the desire of some significant object will have disastrous consequences not only for individuals but for the existing social order. This applies not just to fairy tales but to our social life as well. This is seen in the recurrence of these fairy-tale fears in connection with the market launch of a significant new product, such as the car, radio, telephone, television or mobile phone (see e.g. Pantzar 1996).

Although it is widely acknowledged by now that goods have a significant impact on our lives, they have still not received the attention they deserve in social theory, particularly in *analyses of sociality* (see Preda

1999; Knorr-Cetina 1997). Marx, of course, regarded the commodity as the alienated product of the collective worker's labour, but the main focus of his analyses was on the exchange value rather than the use value of commodities (Marx 1976; see also Haug 1982a). Simmel (and Veblen), on the other hand, drew attention to the use of goods in his examinations of fashion and highlighted the 'specificity of goods' (Simmel 1997 [1900]).

Analyses of our relationships to commodities are conspicuously absent from most post-classical social theory, whether we consider the structural theories inspired by Talcott Parsons or ethnomethodological theories based on the work of Alfred Schütz and Harold Garfinkel. It is not that these theoretical traditions do not accept the existence of commodities, but rather that they do not admit that they have any significant role in social reality. And they do this despite the shared recognition that it is the role of the producer, *Homo faber,* to shape the physical world using his tools, while the consumer, *Homo consumens,* changes that world according to his tastes and preferences.

The situation changed in the 1970s when sociology rekindled its interest in matters of consumption. Not only did it follow anthropology's lead and define consumption items as the most important means of making and maintaining social distinctions, but they were also acknowledged as a key element in identity construction (Warde 1994; Campbell 1996; Ilmonen 2001a). However, the sociology of consumption has always taken a rather narrow view on the use of goods; it has never really been mentioned more than in passing. In this chapter I want to broaden that horizon and show that commodities have a much more important function in our lives than is ordinarily thought; that commodities are not just passive objects that can be applied to some specific purpose. On the contrary, they actively influence our existence and lives. They have an important mediating role in our social networks. In this role they may even serve as a counterforce to individualization and privatization.

Karin Knorr-Cetina (1997, 1) argues that the debate on the 'disembedding of social selves' from human relations ignores the 'ways in which major classes of individuals have tied themselves to object worlds'. She is no doubt right – but then she omits to mention that our relations to objects are different in nature to human relations. Objects don't answer back (at least for the time being) in the same way as other people do.[1] They may nevertheless consume all our attention and become the object of our passionate concerns. How does this happen?

## 9.2   Individualization and sociality

According to Knorr-Cetina (1997), much of the debate that has gone on about the post-modern has focused on the post-social condition. It is part of a metanarrative about individualization. It is not a novel idea that we are living in an age of individualization. Alexis de Tocqueville wrote about it more than 150 years ago, saying that 'individualism is a novel expression, to which a novel idea has given birth'. It must be distinguished from egotism. Individualism is more 'mature and calm' than egotism, but the outcome from both is more or less the same: 'Individualism...disposes each member of the community to sever himself from the mass of his fellow-creatures; and to draw apart with his family and his friends' (de Tocqueville 1969, 506). Once this withdrawal has happened, citizens 'acquire the habit of always considering themselves as standing alone, and they are apt to imagine that their whole destiny is in their own hands'. This involves the risk that the individual confines himself entirely 'within the solitude of his own heart' (ibid., 508).

Since de Tocqueville's days that risk has surfaced from time to time. As Durkheim has famously pointed out, changes in the social division of labour and increasing mobility are setting people free from their old social ties. However, Durkheim (1997 [1893]) was concerned that this process will not necessarily end happily and lead to what he described as 'organic solidarity'. Around the corner lurked the threat of anomie. According to Durkheim (1951 [1897]) the risk of anomie was increased most particularly by consumption and the constant growth of unsatisfied desires.

Durkheim's nightmare of alienation has been repeated primarily in the Anglo-American sociological tradition, particularly in texts concerned with the erosion of community and the end of traditions. Most of them deal with a subject that is nowadays known as social capital. From David Riesman's and colleagues' *The Lonely Crowd* through Peter Berger's and his co-workers' *Homeless Mind* (1974) and Robert Bellah's and his colleagues' *Habits of the Hearts* (1996) to Robert Putnam's *Bowling Alone* (2000), the story has been much the same.

It is customary in these traditions of thought to associate individualization with individualism, which it is feared is accelerated by neo-liberal economic policy. As Knorr-Cetina (1997, 4), echoing Erich Fromm, says, 'the demise of community and traditions also leaves the individual in the lurch – without the psychological means to deal with the great freedom of choice or the contingency of contemporary life as which this freedom rebounds'. This view looks upon society as an aggregate consisting of isolated, asocial and ahistorical psychological particles. Society is like granules of sugar in a bag; or in Nietzsche's words, like 'social sand'.

According to Knorr-Cetina, the post-social condition has nothing to do with individualism or with asocial or non-social relations: 'Rather they are relations specific to late modern societies, which are marked by the interweave of the social as it existed with "other" cultures'. The alien culture relevant here is that of 'knowledge and expertise' (Knorr-Cetina 1997, 5). Without access to 'expert systems' (see e.g. Giddens 1990) the individual is helpless in his choices. This expression accurately describes the current situation in that it does not relate the individual to small crumbs of information but to the 'presence of whole contexts of expert work' (Knorr-Cetina 1997, 5). It is because of this 'presence' that post-social society has also been called 'knowledge society'.

The concept of 'knowledge society' does not just mean that there are more experts and that there is more technological information but there are also more lay interpretations, or as Knorr-Cetina says, 'participant interpretations' about expert knowledge. Take the advice given by nutritionists about healthy eating: this provides an excellent example of a modern situation where we read expert texts, interpret them in our own ways and then apply them to our daily life. If this example can be generalized, what it means is that knowledge and social processes are no longer separate. On the contrary, 'knowledge has become constitutive of social relations' (Knorr-Cetina 1997, 8). According to Knorr-Cetina this changes the status of commodities in our daily lives. They become an important element in our social relations. We only have to think of the telephone, telefax, internet, car or train to understand this. All of them are bound to accelerate individualization. However, in so doing they also help people connect with one another and create 'network sociality' (Wittel 2001). In other words, they act as a counterforce to individualization.

## 9.3 Towards a theory of use: 'work of hybridization'

If the picture sketched above is accurate, our relationship to commodities cannot be located outside the circle of our social life.[2] Even though products are 'non-human actants', they still have the ability to steer our social life. In this role they mediate one type of daily practice into another and connect us to other people (Sartre 1976, 184). They are not indifferent to us because they make our actions possible, whatever the type of commodity: a chair for sitting, a saucepan for cooking (Reckwitz 2002, 253). In some cases such as riding a bicycle and driving a car, the tie between consumer and product is so strong that it is hard to say where the product ends and where we as human beings begin (Preda 1999). According to Bruno Latour (e.g. 1991; Preda 1999), this practical dependence could be called 'work of hybridization' because during the course of this work, objects and people (momentarily) become one.

When man and commodity stand in a relation of co-dependence it is difficult to say which of them ultimately initiates the activity, man or product. It is useful to return to our example of cycling and driving. In principle, both these activities depend in many respects on the condition and properties of the vehicle, for instance, acceleration and steering characteristics. It is only through the use of these vehicles that we have learned how to handle them. Our body has learned how to routinely cycle or drive a car in varying situations (Reckwitz 2002, 251, 258). In the eyes of an outsider, therefore, cycling and driving appear as entirely synchronized activities between the bicycle and car and their drivers. It is only by following activities over time that it is possible to deduce when it is the consumer and when it is the consumption object that steer the 'work of hybridization'. On a cold morning, for instance, if the car doesn't 'want' to start, the driver will just have to wait; ditto on an icy road if the car doesn't 'want' to stop. In these situations the car (and the law of continuity) 'controls' the driver, whether he likes it or not. Otherwise the driver is pretty much the captain of his vehicle.[3]

Time structures, which consist of time sequences and temporal orders, are crucially important to our object relations (see Reckwitz 2002, 255). These structures depend more on product qualities or product functionality than on the symbolic characteristics that have been so central to the sociology of consumption. In fact, all 'work of hybridization' is based on time sequences. Consider the simple process of eating a hamburger (or any other food). It has a point of beginning and a clearly marked ending and sequences in-between. At each stage the hamburger mediates the eating process. Bite by bite we approach it in a slightly different way (see e.g. Law 1992, 381). If instead of eating we turn our attention to listening to a CD, watching television, making a cup of coffee or driving a car, the sequences of our interactions with commodities should become clearer still. The products just mentioned have not just a passive, but also an active impact on our time use. Actor-network theory (ANT) goes so far as to argue (somewhat vaguely) that time order in hybridization work is 'an effect generated by heterogeneous means' (ibid., 382).

Since commodities and human activities are interwoven, the difference between human action and the product's functional qualities is only contingent, as ANT suggests. Goods and human activities constitute a network in which people act and commodities react ad infinitum. 'And, just as human beings have their preferences – they prefer to interact in certain ways rather than in others – so too do the other materials that make up the heterogeneous networks of the social' (Law 1992, 382). Cars and forks can be used as status symbols or for any other purpose (forks to play an instrument, for instance), but this does nothing to change the fact that in their proper uses (driving and eating) they place certain demands upon us.

These demands come from the fact that, firstly, products embody a wide range of *prior experience and current knowledge.* Consumers must have up-to-date skills and know-how in order to be able to use them. The more advanced and sophisticated the products are technically, the more skills they require of consumers. Learning how to use them as a matter of routine practice takes more time than learning simpler products. Secondly, learned practices produce the *emotional level* that is needed to carry out these practices. They reinforce our attitudes towards the commodities we consider our 'own'. They are loaded with emotions that range from strong passions (hate–love) to an attitude of detached indifference.

Thirdly, having fully mastered these learned practices consumers represent a unique junction for those practices. *Commodities mediate these practices to constitute a system that in the future will shape those practices* (Reckwitz 2002, 257). As Gregory Bateson (1972, 318) has argued, tools and commodities in general are one moment in the feedback system of human activity that emerges when we work with them.[4] These networks formed by people and commodities are furthermore liable to become established over time and even to expand (from cars to petrol, from petrol to petrol stations, from petrol stations to motorways and motorway service areas).

In other words, commodities are involved in patterning our social world. For this reason it is wrong to reduce the 'social' only to human actors and their relationships, but the material environment must also be taken into account in its formation, as implied by Jean-Paul Sartre's (1976, 188) concept of 'socio-material'. For the same reason it is also wrong to *separate people and commodities into completely different spheres,* even though they do definitely belong to different *moral* spheres (see Kopytoff 1988, 84). When I say that people and commodities are located at the same level, I do not mean to suggest that people should be treated as tools or other objects and vice versa. Goods have no duties, no rights and responsibilities that are ordinarily accorded to people, but they can be used to promote their moral interests (see Law 1992, 383).

When it is accepted that commodities belong to the same life-circle as people, the methodological asymmetry in our object relations cannot be defended (Preda 1999; Law 1992, 282). This means that, to a certain extent, 'the methodological assumptions that apply to human actors would also apply to things' (Preda 1999) and that subject–subject relations cannot claim superiority over subject–object relations (Reckwitz 2002, 253). This, however, is an exaggeration that has earned ANT some criticism. The theory fails to take account of the fact that, even though there is much variation in subject–object relations, that variation is even greater in subject–subject relations. Besides, in this world of humans, they are regarded as more meaningful than subject–object relations. We show greater affection for our children than for even the most prized of our objects. The symmetry between consumers and commodities should therefore not be confused with an ontological symmetry, for that would lead us to the assumption that commodities have feeling, are intentional and reflective.

Although commodities do not have intentions, the assumption of methodological symmetry means that the material and functional qualities of objects constitute the framework for our interactions with them. The functional qualities of commodities are therefore the most central aspect of their use. For this reason part of the knowledge that is inscribed in commodities includes the functional restrictions they set. However, that knowledge is not complete. We are not aware of all the possible uses of commodities. Edmund Husserl has illustrated this problem by reference to the concepts of *noema* and *noetic*. *Noema* is everything that the consumer knows about the object of consumption. *Noetic*, then, represents the consumer's individual moments of perception (e.g. that a spoon is a piece of cutlery) (Husserl 1964; Juntunen 1986, 74). Our attitude to the object of consumption is dependent on what we know about it and how we perceive it at any one instant as well as on the interaction between our knowledge and perceptions (Grenfell 2004, 26).

Like our knowledge, our perceptions are always incomplete. Being aware of this is crucial to learning the skills we need in the use of commodities. Formal training can provide only limited help; otherwise the only way to learn is by doing it. This follows from our limited knowledge of the functionality of products and restricts our uses of commodities. As we use goods, we also learn more about how they work. This increased knowledge and understanding of products is undefined and personal. Indeed, the outcome of learning by doing has been described as 'indeterminate' or 'tacit' knowledge (Polanyi 1962, 48).

Since our ties with commodities can be very close and strong, Knorr-Cetina (1997, 12) says that they can hardly be described as alienated. In expert work in particular, it seems that if anything, object relations are characterized by the exact opposite, i.e. identification. However, Knorr-Cetina is keen to make a distinction between 'objects of knowledge' and tools and other kinds of goods. This is because she takes a very narrow view of goods other than 'knowledge objects'. She maintains that according to prevailing thinking, goods are not valued for their intrinsic properties but rather for 'what they buy – status, relationships, other objects' (ibid., 11). However, this view is not as dominant as Knorr-Cetina leads us to understand. Much of what she says about 'objects of knowledge' is applicable to other commodities, too.

Besides, there are also commodities whose most important quality may be their symbolic value. This is particularly true of objects that have become totemic in a Durkheimian sense. For instance, such totemic goods as commodified pop stars and football clubs attract people to join the new tribe that is formed around them (fan clubs, collectors' associations). This is of course an old phenomenon, but it has particular relevance in 'knowledge society'. It shows that individualization does not take place in a social vacuum but is associated both with existing institutions and with the world of commodities (Knorr-Cetina 1997, 12). This is another reason why it is wrong to suggest that commodities lie beyond our social interests. On the contrary, we may even experience a sense of solidarity towards objects. This provides a strong foundation for *object-centred sociality*. What Knorr-Cetina means by this phrase is a) 'a sense of bondedness or unity with objects'; b) 'the ought-ness of approaching them in certain ways'; and c) 'states of excitement reaffirming the bondedness' (ibid., 20).

## 9.4 Appropriation of commodities: internalization

It is unclear, however, how to proceed from the stage where commodities have become established as part of our social world to the point that Knorr-Cetina calls object-centred sociality. Sociality among people that is based on good is only a necessary *condition* for sociality with objects. It is necessary, therefore, to be able to explain how the admission that commodities belong to our life-circle leads to object-centred sociality. In the language of market research, we have to be able to explain how the sense of 'me-ness' emerged in relation to commodities. To do that, we have to examine the process of adaptation to goods, an issue that has interested psychologists and social psychologists for a long time. By way of a background to the information they have produced, I start out from Durkheim's idea of totemic thinking.

In his book on the social division of labour, Durkheim (1997 [1893]; see also Beck & Beck-Gernsheim 2002, xxi) maintains that the structural characteristics of differentiating and differentiated societies do not threaten the individual's integration into society, but on the contrary, make it possible. Integration grows out of the need to *coordinate social activities* by establishing social connections between individuals. That need is further reinforced by the demand for increasing *social exchange* based on the division of labour and related specialization. Durkheim later had a compelling desire to elaborate on his account. He had to answer the questions of how the objective social relations and conditions assumed an internalized form and what this internalized form looked like (Morrison 2001, 108).

In order to answer the latter question, Durkheim had to tackle Kant's a priori categories. Whereas in his *Critique of Pure Reason* Kant (1965, 111) said that an understanding of things in the phenomenal world required a priori categories,[5] Durkheim turned this position on its head. He suggested that since people saw themselves as members of different kinds of groups and since they also classified living creatures, primarily animals, in the world around them, these two different modes of classification became merged (Morrison 2001, 110). As a result, pre-modern people began to associate themselves with these animal categories and to produce corresponding symbolic representations, which were called totems.

As we know, Durkheim (1995) believed that totems had great significance not only in primitive societies, but also in advanced European societies. Totemic thinking brought social groups into a relationship with one another. Totems also appeared as material symbols or collective representations (team scarves etc.), which helped to reproduce the existing social fabric. This is the background for why totems, the material symbols of social groups, are treated with such great reverence and respect. To insult them is to insult the groups that respect them. (This explains why in wars it has been important to defend the nation's flag or to hoist the flag in a newly conquered area.)

Durkheim's view has been highly influential. However, he has left many questions unanswered. He did not explain what attitude *individuals* within a given social group took to totemic objects. How did they make them their own? In other words, he left only limited scope for individual variation in the adoption of totemic categories. Their position has probably changed in the wake of the modernization process and individualization. Although they still occur (and new ones are created), for instance, in the form of sports' club symbols or coats of arms of noble families, they no longer have the same coercive effect on group members as they did in pre-modern societies. It can no longer be taken for granted that they will adopt totemic symbols. This applies particularly to commodities in the marketplace, even though they too carry totemic symbols (e.g. Esso's famous tiger advertisement). For this reason it is necessary to analyse how consumers make these goods their 'own' (Ilmonen 2004, 35–36).

Goods are made our own through an *appropriation process*. That can be understood in more than one way, but at least there is a consensus that it only happens after a commodity has been bought. Once the purchase has been made, the commodity exits the marketplace and relinquishes its status as a commodity (the generalized system of equivalence and exchange). At the same time it becomes the property of its buyer (individual, household etc.). At this stage the commodity is singularized and given a 'social life'. It can later be returned to the market (e.g. a second-hand car), thus restoring its status of commodity (Kopytoff 1988, 65; see also Appadurai 1988). However, I shall leave this last stage aside and concentrate only on how singularization might take place.[6]

Lev Vygotsky provides a useful starting point for an examination of the process of appropriation. Vygotsky wanted to find out the general principles governing individual development and related mental processes. His conclusion was quite exceptional in his day: 'Every function in the child's cultural development appears twice: first, on the social level, and later, on the individual level' (Vygotsky 1978, 57). If this principle is generalized to apply to our object relations, it can be said that we first consider the object in relation to the external world of objects and only then try to internalize it. I shall here focus on the latter part of the process and ask how this internalization of objects happens. I am not interested in questions of formal, legal and economic ownership, but rather in the way that we make some object subjectively ours. The phrase 'my home' nicely captures what I have in mind: it shows how the physical object that is a house or a flat is transformed into something personal, into 'home sweet home'.

However, the internalization of commodities is just one step in the appropriation process. It is also important to study how we *project ourselves on external objects* or how we objectify ourselves into them. In other words, it is necessary to explore how we externalize and transfer our desires, our inner emotions and social relations into objects. It is the outcome of this externalization and transfer that market research refers to when it speaks about the *me-ness* of commodities (see Schultz Kleine, Kleine III & Allen 1995). Let me start with the process of internalization.

As mentioned, commodities are only appropriated after the purchase has been made. Market research suggests that consumers become attached to the object almost instantly after acquiring it (see Beggan 1992). This is called the 'instant endowment effect'. However, Michael J. Barone and colleagues (1997, 282–284) have called into question the instantness of this mechanism. In a series of studies involving the exchange of commodities they found no evidence of a lasting increase in object attractiveness. However, even if the valuation of objects does not increase immediately, it may still do so over time. This has been proved experimentally. People develop a strong sense of attachment over time. When the consumer has had the object for a long time, he or she will be increasingly reluctant to give it up (Strahilevitz & Loewenstein 1998, 276, 287–289). Indeed, instead of an instant endowment effect, it would be more accurate to refer simply to an *endowment effect*.

Market research has also attempted to explain this endowment effect. It has first of all been connected with Daniel Kahneman's and Amos Tversky's (Tversky & Kahneman 1991) idea of *loss aversion*. According to them, people are inclined to put more weight on losses than on gains of the same value. This is clearly seen at least in the context of gambling and risk-taking in general (Strahilevitz & Loewenstein 1998, 278). However, it is hard to see how this idea works with such commodities as, say, old walking shoes, even though Strahilevitz and Loewenstein seem to think that loss aversion is equally applicable to all commodities.

Furthermore, the endowment effect has been explained by reference to *familiarity*. The longer someone owns a commodity, the better they learn to know it and interact with it. The more positive the experience, the keener they are to keep it. However, there is no reason to assume that this positive experience will not change over time. It may even be completely reversed as the product wears away, especially if a new generation of products is introduced in the market that offer greater efficiency and in general are more attractive than the old commodities (see Harrison & March 1984). It may also happen that even though the positive experience remains the same, the commodity may still be thought to have negative qualities (see Thaler 1980). They may not outweigh the positive experiences, but may still dissuade consumers from using the old product. For these reasons familiarity cannot, at least on its own, explain people's reluctance to part with their old possessions, even if they no longer work in the best possible way (see Ilmonen 2001b).

So what about taste-change, which has also been put forward as an explanation for the endowment effect? According to Strahilevitz and Lowenstein (1998, 283), 'motivated taste-change suggests that the increases in valuation as a result of ownership and duration of ownership will be mediated by increases in perceived attractiveness'. However, they fail to corroborate this assumption, and they also have no explanation for the growth of 'perceived attractiveness'. It is quite clear that possession alone does not have this effect. Only the active use of commodities can have such a consequence.[7] There are many reasons why only consumption, the recurring use of goods, can contribute to a consumer perception of the commodity that will maintain and even intensify the endowment effect.

In order for us to understand the endowment effect, we need to approach consumption from a slightly different perspective than is ordinarily the case. Consumption is not only about style, fashion or tradition. In Latour's words, it is also 'work'. According to Daniel Miller (1987, 191), this applies particularly to appropriation. *Appropriation work* is a process where the consumer works with an alien object with a specific view to 'de-alienate' it and absorb it as part of his or her social world. Vygotsky suggests that this work involves two steps. The first step involves the *cognitive appropriation* of the commodity, the second its *emotional internalization*. In other words, in the latter stage commodities become loaded with emotional attachment. These steps can also be described in slightly more general terms as a) the recognition of commodities external to our social lives and b) their emotional absorption into our personal lives.

The first step is not really a step at all. It is more a process that breaks down into a number of stages. As has been discussed earlier, many commodities incorporate the existing level of knowledge. Whatever the commodity, knowledge already exists within them (see Preda 1999). This means that the use of commodities requires special skills and related tacit knowledge on the part of the consumer if he or she wishes to take full advantage of their potential (see Polanyi 1962). Even the use of processed foods requires such knowledge. When we consume goods we have to learn to master the skills that attach us to them.

Ordinarily, however, our skills tend to be more limited the more technically sophisticated the product. The concept of affordance is helpful in unravelling this phenomenon. The concept comes from biology but it is also applicable to our object relations. It entails the idea that our environment affords opportunities for action. However, we only see those affordances that tickle our intellectual or physical fancy (Arminen & Raudaskoski 2003, 282). In practice, however, this process moves in the exact opposite direction. John Dewey makes the same point by observing that the only reason why the stimulus attracts our attention is that we already have an existing response (Menand 2002, 330). For instance, when we are holding a hammer in our hand our eyes begin to look for nails. (This is precisely what Husserl had in mind with this concept of noetic.) For this reason it is important to make a distinction between *real and perceived affordances*. Real affordances determine the *boundaries of what is possible,* the confines within which we make our choices.

Goods in the marketplace and their discursive representations, such as advertisements, films and brands, represent existing affordances. We give attention to some of them because we feel drawn towards them. When we choose a certain product we obviously don't know everything about it in advance (the strength of the composites made to use it, its physical properties, its functional flaws). We only have a noema about the product; a notion of what it is good for. The consumer's impression of the commodity's qualities, then, indicates which of its possibilities are put to use (ibid., 284). Take a laptop. Usually only a fraction of its full capacity is used because we have only incomplete knowledge of what it can do. We only learn about its uses when we use the laptop, and not necessarily even then, because we are mainly preoccupied with the *perceived affordances* highlighted by our desires.

Secondly, in the process of applying his or her skills to use a commodity, the consumer is at once reproducing those skills. This reproduction is not just plain repetition, however. In renewing our consumer skills we may also learn new things about the product. No matter how carefully we have read the manual for our new gas cooker, for instance, we will only learn how the oven works through practical experience. As Michel Callon and colleagues (2002, 203) say: 'The qualities of a product depend on the joint work of host actors and there is no reason to believe that consumers do not participate ... in the objectification of those qualities'. As consumers, we learn to recognize what we can do with different commodities. In a word, by using commodities we appropriate them *cognitively as commodities for ourselves.*

Cognitive appropriation is in many cases an on-going process. During the course of that process our relationship to objects changes in the same as Vygotsky (1986) says happens when we move from written text to inner speech or thought. In his analysis of this move, Vygotsky makes a distinction between the *meaning* and *sense* of a word. Meaning refers to the abstract shared understanding of the word, which is defined in dictionaries. Sense, on the other hand, refers to the variable meanings of the concept that we have unconsciously defined in various contexts and that expresses our relationship to the things with which the word is thought to be associated. In other words, meanings are objective and general, whereas the sense of a concept is laden with personal, subjective and emotional experiences. According to Vygotsky, the move from written text to its personal perception means that thought begins to dominate the objective meaning of the concept. In a sense, every individual begins to develop his or her own parole that has its emotional loadings.

As far as I can gather, the Vygotskian step from meaning to sense is analogous to what happens in the use of objects. Nonetheless, the internalization of commodities is not necessarily an individual process but a social one that happens together with other people. For example, when a family of four have bought a house they start to fit it out to make it habitable. The family members must move quite quickly to do this and make their everyday life run smoothly. To begin with, they must form an overall impression of the space they have available. Based on their conclusions they must decide which family members will have which room and allocate different rooms for different functions. Six months later, however, someone may realize that the furniture layout in the house is not very practical. He or she may be able to persuade the other family members that they should to make rearrangements. These changes will help to make the house home, which is no longer just any space but an emotionally highly charged space. In Kopytoff's (1988) words, the house is singularized and made a unique place. Once this has happened the house has a dual value: a value as a commodity that is comparable to other houses in the market and a value as a unique commodity that cannot be compared to others on account of its specificity (Graeber 2001, 32).

It is necessary to stress that the process of internalization does not take place in a cultural void. We learn a great deal from older generations and our friends about how to use commodities. At the same time we learn what sort of attitude we should take towards them and how to use them for our own purposes. As Peter Berger and Thomas Luckmann (1966, 11–58) have pointed out, we have been socialized not only to cultural reality, but we are actually involved in constructing that reality. As a consequence, distinct social cultures and beliefs concerning age, gender, race and religion impact the internalization of commodities.

A good example is provided by the different attitudes of men and women to technical products (see Lupton & Noble 2002, 11–12).

Vygotsky thus sees our thought (or inner speech) as a crossroads of cultural meanings and personal experience. This is what happens when we cognitively appropriate commodities by using them. In this process we improve our skills to use the product. At the same time we gain a more profound experience of the product. That experience shapes our relationship to the commodity both cognitively and emotionally. It becomes more personal. Generally speaking 'appropriation develops a processual, mutually constitutive notion between artefacts and subjectivity' (Lupton & Noble 2002, 7). To revert to the question I asked in connection with Durkheim's collective representations, appropriation causes variation in the attitudes not only of individuals but also social groups towards general meanings that belong to totemic categories. The singularization and appropriation of a commodity resembles a jazz ensemble that plays in many rhythms and tunes rather than a unison aria.

In other words, our interaction with commodities does not leave us indifferent. If they work properly and serve our purposes we are content with them and we invest our emotions in them. And the opposite is true: if we are not happy with them we are liable to reject them. According to Alex Preda (1999), this is consistent with George Herbert Mead's (Deweyian) observation that 'things answer to the attitudes we have formed to them and that our attitudes adjust to things'. As a corollary to the first scenario it can be said that the more we use the commodity, the more likely it is we will commit ourselves. We can also assume that the stronger our involvement in and commitment to the commodity, the more significant a part it will play in our daily life and the stronger the endowment effect.

## 9.5   The externalization of commodities, or how internalized commodities can assume a general meaning

Our involvement in and commitment to a commodity are indicative of the intensity of our feelings towards this object (see Heller 1977, 7). Commitment is by nature a specific process. 'Involvement in something', then, implies two alternatives. According to Heller, involvement is equal to a *feeling*. It can itself be the focus of our attention, but so can the object of involvement. When the emphasis is on the feeling itself, its object fades into the background (Heller 1977, 11–12). The phenomenon is more clearly apparent when we are overcome by some strong emotion such as fear, hatred or love. The same happens when the action associated with our emotion is prevented for whatever reason. The object of involvement, on the other hand, comes to the fore when we focus on resolving a problem, on some specific situation or on the way in which something is happening. However, it is important to realize that regardless of whether the focus of our attention is on the motion or its object; both are always present in our emotions. If one or the other is missing the feeling will be extinguished.

Since our emotions are bound to an external object it follows that no emotion can be detached from making an observation about that object or from the impressions we had of the object before making our observation. On the contrary, our emotions are interwoven with the knowledge we produce about that object and with our perception of that object. *Emotions also have a cognitive component.* They provide *important information* about our relationship to the object of the emotion, which is internalized in experiences and allows us to act in a subjectively meaningful manner in relation to the object of our emotion (see Hochschild 1983, 30–31, 222; Heller 1977, 50).

We are also inclined to project our emotions onto the objects of our consumption. We invest our emotions and desires into the actual objects. As a result they carry part of us, an aura of 'me-ness'. This 'me-ness' is not just a virtual idea. Mass-produced commodities are shaped and earmarked, individually or collectively, through embodied use. For example, 'me' may *decorate or configure them in distinctive ways.* Deborah Lupton and Greg Noble (2002, 11–21) believe that these are two major ways of appropriating PCs, at least in Australian academic settings. Decorating 'includes adding external objects to the computer to achieve a personalizing or aesthetic effect', while configuration means things like naming hard-drive files, changing the desktop image and arranging computer software. It is very likely that these strategies are applicable to most consumption objects and that they vary by gender, age and education, for instance.

However, appropriation strategies should not be taken to mean that involvement necessarily implies a twisted attitude. Rather they are essentially about transcending the functionality of goods. Decorating and configuring objects (or any other appropriation strategy) serve to extend the self outwards in space and to form 'a territory that surrounds the body' (Lupton & Noble 2002, 7), to expand 'me-ness'.

Involvement in and commitment to goods imply then that commodities are not just any objects of consumption. Since we have invested aspects of our 'me-ness' into those commodities, we are inclined to take good care of them, almost as if they were pets. In fact Martin Heidegger (1977) has pointed out that many reflective everyday activities have to do with looking after commodities. These kinds of activities are part of on an on-going process of consumption.[8] Clothes need to be washed, tables cleaned up, cars serviced etc. It is only once commodities have been reduced to little more than rubbish that we reject them and throw them away.

Furthermore, the appropriation of goods not only changes our attitude towards them; it also changes our practices. When we have learned how to use a fairly complicated technical device like a video camera, for instance, we no longer have to pay attention to the cognitive side of how to use it. Shooting video happens more or less routinely. This gives us greater freedom in using the camera because we can now concentrate on what it is we are filming. Once we have reached this stage in the use of our video camera, the actual shooting blends effortlessly with the other activities that are required in the situation. The mental activities of understanding and experiencing the shooting process and knowing how to film become interwoven with a complex web of simultaneous activities such as walking, zooming, checking the lighting conditions.

When we have reached the level where our use of commodities has turned into a routine we do not necessarily regard our actions as consumption at all. Instead, it becomes a by-product of our practices. When we go out for a round of golf we don't think that we are consuming our golf clubs, we just think of the relaxation and health benefits. When we are preparing a meal, we don't think of this process in terms of the consumption of pots and pans: on the contrary, they have a supporting role in the complex series of practices that is called 'cooking'.

The extent to which consumption becomes assimilated into practices obviously varies from one product to the next. On the one hand, there are those very 'fluid' products such as energy and electricity that we use without thinking of them in consumption terms. It is virtually impossible to create a bond of commitment with these kinds of commodities. Such activities as 'cooking' virtually absorb energy consumption into themselves. On the other hand, there are such products as PCs that have a very high degree of control over our practices. Most goods lie somewhere in-between these two extremes. Although some of them may, over time, turn into by-products of a particular activity, we must still continue to pay attention to them every now and then. The only reason we need to do that is to try and improve their functionality. This in itself is an indication of our commitment to these goods.

Although our commitment to goods is personal or group-based it will not necessarily remain hidden to others. Our involvement not only informs us about our relationship to those goods, but if we so want, it also provides information to others about ourselves and our special relationship to the commodity. We may even make this relationship explicit by telling others about our new ways of handling the commodity (developing new recipes and new styles, giving new instructions). Rom Harré (1983, 258) calls this stage 'making known', in which the emphasis is on the productive aspect of the commodity. In this stage we demonstrate to a wider audience our individual way of handling the product. Every step in this direction is always risky because in so doing we let others know what we think about the commodity and our ability to use it (for instance, our ability to cook). In the worst case they may think we are crazy. In the best case we may be praised for a new innovation. When that happens, it is possible that the innovation is accepted in the community as part of its cultural heritage. If this possibility materializes, our innovation will become incorporated as part of our community's common wisdom, which as a social resource benefits the whole community (Ilmonen 2004, 43).

To provide a more formal account of the appropriation process I shall apply Vygostky's and Harré's ideas of the internationalization and externalization of commodities. Harré uses two dimensions to illustrate the process. One is the dimension of 'presentation', the other that of 'realization'. One end of the dimension of 'presentation' consists of public presentation, the other of private presentation (keeping things to ourselves). 'Realization', then, can be either individual or collective (see Figure 9.1).

In sketching this figure for other purposes, Harré (1983, 258) starts out from Vygotskian psychology of language learning in child development.[9] However, language is not a constant system of codes but an ever-changing practice that shapes and modifies the language system. For instance, the language of SMS messages has become far more economical over time. In order to understand these messages we must learn to understand the abbreviations and visual symbols that they now include. Those must first be accepted collectively in order to work as a language. Harré deals with language in the same way. Language, for him, is a developing system that must become established, for a short moment at least, in order to work as a means of communication. For this reason he refers to conventionalization as a process.

From the individual consumer's vantage point conventionalization happens in the marketplace all the time and the circular process

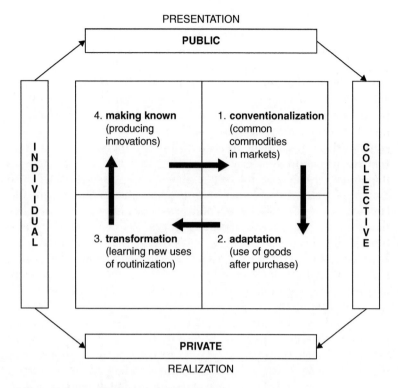

*Figure 9.1*    Appropriation of commodity

may start from any cell in the four-field model. Since my focus here is on the appropriation process, I will start where Harré does. The consumer purchases a good in the marketplace. While the manufacturer has developed it with a specific 'ideal user' in mind, trying to envisage how the product will be typically used, they will rarely be successful. The real user will be some distance away from the imagined 'ideal user' (Woolgar 1991; 2000). The end result will not necessarily be consistent with the manufacturer's expectations because the consumer's appropriation process only begins after they have made the purchase, regardless of whether the commodity is new or conventional (see Miller 1998; Lehtonen 2001). 'Appropriation' refers to the personal or collective appropriation of the commodity. That, in turn, changes the consumer's relationship to the product. The relationship becomes more or less personal.

Let us once again take the bicycle example. Not a mountain bike or a slick racer, but just a completely ordinary bicycle with a few gears. It takes a while for the bicycle to teach its user how to ride it: how to sit in the saddle, how the pedals rotate, how the gears work in relation to the terrain and so on. Once the cyclist has passed this stage, he or she no longer has to pay any attention to the technical side of cycling but can concentrate on enjoying the ride (Ilmonen 2001b, 21–22). As a result the cyclist's approach to the bicycle and its use takes on personal or group-based features. We may mark the bicycle in some way, for instance by installing a distinctively coloured shopping basket, or decorate it by painting, which is often done with old bicycles.

These singularizing decorations may include tribal symbols, like the colours, badges or names of a football club. In the best case this marking may include innovative elements, such as the development of a new type of taillight. 'Making known' does not necessarily require this, however. The main purpose is to show others that the user is in control of the bicycle. But sometimes this is not enough. The user may also need documentation, a driving licence or a gun licence to prove that he or she is a proper consumer of certain special products (cars, motorcycles, guns).

Let me take another example to 'make myself known'. Doing the groceries is one of our everyday practices. It is a common source of headache whether we should buy certain ingredients or make do with processed foods. In either case the next step is to decide how to prepare the food and what additional items are needed. In making these decisions we may resort to some familiar recipe. However, we might not be able to use the recipe as such because not all family members like it or can eat it because of an allergy. We therefore have to make adjustments to the recipe in order to satisfy the tastes and special needs of all family members. Since we might not all be master chefs à la Bocuse, we have to rely on the method of trial and error. After a few successes we might be personally content that we have produced something new and feel that it is worthwhile to share our innovation with friends and neighbours. If they, too, like the new recipe, they in turn might recommend it to friends. Thus the recipe gradually becomes conventionalized and continues on its path of circulation.

Some major corporations even have mechanisms in place to systematically take advantage of consumer input in their product development. Whether these innovations are actually put to use depends on how keen consumers are to adopt them (see Klein 2000). Callon and colleagues (2002, 203) summarize the point thus: 'The products they buy are tested in their home; collective evaluations are made; learning takes place, which gives rise to evaluations. More broadly, our consumers are caught in social networks in which tastes are formed, discussed and mitigated'. These networks are mediated by commodities. They therefore play a significant part in our social life. However, not all commodities achieve this status. Therefore it is probably right to say that 'in the economy of qualities, competition turns around the attachments of consumers to products whose qualities have progressively been defined with their active participation' (ibid., 212). If the attempt to commit consumers to products by marketing, for instance, fails to succeed, then consumption objects will not be appropriated. Instead, they will remain in the position of goods until they are rejected as waste.

# Notes

## 1  The Sociology of Consumption: a Brief History

1. Paul Lazarsfeld says the first social scientist who collected observations for the explicit purpose of testing his theoretical ideas was French engineer Frédéric Le Play (1806–1882) (Töttö 2000, 171).

## 2  Markets and the Neo-liberal Utopia of Omnipotent Markets

1. Anthony Giddens (2000, 29), a former advisor to Tony Blair, argues that it is impossible to say 'no' to the markets. The only realistic alternative is to get capitalism to work in people's best interests economically, socially and culturally by 'modernizing social democracy'. This, to an attentive reader, smacks very much of demagogy, for it is hard to understand how capitalism could be made humane simply by reforming social democracy. Surely this requires other deep-going changes, such as a revamping of the World Bank and other similar institutions, the international money markets and global companies' business practices?
2. At this juncture it is useful to recall that not all proponents of the Scottish Enlightenment were opposed to the state institution as such but rather to the English crown and state (Paterson 2000, 43–47).
3. Smith staunchly defended the Navigation Acts that protected British shipping and trade from foreign competition and brought accumulating wealth to Britain. He also took the view that protectionism should be countered by protectionism (Aldridge 2005, 51).
4. In the seventeenth century the prevailing thinking still was that trade and routine economy should not be treated in the same way. State control was to be exercised first and foremost over trade. Indeed, in this respect all hope was invested in the state. Money was not to be allowed to become the 'tyrant of trade' (Meuret 1988, 234, 236).
5. Here, Friedman differs in his thinking from Adam Smith, who refers not to the maximization of personal benefits but rather to acting in ways that make welfare accessible to all.
6. A number of economists returning to Germany after World War II mounted a critique that went further than Adorno's and Horkheimer's comments on the market and rational action. These Ordoliberals argued that one of the reasons for the German catastrophe was the absence of a genuinely free market. They advocated a competition-based market, but under specific institutional conditions. Institutional and legal arrangements, they suggested, had to be put in place that were enough to correct any distortions caused by the free market, but not to steer the market. Intervention would be legitimate to address employment, health and housing policy issues, for instance.

By way of a counterbalance, organizations outside the market were to be reconstructed on a business model (Dean 1999, 56–57). The Ordoliberal movement goes to show that there was not just one, but many different neo-liberalisms, even though they did share similarities. For instance, the latter aspect of Ordoliberal thinking was closely associated with the Chicago School of Economics, which is often considered the most archetypical example of neo-liberal thinking.

7. In fact the same argument can be applied against all marketization. For instance, studies on the privatization of British Rail showed that marketization destroyed much of the workplace culture that had helped to make the railways run so smoothly (Aldridge 2005, 54).

8. A Pareto optimum is a condition of equilibrium that can no longer be adjusted without adversely affecting the position of at least some party. Mary Douglas (1986, 48) says that anthropologists had an exhaustive debate on social equilibrium models as early as the 1950s. They concluded that there are no compelling grounds to assume that there is any tendency in the economic world towards equilibrium at aggregate level, let alone that such an equilibrium would actually be achieved.

9. Neo-liberal economic theory does offer one example of economic equilibrium analysis, i.e. the famous Bayesian rule of expected utility. Expected utility is purely *subjective* by nature but this does not seem to bother economists working to develop their models. They assume that the expectations of all economic agents are based on the same information and on similar subjective expectations (Beckert 1996, 811). This does not make very much sense because businesses do not compete in the same markets nor do they operate in the same economic sector. This means that information that is important to IBM or Nokia is meaningless to the corner florist's shop. The same goes for the subjective expectations of the former and the latter: it is hard to see how they could ever coincide.

10. The very earliest advocates of negative freedom and the order created by capitalism can in fact be traced as far back as fifteenth-century Italian city states (e.g. Cusanus and della Mirandola), before capitalism had been established as an economic system (Sahlins 2000, 535–537).

11. There were in fact some endeavours within mercantilism to remove local protective duties and to create a national market. Jean-Baptiste Colbert, Finance Minister for Louis XIV in the late seventeenth century, set out to create a unified economic system but failed because the French Crown was chronically short of cash. Consequently he was unable to get rid of regional duties. Colbert's successor, Jacques Turgot, was in turn committed to creating a system of internal free trade but he had no further success (Cameron 1993, 151).

12. In their study of a small number of companies in pharmaceuticals and scientific instruments, Malcolm Chapman and Peter J. Buckley (1997, 240–241) found that none of them followed Williamson's transaction cost theory. In fact most managers had never even heard of the theory, nor did they perform cost calculations when they were thinking of outsourcing some function. Decisions were usually based on gut feelings, and they were influenced not only by cost considerations but also by trust and personal relations with

the people in charge of the units being outsourced and by current fashion and political motives.

13. It is hardly surprising then that, with one single exception, Callon (1998) was unable to locate studies for his book that would have shown under what conditions *Homo economicus* is created. Even stock brokers rarely live up to this concept. A unique set of circumstances is needed for *Homo economicus*, in the economic theory sense, to emerge, including mutually independent sellers and sales items that cannot be associated with any particular seller.

14. Pasi Sorjonen (2004, 5) says that economic forecasts don't work because a) the forecast models are defective (they cannot explain even past developments), b) the assumptions on which the models are based do not hold, c) the assumptions about economic policy are wrong and d) there are problems with the statistics used.

15. It is an interesting conceptual conjuring trick that this mismatch between economic reality and the real world is called a market failure when what we really have is a model failure (see Carrier 1997, 16). Neo-liberal economic theory refuses to accept this but instead wants to turn our attention to what are called 'market imperfections' (Aldridge 2005, 67). The point being made here is that the state and trade unions, for instance, are effectively hampering the complete and unrestrained freedom of the markets – although no one knows exactly what this ultimate ideal would look like in reality. Therefore the World Bank and others take the United States and the US economy and say this is it, this is the ideal. Anything that deviates from this norm is called an 'imperfection', and advice is dished out accordingly. Japan, for instance, was told that it needs to embark on institutional reform to achieve optimal economic performance, even though the Japanese economy was in robust health before the recession (Boyer 2005, 525). Similar advice is offered to EU countries, too (except the UK and Ireland).

# 4   Want, Need and Commodity

1. Ann-Mari Sellerberg (1978, 46) has reported on studies in which pre-teenage American children were allowed to pick and choose whatever they wanted from a department store. The assumption was that the children would mainly go for sweets and toys. Not so. Sweets and toys were certainly included among the items that the children put in their shopping trolleys, but otherwise they were largely filled with the same items as their parents would have picked, i.e. food and other daily necessities. The researchers' interpretation was that the children had learned from their parents which goods are understood as objects of everyday needs.

2. Lacan's understanding of desire does not differ very much from John Locke's. Locke describes desire as an uncomfortable state of mind because it constantly turns one's thoughts to something desirable that is not there (see Berry 1994, 113).

3. It is exciting to notice that neo-classical economic theory is once again, no doubt unintentionally, moving towards the model of tradition-directed society. This theory has it that consumers seek to maximize their benefits (income–price ratios) in such a way that their preferences (desires) remain

unchanged. Consumer behaviour, according to this theory, is explained not so much by benefit maximization as by consumers' shifting preferences. Therefore only the maximization of benefits is understood in this frame of thinking as rational activity. By contrast, the satisfaction of new preferences (desires) is regarded as irrational. In the world of expanding consumption, this thinking makes little sense.

4. Aristotle refers to King Midas, who prayed that everything he touched might turn to gold – and his prayer was answered. Legend has it that King Midas starved to death.

5. Even though Ferdinand Tönnies associates his concept of *Gesellschaft* with urban life, cities have existed throughout recorded history, and his concept of *Gemeinschaft* seems to be well applicable to most Italian city-states.

6. A few years ago I happened to hear a radio interview of a severely alcoholic man. He kept repeating that his drinking had long since ceased to be a pleasure. The best part was the split moment before he cracked open the bottle. At that point, the interviewee said, it was still possible to imagine all the pleasures associated with drinking. The drinking and the inebriation, on the other hand, had lost all their sparkle.

7. Novelists have realized this a long time ago. In Anton Chekhov's (2008, 149) fine short story *The Siren*, court secretary Zhilin says that in every meal the 'imagination plays a big part, too...anything learned or intellectual always spoils the appetite...On your way home try to think of your decanter and appetizer, nothing else.'

8. Roberta Sassatelli (2001, 99–103) refers in this sense to 'tamed hedonism'.

## 6  The Use and Meanings of Money

1. The euro forms an interesting exception to state money in that it is not secured by any guarantee system. For this reason it came under attack from currency speculators and in 2000 lost 30 per cent of its value against the US dollar. This was presumably based on the relatively poor shape of the eurozone economy at the time, but the value of the euro was also shaken by the phenomenon known as 'negative psychology': its value dropped because there were no hard and fast criteria against which to measure it. At the time, the euro was not money in the proper sense of the word (Dodd 2005, 564).

2. Ironically enough, Vladimir Lenin took the position that the best way to destroy an economic system was to ruin its currency. Keynes shared this view in his *Economic Consequences*, which explored the economic effects of World War I (see Ferguson 1999).

3. Ben Fine and Costas Lapavitsas (2000, 369) criticize the distinction made by Polanyi and later by Vivian Zelizer between 'general money' and money dedicated for 'limited purposes'. They argue that this distinction conflicts with the general theory of money. But they are barking up the wrong tree. Neither Polanyi nor Zelizer are suggesting that general money cannot be used as a general means of exchange. They are simply saying that this kind of money is earmarked for some specific purpose, 'prolonged need satisfaction'.

# 7 Mechanisms of Consumption Choice and Their General Cultural Framework

1. E.P. Thompson (1983, 202) draws attention to how traditional festivals of the Anglican Church differed from the peasantry's. While the former were typically between Christmas and Easter, the latter were held all year round, although predominantly in the autumn, in connection with the beginning and end of harvest.

2. It is important not to confuse this with the theory of rational choice that dominates much of economic-consumption research. The theory of rational choice is concerned to identify the most economical or efficient ways of implementing preferences, but the preferences themselves are taken as given. In this sense the theory approximates ordinary routine behaviour (Pantzar 1996, 5).

3. For Giddens, routine is a historical concept. In feudal class society, routine is embedded in tradition. Routine only becomes a specific form of conduct in capitalist class society, when tradition begins to lose its grip (Giddens 1979, 221). This position is hard to defend, however. Even in feudal society not all routine action was traditional, nor were all traditional practices simply a matter of routine, but they involved individual variation as well.

4. Jeffrey Alexander criticizes Bourdieu's theory of practices for failing to accommodate the self. Consequently, Alexander says, the theory is 'too practical'. He might have a point. In one respect, however, Alexander's critique is misplaced. He argues that Bourdieu 'employs his special kind of sociologized biologism', as for him 'a practical belief is not a state of mind...but rather a state of body' (Alexander 1995, 144). This clearly is an overinterpretation of Bourdieu, whose aim is simply through practices to transform states of mind, intended performances, into states of the body. Cultivation of the body, in order words, incorporates a state of mind, a notion of how the optimal athletic performance is achieved.

5. In tracing the changes that took place in the consumption behaviour of the wealthiest strata from the fifteenth to the seventeenth century, Fernand Braudel considers an interesting question that continues to occupy scholars today, namely which comes first, supply or demand? Jean-Baptiste Say is thought to have solved this question by the early nineteenth century. His idea is known as *Say's Law*, which states that supply in the market automatically creates its own demand. This law was considered valid until the 1930s, when Keynes turned it on its head. According to Braudel, however, the historical evidence supports the validity of Say's Law. Manufacturing output increased at least fivefold from the seventeenth to the nineteenth century. In part for this reason, John Stuart Mill and Charles Gide subscribed to Say's Law in the nineteenth century. Nevertheless, Braudel suggests that the law has only limited historical validity, and that in fact it is not a law at all. He points out that the changes in consumption before the Industrial Revolution were driven by demand. The setting was only reversed with industrial production, although there are differing views on that as well. Jacques Turgot, for instance, took the view that the Industrial Revolution was based precisely on the growth of demand (Braudel 1982, 181–183).

6. In fact, based on Bourdieu's data it is fair to say that class differences in food consumption are positively marginal. This is clear in a comparison of the food budgets of the working class and the professional-managerial class (Bourdieu 1984, 181–189):

|  | working class | professional-managerial class |
|---|---|---|
| meat | 9.8% | 8.1% |
| fat | 5.3% | 4.3% |
| vegetables | 5.3% | 5.4% |
| fruit | 2.4% | 3.1% |

   Based on these expense items it is far-fetched to conclude, as Bourdieu does, that the adaptation of the working-class taste to bare necessities leads to heavy foodstuffs and the bourgeoisie's freedom of choice is conducive to light food choices. The differences observed by Bourdieu actually only apply to the consumption of cultural services and goods.

7. Bourdieu has not given very much thought to this in his theory of *habitus*. He pays hardly any attention at all to individual variation in *habitus* or to other kinds of collective variation than class-based variation. He also ignores gender and age-related variation in *habitus*, despite their obvious significance (Lau 2004, 273; Rahkonen & Purhonen 2004, 173–178).

8. Interestingly, consumers in the eurozone are more or less unanimous in their assessment that prices have gone up since joining the new currency, even though the statistics suggest otherwise. This is obviously explained in part by consumers' low price awareness but also by some marked price hikes in everyday consumption items in the wake of the euro (e.g. a cup of coffee, a pint of beer at the pub), but these items have been dropped from the consumer price index.

9. In a sense this principle runs in the opposite direction to the theory of consumer choice; I owe this observation to Mika Pantzar.

# 8   Consumption As Ideological Discourse

1. There are, of course, many other ways to define ideology. Most definitions, however, emphasize that a) society is hierarchically ordered and b) the elite(s) of these hierarchies are capable of imposing their own sensemaking of reality, regardless of how appropriate it is. However, ideology is not just the way that dominant elites perceive reality, but even those who are governed have their own ideologically loaded views, as Margaret Archer (echoing Antonio Gramsci) points out. Indeed, Andrew Wernick's (1991, 31) view of ideology can also be defended. Wernick says that ideology refers to the level of reality at which people orient to reality. It consists of symbols, differences and ideals as well as thought systems into which they are organized.

2. It is virtually impossible to escape these kinds of classifications. Take the famous French chef Alain Senderens, who decided to close his Michelin three-star restaurant Lucas Carton because he wanted to dissociate himself from the whole rating system. He therefore re-opened a cheaper restaurant – and was straightaway awarded two Michelin stars in 2006.

3. Naomi Klein (2000) says that in the United States this has now gone so far that brands have their own schools and educational institutions. She refers to Coca Cola, Pepsi Cola, Adidas and Nike universities.

4. I could have used the term subculture rather than microculture, but decided against it because the prefix 'sub' can be understood in many different ways. As Ulf Hannerz 1992) points out, 'sub' can mean that the culture of a particular social group is part of mainstream culture. It can also be taken to mean a counterculture to the dominant mainstream culture. To avoid this sort of confusion it makes sense to use a term that takes account of the specificity contained within the subculture as well as its position vis-à-vis mainstream culture. Hannerz suggests that the concept of microculture serves this purpose very well (ibid., 77). It allows us to take account of the distinctive features of the group's culture and its position vis-à-vis mainstream culture. That position can be a subordinated one, but also separate and as equally valued as the prevailing culture.
5. Former British Prime Minister Margaret Thatcher is said to have been the absolute master of this art, but judging by TV pictures US Secretary of State Condoleezza Rice hardly pales in comparison.

# 9   Consumption As Use: Our Relationship to Commodities

1. The Japanese have apparently developed toilets that provide feedback on their user's actions, for instance, they analyse feces to determine what people have been eating and suggest any dietary changes that may be necessary in view of current health recommendations.
2. Disposable goods are excluded from this analysis.
3. In fact some car manufacturers are already bringing out models that do not immediately respond to the driver's actions. They may, for example, slow down on corners regardless of the driver's intentions.
4. Bateson (1972, 318) was interested in developing a systemic perspective on the interaction between humans and non-human materials. He took the view that in the felling of a tree, for example, man and tree constituted one type of feedback system. The tree has an active role in this process in that man must constantly take account of the changes happening in the tree that is going to be cut down if he wants to do the job safely. According to Bateson, the Western observer does not, however, view the felling of the tree in these terms. Instead he says, 'I cut down the tree' and even believes that there is a delimited agent, a 'self' separate from the tree that is felled.
5. What Kant meant by this was that people's social life was preceded by thought categories. Lévi Strauss, whose name has appeared here and there in this book, based his anthropology on this Kantian idea.
6. A few words of warning are in order. Not all commodities are singularized. This applies to disposable goods and some everyday commodities such as washing powder and clothes' pegs.
7. It is worth pointing out that the subjects in Strahilevitz's and Loewenstein's experiment did not have the chance to actually use the commodities in question (ibid., 286).
8. It is telling that this type of activity is called 'housework' rather than consumption, even though consumption naturally requires much work.

9. Mary Archer (2002, 114–117) has challenged this premise. She argues that private practices precede collective realization. It is hard to say who is in the right. However, both are more interested in a morphological analysis of child development than in how we, in our role as consumers, confront the existing world of goods. Since my concern here is with the latter aspect and since my specific focus is on the appropriation of goods, I shall here go with Vygotsky's and Harré's theory.

# References

Abbott, Pamela & Wallace, Claire (1990) *An Introduction to Sociology: Feminist Perspectives*. London: Routledge.

Abolafia, Mitchel (1998) Markets as Cultures: An Ethnographic Approach, in M. Callon (ed.) *The Laws of the Markets*. Oxford: Blackwell, 69–85.

Adorno, Theodor W. & Horkheimer, Max (1979) *Dialectic of Enlightenment*. London: Verso.

Aldridge, Alan (2005) *The Market*. Cambridge: Polity.

Alexander, Jeffrey (1995) *Fin de Siècle Social Theory: Relativism, Reduction and the Problem of Reason*. London: Verso.

Alho, Olli (1988) *Hulluuden puolustus ja muita esseitä*. Keuruu: Otava.

Allardt, Erik (1986) Elämäntapa, harkinta ja muoti ihmisten valintojen perustana, in K. Heikkinen (ed.) *Kymmenen esseetä elämäntavasta*. Helsinki: Yleisradio, 5–12.

Althusser, Louis (1976) *Positions*. Paris: Editions Sociales.

Appadurai, Arjun (1988) Introduction: Commodities and the Politics of Value, in A. Appadurai (ed.) *The Social Life of Things: Commodities in Cultural Perspective*. Cambridge: Cambridge University Press, 3–63.

Archer, Margaret (1988) *Culture and Agency: The Place of Culture in Social Theory*. Cambridge: Cambridge University Press.

Archer, Margaret (2002) *Being Human: The Problem of Agency*. Cambridge: Cambridge University Press.

Aristotle (1992) *The Politics*. London: Penguin Books.

Arminen, Ilkka & Raudaskoski, Hannu (2003) Tarjoumat ja tietotekniikan tutkimus. *Sosiologia* 40:4, 279–295.

Arvastson, Gösta (1987) *Maskinmänniskan: Arbetets förvandlingar i 1900-talets storindustri*. Göteborg: Korpen.

Asplund, Johan (1991) *Essä om Gemeinschaft och Gesellschaft*. Göteborg: Korpen.

Autio, Johanna, Marjamäki Kirsti & Peura-Kapanen Liisa (1985) *Nuoret kuluttajina. Osa 1: Nuorten henkilökohtaiset menot sekä kotitalouksien kulutusrakenne*. Helsinki: Kotitalous- ja kuluttaja-asiain tutkimuskeskus.

Bahtin, Mihail (1995) *François Rabelais: keskiajan ja renessanssin nauru*. Helsinki: Taifuuni.

Barone, Michael J., Shimp, Terence A. & Sprott, David E. (1997) Mere Ownership Revisited: A Robust Effect? *Journal of Consumer Psychology* 5:3, 257–284.

Barrett, Michèle (1988) *Women's Oppression Today: The Marxist/feminist Encounter*. London: Verso.

Barthes, Roland (1967) *Elements of Semiology*. Bungay: Jonathan Cape.

Barthes, Roland (1979) Toward a Psychosociology of Contemporary Food Consumption, in R. Foster & O. Ranum (eds) *Food and Drink in History: Selections from the Annales*. Baltimore: Johns Hopkins University Press, 166–173.

Barthes, Roland (1983) *The Fashion System*. New York: Hill and Wang.

Bateson, Gregory (1972) *Steps to an Ecology of Mind*. New York: Ballantine Books.

Baudelaire, Charles (2006 [1869]) *Le Spleen de Paris*. Paris: Gallimard.

Baudrillard, Jean (1988) *Selected Writings*. Cambridge: Polity Press.

Bauman, Zygmunt (1992) *Intimations of Postmodernity*. London: Routledge.

Beck, Ulrich & Beck-Gernsheim, Elisabeth (2002) *Individualization: Institutionalized Individualism and Its Social and Political Consequences*. London: Sage.

Becker, Ulrich & Nowak, Horst (1981) The Everyday-Life Approach as a New Perspective in Opinion and Marketing Research. *Marketing and Research Today*, January. Amsterdam, Esomat, 20–29.

Beckert, Jens (1996) What is Sociological about Economic Sociology? Uncertainty and the Embeddedness of Economic Action. *Theory and Society* 25, 803–840.

Beggan, James K. (1992) On the Social Nature of Nonsocial Perception: The Mere Ownership Effect. *Journal of Personality and Social Psychology* 62:2, 229–237.

Belk, Russell & Wallendorf, Melanie (1988) Sacred and Profane Aspects of Money in Consumption. Paper presented at Sociology of Consumption Conference, Oslo, 1–25.

Bell, Catherine (1992) *Ritual Theory, Ritual Practice*. Oxford: Oxford University Press.

Bell, Daniel (1990) Interview, in R. Swedberg (ed.) *Economics and Sociology: Redefining their Boundaries*. Princeton: Princeton University Press.

Bellah, Robert, Madsen, Richard, Sullivan, William, Swidler, Ann & Tipton, Steven (1996) *Habits of the Heart: Individualism and Commitment in American Life*. Updated version. Berkeley: University of California Press.

Benjamin, Walter (2003 [1939]) *Paris, capitale du XIXe siècle*. Paris: Allia. [Paris: the Capital of the Nineteenth Century]

Bennett, Merrill K. (1954) *The World's Food: A Study of the Interrelations of World Populations, National Diets, and Food Potentials*. New York: Harper.

Berger, Peter & Luckmann, Thomas (1966) *The Social Construction of Reality: A Treatise in the Sociology of Knowledge*. New York: Anchor Books/Doubleday.

Berger, Peter, Berger, Brigitte & Kellner, Hansfried (1974) *The Homeless Mind: Modernization and Consciousness*. New York: Vintage Books.

Berlin, Isaiah (2001) *Vapaus, ihmisyys ja historia*. Helsinki: Gaudeamus.

Berry, Christopher J. (1994) *The Idea of Luxury: A Conceptual and Historical Investigation*. Cambridge: Cambridge University Press.

Blumer, Herbert (1969) Fashion: From Class Differentiation to Collective Selection. *The Sociological Quarterly* 10:3, 275–289.

Boudon, Raymond (1981) *The Logic of Social Action: An Introduction to Sociological Analysis*. London: Routledge & Kegan Paul.

Bourdieu, Pierre (1978) Réponses à quelques objections. *Actes de la Recherche en Sciences Sociales* 23, 67–69.

Bourdieu, Pierre (1980) *Questions de sociologie*. Paris: Les Éditions de Minuit.

Bourdieu, Pierre (1984) *Distinction: A Social Critique of the Judgment of Taste*. Cambridge: Harvard University Press.

Bourdieu, Pierre (1986) *Kultursociologiska texter*. Stockholm: Salamander.

Bourdieu, Pierre (1990) *In Other Words. Essays Towards a Reflexive Sociology*. Cambridge: Polity Press.

Bourdieu, Pierre (1998) *Acts of Resistance: Against the New Myth of Our Time*. Cambridge: Polity Press.

Bourdieu, Pierre (2005) *Social Structures of the Economy*. Cambridge: Polity Press.

Boyer, Robert (2005) How and Why Capitalisms Differ. *Economy and Society* 34:4, 509–557.

Braudel, Fernand (1982) *Wheels of Commerce: Capitalism and Material Life 1400–1800.* London: Collins.

Burke, Peter (1983) *Folklig kultur: Europa 1500–1800.* Malmö: Författarförlaget.

Burt, Ronald (1993) The Social Structure of Competition, in R. Swedberg (ed.) *Explorations in Economic Sociology.* New York: Russel Sage Foundation, 63–103.

Callon, Michel (1998) *The Laws of the Markets.* Oxford: Blackwell.

Callon, Michel (1999) Actor-Network Theory: The Market Test, in J. Law and J. Hassard (eds) *The Actor Network Theory and After.* Oxford: Blackwell Publishers, 181–195.

Callon, Michel, Méadel, Cécile & Rabeharisoa, Vololona (2002) The Economy of Qualities. *Economy and Society* 31:2, 194–217.

Cameron, Rondo (1989) *A Concise Economic History of the World: From Paleolithic Times to the Present.* New York: Oxford University Press.

Camic, Charles (1986) The Matter of Habit. *American Journal of Sociology* 91:5, 1039–1087.

Campbell, Colin (1987) *The Romantic Ethic and the Spirit of Modern Consumerism.* Oxford: Basil Blackwell.

Campbell, Colin (1996) *The Myth of Social Action.* Cambridge: Cambridge University Press.

Carlsen, Jørgen, Schanz, Hans-Jørgen, Schmidt, Lars-Henrik & Thomsen, Hans-Jørgen (1980) *Kapitalisme, behov og civilisation 1–2.* Århus: Modtryck.

Carrier, James (1997) Introduction, in J. G. Carrier (ed.) *Meanings of the Market: The Free Market in Western Culture.* Oxford: Berg, 1–68.

Castells, Manuel (1996) *Information Age: Economy, Society and Culture. Vol. 1. The Rise of the Network Society.* Massachusetts & Oxford: Blackwell.

Castiglione, Baldesar (1959) *The Book of the Courtier.* New York: Anchor Books.

Chadwick, Martin (1988) *Gender and Symbol in Advertising Imagery: A Comparison of Goffman and Williamson.* Papers in Sociology and Anthropology No. 5. Manchester: University of Salford.

Chaney, Dick (2002) *Cultural Change and Everday Life.* Hampshire: Palgrave.

Chapman, Malcolm & Buckley, Peter (1997) Markets, Transaction Costs, Economists and Social Anthropologists, in J. Carrier (ed.) *Meanings of the Market: Free Market in Western Culture.* Oxford: Berg, 224–250.

Chekhov, Anton (2008) *The Comic Stories.* London: Carlton Publishing Group.

Child, Julia, Bertholle, Louisette & Beck, Simone (2009) *Mastering the Art of French Cooking.* New York: Alfred A Knoph Inc.

Christensen, Christa L. (1986) Krop og form i et spørgsmål om stil, in C. L. Christensen & C. Lykke (eds), *Slidser. En bok om mode.* Århus: Modtryck, 55–74.

Christensen, C. L. & Lykke, C. (eds) *Slidser. En bok om mode.* Århus: Modtryck.

Clarke, John & Critcher, Chas (1985) *The Devil Makes Work: Leisure in Capitalist Britain.* Houndmills: MacMillan.

Classen, Constance, Howes, David & Synnott, Anthony (1994) *Aroma: The Cultural History of Smell.* London: Routledge.

Clastres, Pierre (1989) *Society Against the State: Essays in Political Anthropology.* New York: Zone Books.

Connerton, Paul (1989) *How Societies Remember.* Cambridge: Cambridge University Press.

Crompton, Rosemary (2002) Employment, Flexible Working and the Family. *British Journal of Sociology* 53:4, 537–558.

Dalton, George (1971) Ekonomisk teori och primitiva samhällen, in T. Gerholm (ed.) *Prolog till en marxisrisk antropologi: En diskussion om teori och metod.* Stockholm: Pan/Norstedts.

Dean, Mitchell (1999) *Governmentality: Power and Rule in Modern Society.* London: Sage.

Deaton, Angus & Muellbauer, John (1986) *Economics and Consumer Behaviour.* Cambridge: Cambridge University Press.

Delhaye, Christine (2002) The Development of Consumption Culture and Individualisation of Female Identity. Fashion Discourse in the Netherlands 1880–1900. *Journal of Consumer Culture* 6:1, 87–115.

Dewey, John (1958) *How We Think.* Boston: D.C. Heath Publishers.

Dodd, Nigel (2005) Reinventing Monies in Europe. *Economy and Society* 34:4, 558–583.

Douglas, Mary (1966) *Purity and Danger: An Analysis of Concepts of Pollution and Taboo.* London: Routledge & Kegan Paul.

Douglas, Mary (1984) Standard Social Uses of Food: Introduction, in M. Douglas (ed.) *Food in the Social Order.* New York: Russell Sage Foundation.

Douglas, Mary (1986) *How Institutions Think.* New York: Syracuse University Press.

Douglas, Mary (1991) *Implicit Meanings: Essays in Anthropology.* London: Routledge.

Douglas, Mary (1996) *Thought Styles: Critical Essays on Good Taste.* London: Sage.

Douglas, Mary & Gross, Jonathan (1981) Food and Culture: Measuring the Intricacy of Rule Systems. *Social Science Information* 20:1, 1–35.

Douglas, Mary & Isherwood, Baron (1980) *The World of Goods: Towards an Anthropology of Consumption.* Bungay: Penguin Books.

Du Gay, Paul & Pryke, Michael (2002) *Cultural Economy: Cultural Analysis and Commercial Life.* London: Sage.

Durkheim, Emile (1951 [1897]) *Suicide.* New York: Free Press of Glenco.

Durkheim, Emile (1983) *Pragmatism and Sociology.* Cambridge: Cambridge University Press.

Durkheim, Emile (1995) *The Elementary Forms of Religious Life.* New York: Free Press.

Durkheim, Emile (1997 [1893]) *The Division of Labor in Society.* New York: Free Press.

Eco, Umberto (1971) *Den frånvarande strukturen: Introduktion till den semiotiska forskningen.* Lund: Bo Cavefors Bokförlag.

Eco, Umberto (1987) *Travels In Hyperreality.* London: Pan Books.

Ehn, Billy & Löfgren, Orvar (1986) *Kulturanalys: Ett etnologisk perspektiv.* Stockholm: Liber.

Elias, Norbert (1978a) *What is Sociology?* London: Hutchinson.

Elias, Norbert (1978b) *The Civilizing Process. Vol. 1: History of Manners.* Oxford: Basil Blackwell.

Elias, Norbert (1982) *The Civilizing Process, Vol 2: State Formation and Civilization.* Oxford: Basil Blackwell.

Englund, Peter (2004) *Hiljaisuuden historia.* Helsinki: WSOY.

Eskola, Antti (1982) *Vuorovaikutus, muutos, merkitys.* Helsinki: Tammi.

Ewen, Stuart (1976) *Captains of Consciousness.* New York: Basic Books.

Ewen, Stuart (2000) Marketing Dreams: The Political Elements of Style, in A. Tomlinson (ed.) *Consumption, Identity & Style*. London: Routledge, 41–56.

Eyerman, Ron & Jamison, Andrew (1991) *Social Movements: A Cognitive Approach*. Cambridge: Polity Press.

Falk, Pasi (1990) Modernin hedonismin paradoksi. *Sosiologia* 27:2, 108–124.

Falk, Pasi (1995) *The Consuming Body*. London: Sage.

Falk, Pasi & Mäenpää, Pasi (1997) *Lottomiljonäärit: tutkimus suomalaisista lottovoittajista*. Helsinki: Gaudeamus.

Featherstone, Mike (1991) *Consumer Culture & Postmodernism*. London: Sage.

Feldman, Saul & Thielbar, Gregory (eds) (1976) *Life Styles: Diversity in American Society*. Boston: Little & Brown.

Ferguson, Niall (1999) *The Pity of War*. London: Penguin Books Ltd.

Fiddes, Nigel (1991) *Meat: A Natural Symbol*. London: Routledge.

Fine, Ben & Lapavitsas, Costas (2000) Markets and Money in Social Theory: What Role for Economics? *Economy and Society* 29:3, 357–382.

Foucault, Michel (1970) *The Order of Things: An Archaeology of the Human Sciences*. Bristol: Tavistock.

Foucault, Michel (1977) *Discipline and Punish: The Birth of the Prison*. New York: Random House.

Foucault, Michel (1978) *The History of Sexuality. Volume 1: An Introduction*. London: Allen Lane.

Fourier, Charles (1983) *Slaget om de små pastejerna: Skrifter i urval*. Stockholm: Federativ.

Frank, Thomas (1997) *The Conquest of Cool: Business Culture, Counterculture, and the Rise of Hip Consumerism*. Chicago: The University of Chicago Press.

Frankl, Viktor E. (1978) *The Unheard Cry for Meaning: Psychotherapy and Humanism*. New York: Simon & Schuster Inc.

Freud, Sigmund (2004) *Civilization and Its Discontents*. London: Penguin Books.

Friedman, Milton ([1962] 1982) *Capitalism and Freedom*. Chicago: University of Chicago Press.

Friedman, Milton & Friedman, Rose (1982) *Free to Choose: A Personal Statement*. Hammondsworth: Pelican Books.

Fuller, Linda & Smith, Vicki (1991) Consumer Reports: Management by Customers in a Changing Economy. *Work, Employment and Society* 5:1, 1–16.

Gadamer, Hans-Georg (2004) *Hermeneutiikka: Ymmärtäminen tieteissä ja filosofiassa*. Tampere: Vastapaino.

Galperin, Pjotr (1979) *Johdatus psykologiaan*. Pori: Kansankulttuuri.

Ganssman, Heiner (1988) Money – a Symbolically Generalised Means of Communication? On the Concept of Money in Recent Sociology. *Economy and Society* 17:3, 285–316.

Garine, Igor de (1976) Food, Tradition and Prestige, in D. Walcher, N. Kretchmer, H. L. Barnett (eds) *Food, Man and Society*. New York: Plenum Press, 150–171.

Gartman, David (1991) Culture as Class Symbolization or Mass Reification? A Critique of Bourdieu's Distinction. *American Journal of Sociology* 97:2, 421–447.

Giddens, Anthony (1979) *Central Problems in Social Theory: Action, Structure and Contradiction in Social Analysis*. London: MacMillan.

Giddens, Anthony (1984) *The Constitution of Society*. Oxford: Polity Press.

Giddens, Anthony (1990) *The Consequences of Modernity*. Cambridge: Polity Press.

Giddens, Anthony (2000) *The Third Way and its Critics*. Cambridge: Polity Press.

Gilbert, Emily (2005) Common Cents: Situating Money in Time and Place. *Economy and Society* 34:3, 357–388.

Godelier, Maurice (1987) *Antropologia ja materialismi*. Tampere: Vastapaino.

Godelier, Maurice (1999) *The Enigma of the Gift*. Chicago: The University of Chicago Press.

Goldman, Robert & Papson, Stephen (1998) *Nike Culture: The Sign of the Swoosh*. London: Sage.

Goode, Judith, Theophano, Janet & Curtis, Karen (1984a) A Framework for the Analysis of Continuity and Change in Shared Sociocultural Rules for Food Use: The Italian-American Pattern, in *Ethnic and Regional Foodways in The United States: The Performance of Group Identity*. Knoxville: The University of Tennessee Press, 66–88.

Goode, Judith, Curtis, Karen & Theophano, Janet (1984b) Meal Formats, Meal Cycles and Menu Negotiation in the Maintenance of an Italian-American Community, in. M. Douglas (ed.) *Food in the Social Order: Studies in Food and Festivites in Three American Communities*. New York: Russell Sage Foundation, 143–218.

Goody, Jack (1984) *Cooking, Cuisine and Class: A Study in Comparative Sociology*. Cambridge: Cambridge University Press.

Graeber, David (2001) *Toward an Anthropological Theory of Value: The False Coin of Our Dreams*. New York: Palgrave.

Granovetter, Mark (1973) The Strength of Weak Ties. *American Journal of Sociology* 78:6, 1360–1379.

Grenfell, Michael (2004) *Pierre Bourdieu: Agent Provocateur*. Manchester: Continuum.

Gronow, Jukka (1990) Mitä on hyvä maku? *Sosiologia* 27:2, 95–107.

Gronow, Jukka (1996) Valistusfilosofia ja poliittinen taloustiede: Yhteiskunta omalakisena järjestelmänä, teoksessa, in J. Gronow, A. Noro & P. Töttö (eds) *Sosiologian klassikot*. Helsinki: Gaudeamus, 31–60.

Gronow, Jukka (1997) *The Sociology of Taste*. London: Routledge.

Gronow, Jukka (1998) In Food we do *not* trust. Kulutuksen vaarat ja riskit. *Tiede & Edistys* 23:1, 1–10.

Gronow, Jukka & Warde, Alan (eds) (2001) *Ordinary Consumption*. London: Routledge.

Guzman, Maria (2003) Når dyr blir kjøtt: Skeptiske forbrukere og kampen om etisk produksjon, in E. Jacobsen, R. Almås & J. P. Johnsen (eds) *Den politiserte maten*. Oslo: Astrakt förlag, 289–314.

Halbwachs, Maurice (1992) *On Collective Memory*. Chicago: University of Chicago Press.

Hallenberg, Helena (2004) *Apteekki keittiössä: Ruokavalio kiinalaisessa terveyden-hoidossa*. Helsinki: Tammi.

Halpern, David (2005) *Social Capital*. Cambridge: Polity Press.

Hannerz, Ulf (1992) *Cultural Complexity: Studies in the Social Organization of Meaning*. New York: Columbia University Press.

Harré, Rom (1983) *Personal Being*. Oxford: Basil Blackwell.

Harris, Marvin (1986) *Good to Eat: Riddles of Food & Culture*. London: Allen & Unwin.

Harris, Marvin (1990) Emics and Etics Revisited, in T. H. Headland, K. Pike & M. Harris (eds) *Emics and Etics: The Insider/ Outsider Debate*. Newbury Park: Sage, 28–47.

Harrison, J. Richard & March, James G. (1984) Decision Making and Postdecision Surprises. *Adimistrative Science Quarterly* 29:1, 26–42.

Haug, Wolfgang F. (1982a) *Luentoja Marxin pääomasta*. Helsinki: Kansankulttuuri.

Haug, Wolfgang F. (1982b) *Mainonta ja kulutus*. Jyväskylä: Vastapaino.

Haug, Wolfgang F. (1986) *Critique of Commodity Aesthetics*. Minneapolis: University of Minnesota Press.

Havel, Vaclav (1991) *En dåre i Prag*. Stockholm/Stehag: Symposion Bokförlag.

Hayek, Friedrich (1949) *Individualism and Economic Order*. London: Routledge & Kegan Paul.

Hayek, Friedrich (1960) *The Constitution of Liberty*. London: Routledge & Kegan Paul.

Hayek, Friedrich (1994) *The Road to Serfdom*. Chicago: Chicago University Press.

Heelas, Paul, Lash, Scott & Morris, Paul (1996) *Detraditionalization: Critical Reflections on Authority and Identity*. Oxford: Blackwell.

Heidegger, Martin (1977) *Sein und Zeit*. Frankfurt: Vittoria Klosterman.

Heine, Peter (1994) The Revival of Traditional Cooking in Modern Arabic Cookbooks, in S. Zubaida & R. Tapper (eds) *Culinary Cultures of the Middle East*. London: I.B. Tauris, 143–152.

Heinonen, Visa (2003) James päällä joka säällä: Suomalaisen nuorisomainonnan historiaa, in S. Aapola & M. Kaarninen (eds) *Nuoruuden vuosisata: Suomalaisen nuorison historia*. Helsinki: SKS, 455–479.

Heller, Agnes (1977) *Instinkt, Aggression, Charakter: Einleitung zu einer marxistischen Sozialanthropologie*. Hamburg: VSA.

Heller, Agnes (1978) *Das Alltagsleben: Versuch einer Erklärung der individuellen Reproduktion*. Frankfurt am Main: Suhrkamp.

Heller, Agnes (1979) *Theory of Feelings*. Assen: Van Gorcum.

Heller, Agnes (1980) *Theorie der Bedürfnisse bei Marx*. Hamburg: VSA-Verlag.

Hirdman, Yvonne (1983) *Magfrågan: Mat som mål och medel. Stockholm 1870–1920*. Stockholm: Raben & Sjögren.

Hirsch, Fred (1977) *Social Limits of Growth*. London: Routledge & Kegan.

Hirschman, Alfred O. (1977) *The Passions and the Interests: Political Arguments for Capitalism before Its Triumph*. Princeton: Princeton University Press.

Hobbes, Thomas (1991) *Leviathan*. Cambridge: Cambridge University Press.

Hobsbawm, Eric (1988a) Introduction: Inventing Traditions, in E. Hobsbawn & T. Ranger (eds) *The Invention of Tradition*. Cambridge: Cambridge University Press, 1–14.

Hobsbawm, Eric (1988b) Mass Producing Traditions: Europe 1820–1914, in E. Hobsbawm & T. Ranger (eds) *The Invention of Tradition*. Cambridge: Cambridge University Press, 263–309.

Hochschild, Arlie (1983) *The Managed Heart: Commercialization of Human Feeling*. Berkeley: University of California Press.

Houthakker, H. S. (1957) An International Comparison of Household Expenditure: Commenting the Centenary of Engel's Law. *Econometrica* 25, 532–551.

Hradil, Stefan (1989) System und Akteur: Eine empirische Kritik der soziologischen Kulturtheorie Pierre Bourdieus, in K. Eder (ed.) *Klassenlage, Lebensstil und kulturelle Praxis: Beiträge zur Auseineisetzung mit Pierre Bourdieus Klassentheorie.* Frankfurt a/M: Suhrkamp, 111–142.

Hume, David (1987[1742]) *Essays, Moral, Political, and Literary.* Edited by Eugene F. Miller. Liberty Fund, Indianapolis 1987.

Husserl, Edmund (1964) *The Idea of Phenomenology.* The Hague: Martinus Nijhoff.

Ilmonen, Kaj (1984) *Behov bland punkare och byrokrater: Essäer från en konsumentforskares Arbetsbord.* Stockholm: Koperativa Institutet.

Ilmonen, Kaj (1985) *Tarpeiden järjestelmä ja järjestelmän tarpeet.* Helsinki: Kulutusosuustoiminnan keskusliitto.

Ilmonen, Kaj (1986) Uuden yhteiskunnan etsijä – Charles Fourier. *Politiikka* 28:3, 201–207.

Ilmonen, Kaj (1990) Tuotanto ja kulutus – toistensa peilikuvia. *Sosiologia* 27:2, 85–94.

Ilmonen, Kaj (1991a) Change and Stability in Finnish Eating Habits, in Elisabeth L. Furst, Lotte Holm and Unni Kjaernes (eds) *Palatable worlds. Sociocultural Food Studies.* Oslo: Solum.

Ilmonen, Kaj (1991b) Ritualismi ja suomalainen työväenliike, in U. M. Peltonen & K. Stenvall (eds) *Myytit ja symbolit.* Tampere: Työväen historian ja perinteen tutkimuksen seura, 18–46.

Ilmonen, Kaj (1993) *Tavaroiden taikamaailma: Sosiologinen avaus kulutukseen.* Tampere: Vastapaino.

Ilmonen, Kaj (1999) Työelämä ja tunteet, in S. Näre (ed.) *Tunteiden sosiologiaa.* Helsinki: SKS, 299–324.

Ilmonen, Kaj (2001a) The Sociology of Consumption, in *International Encyclopedia of the Social and Behavioral Sciences.* Amsterdam: Elsvier, 2687–2690.

Ilmonen, Kaj (2001b) Sociology, Consumption and Routine, in J. Gronow & A. Warde (eds) *Ordinary Consumption.* London: Routledge, 9–24.

Ilmonen, Kaj (2004) The Use and Commitment to Goods. *Journal of Consumer Culture* 4:1, 27–50.

Ilmonen, Kaj & Jokinen, Kimmo (2002) *Luottamus modernissa maailmassa.* Jyväskylä: SoPhi.

Ilmonen, Kaj & Pantzar, Mika (1985) *Ruoan valinta, ruoan merkitykset ja tulot.* Helsinki: TTT-tutkimusselosteita 33.

Ilmonen, Kaj & Pantzar, Mika (1986) Determinants in the Modern Choice of Food. *Journal of Consumer Studies and Home Economics* 10:4, 97–110.

Ilmonen, Kaj & Pantzar, Mika (1989) Yhteiskunnallisen sukupuolen tuottaminen ja kulutus. TTT-Katsaus I, 65–77.

Ingham, Geoffrey (2004) *The Nature of Money.* Cambridge: Polity Press.

Isotalus, Päivi (2004) *Sanan säilä on vahva ase markkinoilla.* Helsingin Sanomat 4.2.

Jacobsen, Eivind & Kjaerness, Unni (2003) Sikker mat til forbrukerne, in E. Jacobsen, R. Almås & J. P. Johnsen (eds) *Den politiserte maten.* Oslo: Abstrakt forlag, 245–274.

Jelliffe, Derrick B. (1967) Parallel Food Classifications in Developing and Industrial Countries. *The American Journal of Clinical Nutrition* 20:3, 279–281.

Joas, Hans (1996) *The Creativity of Action.* Chicago: The University of Chicago Press.

Jonsson, Ernst (1979) *Konsten att förföra konsumenten.* Stockholm: Raben & Sjögren.

Julkunen, Raija (2001) *Suunnanmuutos: 1990-luvun sosiaalipoliittinen reformi Suomessa.* Tampere: Vastapaino.

Juntunen, Matti (1986) *Edmund Husserlin filosofia.* Helsinki: Gaudeamus.

Kalcik, Susan (1984) Ethnic Foodways in America: Symbol and the Performance of Identity, in L. K. Brown & K. Mussel (eds) *Ethnic and Regional Foodways in The United States: The Performance of Group Identity.* Knoxville: The University of Tennessee Press, 37–65.

Kangas, Risto (2001) *Yhteiskunta.* Tutkijaliitto: Helsinki.

Kant, Immanuel (1965) *Critique of Pure Reason.* New York: St. Martins Press.

Keynes, John Maynard (1962) *Essays in Persuasion.* New York: Norton.

Keynes, John Maynard (1964) *The General Theory of Employment, Interest and Money.* New York: Harcourt Brace.

Klein, Naomi (2000) *No Logo: Taking Aim at the Brand Bullies.* Toronto: Knopf.

Klinge, Matti (1972) *Vihan veljistä valtiososialismiin.* Helsinki: WSOY.

Knorr Cetina, Karin (1997) Sociality with Objects: Social Relations in Postsocial Knowledge Societies. *Theory, Culture & Society* 14:4, 1–30.

Knudsen, Britta (1986) I Modets tegn – om modet som kultur, in C. L. Christensen & C. Lykke (eds), *Slidser. En bok om mode.* Århus: Modtryck, 33–54.

Konsumentverket (1986) *Konsumption i förändring: en sammanställning.* Stockholm: Konsumentverket.

Kopytoff, Igor (1988) The Cultural Biography of Things: Commodifications as Process, in A. Appadurai (ed.) *Social Life of Things.* Cambridge: Cambridge University Press, 64–91.

Krause-Jensen, Esben (1983) *Nomadfilosofi.* Viborg: Sjakalen.

Krueger, David (1986) Money, Success and Success Phobia, in D. Krueger (ed.) *The Last Taboo: Money as Symbol and Reality in Psychotherapy and Psychoanalysis.* New York: Brunner-Mazel.

Kurlansky, Mark (2003) *Salt. A World History.* New York: Vintage.

Lacan, Jacques (1982) *Ecrits: A Selection.* Bristol: Tavistock Publications.

Lagerspetz, Eerik (2004) Talouden moraali, moraaliton talous ja F. A. Hayekin uusliberalismi, in I. Kauppinen (ed.), *Moraalitalous.* Tampere: Vastapaino, 92–134.

Lasch, Christopher (1980) *The Culture of Narcissism: American Life in an Age of Diminishing Expectations.* New York: Warner Books.

Lash, Scott (1990) *Sociology of Postmodernism.* London: Routledge.

Latour, Bruno (1991) *Nous n'avons jamais été modernes: Essai d'anthropologie symétrique.* Paris: Èditions la Découverte.

Lau, Raymond W. K. (2004) Habitus and the Practical Logic of Practice: An Interpretation. *Sociology* 38:2, 369–387.

Laurila Eino H (& Kallinen, Tauno) (1985) *Kulutus Suomen kansantaloudessa vuosina 1900–1975.* Helsinki: ETLA, B 42.

Law, John (1992) Notes on the Theory of the Actor-Network: Oredering, Strategy, and Heterogeneity. *Systems Practice* 5:4, 379–393.

Lazarsfeld, Paul (1982) *The Varied Sociology of Paul F. Lazarsfeld.* Writings Collected and Edited by P. L. Kendall. New York: Columbia University Press.

Leach, Edmund (1968) *Ritual,* in *International Encyclopedia of the Social Sciences, Vol. 13.* New York: MacMillan and Free Press, 520–526.

Lefebvre, Henri (1971) *Everyday Life in the Modern World.* New York: Harper Torchbooks.

Lehtonen, Turo-Kimmo (2001) Dancing on the Tightrope: Everyday Aesthetics in the Practices of Shopping, Gym Exercise and Art Making. *European Journal of Cultural Studies* 4:1, 63–83.

Leidner, Robin (1993) *Fast Food, Fast Talk: Service Work and the Routinization of Everyday Life.* Berkeley: University of California Press.

Leontiev Aleksei N. (1978) *Activity, Consciousness, Personality.* Englewood Cliffs, NJ: Prentice Hall.

Lévi-Strauss, Claude (1962) *La pensée sauvage.* Paris: Plon.

Lévi-Strauss, Claude (1969) *The Elementary Structure of Kinship.* Boston: Beacon Press.

Lévi-Strauss, Claude (1986) *Structural Anthropology 1–2.* Aulesbury: Peregrine Books.

Löfgren, Orvar (1990) Consuming Interests, in Orvar Löfgren (ed.) *Culture and History.* Copenhagen: Akademisk förlag.

Lovejoy, Arthur (1960) *Great Chain of Being: A Study of the History of an Idea.* New York: Harper & Row.

Lukács, George (1971) *History and Class Consciousness: Studies in Marxist Dialectics.* Cambridge: The MIT Press.

Lupton, Deborah (1996) *Food, The Body and The Self.* London: Sage.

Lupton, Deborah & Noble, Greg (2002) Mine/Not mine: Appropriating Personal Computers in the Academic Workplace. *Journal of Sociology* 38:1, 5–23.

MacFarlane, Alan (1987) *The Culture of Capitalism.* Oxford: Basil Blackwell.

Maffesoli, Michel (1995) *Maailman mieli: Yhteisöllisen tyylin muodoista.* Helsinki: Gaudeamus.

Mäkelä, Johanna (1996) Kunnon ateria: Pääkaupunkiseudun perheellisten naisten käsityksiä. *Sosiologia* 33:1, 12–22.

Mäkelä, Johanna (2000) Cultural Definition of the Meal, in N. Meiselman & F. Herbert (eds) *Dimensions of the Meal: The Science, Culture, Business, and Art of Eating.* Gaithersburg: Aspen Publishers, 7–18.

Mäkelä, Johanna (2002) *Syömisen rakenne ja kulttuurinen vaihtelu.* Helsinki: Kuluttajatutkimuskeskus.

Malinowski, Bronislaw (1960) *A Scientific Theory of Culture and Other Essays.* New York: Oxford University Press.

Malinowski, Bronislaw (1992) *Argonauts of the Western Pacific.* London: Routledge.

Mandeville, Bernard (1988) *The Fable of Bees or Private Vices, Public Benefits.* 2 Vols. Indianapolis: Liberty Classics.

Mantzavinos, Chrysostomos (2004) *Individuals, Institutions, and Markets.* Cambridge: Cambridge University Press.

Marcuse Herbert (1964) *One-dimensional Man.* London: Ark Paperbacks.

Marx, Karl (1959) *Economic and Philosophical Manuscripts of 1844.* Moscow: Progress Publishers.

Marx, Karl (1976) *Capital: Volume one.* Harmondsworth: Penguin Books.

Mason, Roger (1981) *Conspicuous Consumption: A Study of Exceptional Consumption Behaviour.* Guilford: Gower.

Mauss, Marcel (1990) *The Gift*. London: Routledge.

McCracken, Grant (1988) *Culture and Consumption*. Bloomington: Indiana University Press.

Menand, Louis (2002) *The Metaphysical Club*. London: Flamingo.

Mennell, Stephen (1985) *All Manners of Food: Eating and Taste in England and France from the Middle Ages to the Present*. Oxford: Basil Blackwell.

Mennell, Stephen (1989) *Norbert Elias: Civilization and the Human Self-Image*. Oxford: Basil Blackwell.

Mennell, Stephen (1991) On the Civilizing of Appetite, in M. Featherstone, M. Hapworth & B. S. Turner (eds) *Body: Social Processes and Cultural Theory*. London: Sage, 126–156.

Mennell, Stephen, Murcott, Ann & van Otterloo, Anneke (1992) *The Sociology of Food: Eating, Diet and Culture*. London: Sage.

Merleau-Ponty, Maurice (1963) *The Structure of Behaviour*. Boston: Beacon Press.

Meuret, Daniel (1988) A Political Genealogy of Political Economy. *Economy and Society* 17:2, 226–250.

Meyer Heintz-Dieter (2000) Taste Formation of Rhetorics and Institutions. *International Sociology* 15:1, 33–56.

Miller, Daniel (1987) *Material Culture and Mass Consumption*. Oxford: Basil Blackwell.

Miller, Daniel (1998) *A Theory of Shopping*. Cambridge: Polity Press.

Miller, Max (1989) Systematisch verzerrte Legitimationsdiskurse: Einige kritische Überlegungen zu Bourdieus Habitustheorie, in K. Eder (ed.) *Klassenlage, Lebensstil und Kulturelle Praxis. Beiträge zur Auseinandersetzung mit Pierre Bourdieus Klassentheorie*. Frankfurt a/M: Suhrkamp, 191–220.

Mills C. Wright (1976) Status Panic, in S. Feldman & G. Thielbar (eds) *Life Styles: Diversity in American Society*. Boston: Little & Brown.

Mintz Sidney W. (1985) *Sweetness and Power: The Place of Sugar in Modern History*. New York: Viking Penguin.

Misztal, Barbara (1996) *Trust in Modern Societies*. Cambridge: Polity Press.

Misztal, Barbara (2003) *Theories of Social Remembering*. Glasgow: Open University Press.

Morrison, Kenneth (2001) The Disavowal of the Social in the American Reception of Durkheim. *Journal of Classical Sociology* 1:1, 95–125.

Murcott, Ann (1982) On the Social Significance of the 'Cooked Dinner' in South Wales. *Social Science Information* 21:4/5, 677–696.

Murcott, Ann (1986) You Are What You Eat. Anthropological Factors Influencing Food Choice, in C. Riston, L. Gofton & J. McKenzie (eds) *The Food Consumer*. Chichester: John Wiley, 107–125.

Nietzsche, Friedrich (2006) *Thus Spoke Zarathustra*. Cambridge: Cambridge University Press.

Noro, Arto (1986) Simmel, muoti ja moderni. Johdatus 'moderniin', in G. Simmel (ed.), *Muodin filosofia*. Rauma: Odessa, 7–18.

Noro, Arto (1991) *Muoto, moderniteetti ja 'kolmas': Tutkielma Georg Simmelin sosiologiasta*. Helsinki: Tutkijaliitto.

Packard, Vance (1966) *The Waste Makers*. Aulesbury: Pelican Book.

Packard, Vance (1970) *Hidden Persuaders*. Hammondsworth: Penguin.

Pahl, Jan (1989) *Money and Marriage*. London: MacMillan.

224    *References*

Pahl, Jan (1990) Household Spending: Personal Spending and the Control of Money in Marriage. *Sosiology* 24:1, 119–138.
Pahl, Ray (2000) *On Friendship*. Padstow: Polity.
Pantzar, Mika (1996) Rational Choice of Food: On the Domain of the Premises of the Consumer Choice Theory. *Journal of Consumer Studies and Home Economics* 20:1, 1–20.
Parsons, Talcott & Smelser, Neil (1956) *Economy and Society: A Study in the Integration of Economic and Social Theory*. New York: The Free Press.
Paterson, Lindsay (2000) Civic Society and Democratic Renewal, in S. Baron, J. Field & T. Schuller (eds) *Social Capital: Critical Perspectives*. Oxford: Oxford University Press, 39–55.
Piaget, Jean (1974) *Sociologiska förklaringar*. Lund: Argos.
Pike, Kenneth (1990) On the Emics and Etics of Pike and Harris, in T. N. Headland, K. L. Pike & M. Harris (eds) *Emics and Etics: The Insider/Outsider Debate*. Newbury Park: Sage, 28–47.
Pirenne, Henri (1967) Aspects of Medieval European Economy, in G. Dalton (ed.), *Tribal and Peasant Economies: Readings in Economic Anthropology*. Garden City: Natural History Press, 418–437.
Plato (2006) *The Republic*. New Haven: Yale University Press.
Polanyi, Karl (1957) *The Great Transformation: The Political and Economic Origins of Our Time*. Boston: Beacon Press.
Polanyi, Karl (1971) *Primitive, Archaic and Modern Economies*. Boston: Beacon Press.
Polanyi, Michael (1962) *Personal Knowledge: Towards a Post-Critical Philosophy*. Chicago: The University of Chicago Press.
Povlsen, Karen K. (1986) Modens imaginationer, in C. L. Christensen & C. Lykke (eds) *Slidser: En bog om mode*. Århus: Modtryk, 121–143.
Prättälä, Ritva (1989) Young People and Food: Socio-Cultural Studies on Food Consumption Patterns. Helsinki: Department of Nutrition, University of Helsinki.
Prättälä, Ritva (2003) Naisten ja miesten ruoka, in L. Luoto, K. Viinikainen & I. Kulmala (eds) *Sukupuoli ja terveys*. Tampere: Vastapaino, 210–216.
Prättälä, Ritva, Pelto, Gretel, Pelto, Pertti, Ahola, Marit & Räsänen, Leena (1993) Continuity and Change in Meal Pattern: The Case of Urban Finland. *Ecology of Food and Nutrition* 31, 87–100.
Preda, Alex (1999) The Turn to Things: Arguments for a Sociological Theory of Things. *Sociological Quarterly* 40:2, 347–366.
Préteceille, Edmond & Terrail, Jean-Pierre (1986) *Capitalism, Consumption and Needs*. Oxford: Basil Blackwell.
Putnam, Robert (2000) *Bowling Alone: The Collapse and Revival of American Community*. New York: Simon & Schuster.
Rahkonen, Keijo & Purhonen, Semi (2004) Kulttuuripääoma ja hedonistinen kuluttaminen Suomessa: Empiirisesti orientoitunut jälkikirjoitus 1990-luvun kulutussosiologiaan, in P. Jokivuori & P. Ruuskanen (eds) *Arjen talous. Talous, tunteet ja yhteiskunta*. Jyväskylä: SoPhi, 157–184.
Raijas, Anu (2000) Erilaisten kotitalouksien kulutusmuutokset 1990-luvun kulutustutkimuksen valossa, in K. Hyvönen, A. Juntto, P. Laaksonen & P. Timonen (eds) *Hyvää elämää: 90 vuotta suomalaista kulutustutkimusta*. Helsinki: Tilastokeskus & Kuluttajatutkimuskeskus, 48–56.

Rao, Hayagreeva, Monin, Phillipe & Durand, Rodolphe (2003) Institutional Change in Toque Ville: Nouvelle Cuisine as an Identity Movement in French Gastronomy. *American Journal of Sociology* 108:4, 795–843.

Räsänen, Pekka (2005) Tieto- ja viihdekulutuksen muotoutuminen eri väestöryhmissä. *Sosiologia* 42:1, 19–34.

Reckwitz, Andreas (2002) Towards a Theory of Social Practices. A Development in Cultural Theorizing. *European Journal of Social Theory* 5:2, 234–264.

Riesman, David (1969) *The Lonely Crowd*. New Haven: Yale University Press.

Riesman, David & Lerner, David (1965) Self and Society: Reflections on Some Turks in Transition, in D. Riesman (ed.), *Abundance for What? and Other Essays*. Garden City: Anchor Books.

Rinaldi, Mariangela & Vicini, Mariangela (2000) *Buon Appetito, Your Holiness: The Secrets of Papal Table*. Kent: Pan Books.

Roden, Claudia (1994) Jewish Food in Middle East, in S. Zubaida & R. Tapper (eds) *Culinary Cultures of the Middle East*. London: I.B. Tauris, 153–158.

Rojek, Chris (1985) *Capitalism & Leisure Theory*. London: Tavistock Publications.

Rose, Gillian (1978) *The Melancholy Science: An Introduction to the Thought of Theodor Adorno*. London: The Macmillan Press.

Rousseau, Jean-Jacques (1985) Discours sur l'origine et les fondements de l'inégalité parmi les hommes, *Oeuvres complètes III*. Paris: Gallimard.

Sahlins, Marshall (1976) *Culture and Practical Reason*. Chicago: The University of Chicago Press.

Sahlins, Marshall (1985) *The Islands of History*. Chicago: The University of Chicago Press.

Sahlins, Marshall (2000) *Culture in Practice. Selected Essays*. New York: Zone Books.

Sartre, Jean Paul (1976) *Critique of Dialectical Reason*. London: New Left Books.

Sassatelli, Roberta (2001) Tamed Hedonism: Choice, Desires, and Deviant Behaviour, in J. Gronow & A. Warde (eds) *Ordinary Consumption*. London: Routledge, 93–106.

Sayer, Andrew (2003) (De)commodification, Consumer Culture, and Moral Economy. *Environment and Planning D: Society and Space* 21, 341–357.

Schaper, Eva (1987) The Pleasures of Taste, in E. Schaper (ed.) *Pleasure, Preference and Value: Studies in Philosophical Aesthetics*. Cambridge: Cambridge University Press, 39–56.

Scherhorn, Gerhard (1990) The Addictive Trait in Buying Behaviour. *Journal of Consumer Policy*, 13, 33–51.

Schivelbusch, Wolfgang (1992) *Tastes of Paradise*. New York: Pantheon Books.

Schultz Kleine, Susan, Kleine III, Robert & Allen, Chris (1995) How Is a Possession 'Me' or 'Not Me'? Characterizing Types and an Antecedent of Material Possession Attachment. *Journal of Consumer Research* 22:3, 327–343.

Schulze, Gerhard (1992) *Die Erlebnisgesellschaft: Kultursoziologie der Gegenwart*. Frankfurt a/M: Campus.

Schutz, Alfred (1962) *Collected Papers*. Vol. I. The Hague: Martinus Nijhoff.

Scott, Alan (1996) Bureaucratic Revolutions and Free Market Utopias. *Economy and Society* 25:1, 89–110.

Scott, John (2002) Social Class and Stratification in Late Modernity. *Acta Sociologica* 45:1, 23–35.

Seies, Eeva-Riitta (1986) Tulossa: Involvement. *Talouselämä* 18, 87–88.

Sellerberg, Ann-Mari (1978) *Konsumptionens sociologi*. Lund: Universitetsförlaget.

Sellerberg, Ann-Mari (1987) *Avstånd och attraktion: Om modets växlingar.* Uddevalla: Carlssons.

Sen, Amartya (1983) Economics and the Family. *Asian Development Review* 1, 14–26.

Sennett, Richard (1976) *The Fall of Public Man: On the Social Psychology of Capitalism.* New York: Random House.

Sève, Lucien (1975) *Marxisme et theorie de la personalité.* Paris: Editions Sociales.

Shakespeare, William (1971) *Timon of Athens: Shakespeare Complete Works.* London: Oxford University Press.

Shephard, Sue (2000) *Pickled, Potted and Canned: The Story of Food Preserving.* London: Headline.

Shils, Edvard (1981) *Tradition.* Chicago: The University of Chicago Press.

Shove, Elizabeth (2003) *Comfort, Cleanliness and Convenience: The Social Organization of Normality.* Oxford: Berg.

Siikala, Jukka (1985) Nimet, myytit ja yhteiskunta. *Tiede & Edistys* 10:2, 132–136.

Simmel, Georg (1950) *The Sociology of Georg Simmel.* Ed. by Kurt H. Wolff. New York: Free Press.

Simmel, Georg (1978) *The Philosophy of Money.* London: Routledge & Kegan Paul.

Simmel, Georg (1981) *Hur är samhället möjligt? och andra essäer.* Göteborg: Korpen.

Simmel, Georg (1997 [1900]) The Philosophy of Fashion, in D. Frisby and M. Featherstone (eds) *Simmel on Culture.* London: Sage.

Simmel, Georg (2005) *Suurkaupunki ja moderni elämä: Kirjoituksia vuosilta 1895–1917.* Helsinki: Gaudeamus.

Simon, Herbert (1945) *Administrative Behavior.* New York: MacMillan.

Slater, Don (2002) Capturing markets from the Economists, in P. de Guy & M. Pryke (eds) *Cultural Economy: Cultural Analysis and Commercial Life.* London: Sage, 59–75.

Slater, Don & Tonkiss, Fran (2001) *Market Society: Markets and Modern Social Theory.* Cambridge: Polity Press.

Smart, Barry (1999) *Facing Modernity. Ambivalence, Reflexivity and Morality.* London: Sage.

Smart, Barry (2003) *Economy, Culture and Society: A Sociological Critique of Neo-Liberalism.* Buckingham: Open University Press.

Smelt, Simon (1980) Money's Place in Society. *British Journal of Sociology* 91:2, 204–223.

Smith, Adam (1904) *The Wealth of the Nations.* London: Methuen & Co.

Smith, Adam (1982) *The Theory of Moral Sentiments.* Indianapolis: Liberty Classics.

Sombart, Werner (1967 [1922]) Luxury and Capitalism, Ann Arbor: university of Michigan Press.

Sorjonen, Pasi (2004) Taloutta ei voi ennustaa – ainakaan ilman tilastoja. STAT. FI i, 4–6.

Stigler Georg J. (1954) The Early History of Empirical Studies of Consumer Behaviour. *Journal of Political Economy* 62:2, 95–113.

Strahilevitz, Michael & Loewenstein, George (1998) The Effect of Ownership History on the Valuation of Objects. *Journal of Consumer Research* 25:3, 276–289.

Sulkunen, Pekka (2004) Voimme olla addiktoituneita mihin tahansa: Onko addiktio vain käsite vai todellinen asia? in P. Jokivuori & P. Ruuskanen (eds) *Arjen talous: Talous, tunteet ja yhteiskunta.* Jyväskylä: SoPhi, 139–156.

Tannahill, Raya (1975) *Food in History.* Bungay: Paladin.

Tarde, Gabriel de (1890) *Les Lois de L'imitation: etude sociologique,* Paris Felix Alcan.

Thaler, Richard (1980) Toward a Positive Theory of Consumer Choice. *Journal of Economic Behaviour and Organization* 1 (March), 39–60.

Thomas, William I & Znaniecki, Florian (1958) *The Polish Peasant in Europe and America.* New York: Dover.

Thompson, Edward P. (1983) *Herremkt och folkligt kultur.* Malmö: Författarförlaget.

Thrift, Nigel (2005) *Knowing Capitalism.* London: Sage.

Tigerstedt, Christoffer & Törrönen, Jukka (2005) Muuttuvatko suomalaiset juomatavat? Kulttuurisen lähestymistavan jäljillä. *Sosiologia* 42:1, 35–49.

Tocqueville, Alexis de (1969) *Democracy in America* Vol. 2. New York: Doubleday.

Tönnies, Ferdinand (1920) *Gemeinschaft und Gesellschaft: Grundbegriffe der reinen Soziologie.* Berlin: Verlag Karl Curtius.

Töttö, Pertti (2000) *Pirullisen positivismin paluu: Laadullisen ja määrällisen tarkastelua.* Tampere: Vastapaino.

Turner, Bryan (1986) Simmel, Rationalisation and the Sociology of Money. *Sociological Review* 34:1, 93–114.

Turner, John C. (1987) *Rediscovering the Social Group: A Self-Categorization Theory.* Oxford: Basil Blackwell.

Turner, Stephen (1994) *The Social Theory of Practices: Tradition, Tacit Knowledge and Presuppositions.* Cambridge: Polity Press.

Tversky, Amos & Kahneman, Daniel (1991) Loss Aversion in Riskless Choice: A Reference-Dependent Model. *Quarterly Journal of Economics* 106:4, 1039–1061.

Twigg, Julia (1984) Vegetarianism and Meaning of Meat, in A. Murcott (ed.) *The Sociology of Food and Eating: Essays on the Sociological Signification of Food.* Aldershot: Gover.

Varjonen, Johanna (2001) *Elämyksiä, terveyttä, vaihtelua. 2000-luvun ruokatottumukset.* Helsinki: Kuluttajatutkimuskeskus, julkaisuja 3.

Veblen, Thorstein (1994) *Theory of the Leisure Class.* New York: Dover Publications.

Vygotsky, Lev (1978) *Mind in Society.* Harvard, MA: Harvard University Press.

Vygotsky, Lev (1986) *Thought and Language.* Cambridge, MA: The MIT Press.

Warde, Alan (1994) Consumption, Identity-Formation and Uncertainty. *Sociology* 28:4, 877–898.

Warde, Alan (1997) *Consumption, Food and Taste: Culinary Antinomies and Commodity Culture.* London: Sage.

Warde, Alan & Martens, Lydia (2000) *Eating Out.* Cambridge: Cambridge University Press.

Weber, Max (1964) *The Theory of Social and Economic Organization.* New York: Free Press.

Weber, Max (1978) *Economy and Society.* Berkeley: University of California Press.

Wernick, Andrew (1991) *Promotional Culture: Advertising, Ideology and Symbolic Expression.* London: Sage.

Whitehead, T. L. (1984) Sociocultural Dynamics and Food Habits in a Southern Community, in M. Douglas (ed.) *Food in the Social Order: Studies of Food and Festivities in Three American Communities.* New York: Russell Sage Foundation, 97–142.

Williams, Raymond (1977) *Marxism and Literature.* Oxford: Oxford University Press.

Williamson, Oliver (1975) *Markets and Hierarchies: Analysis and Antitrust Implications.* New York: MacMillan.

Willis, Paul (1977) *Learning to Labour: How Working Class Kids Get Working Class Jobs.* Farnborough: Saxon House.

Wilska, Terhi-Anna (2002) Me – A Consumer? Consumption, Identities and Lifestyles in Today's Finland. *Acta Sociologica* 45:3, 195–210.

Wilson, Elisabeth (1985) *Adorned in Dreams: Fashion and Modernity.* Tiptree: Virago Press.

Wittel, Andreas (2001) Toward a Network Sociality. *Theory, Culture & Society* 18:6, 51–76.

Wittgenstein, Ludwig (1969) *On Certainty.* Oxford: Basil Blackwell.

Woolgar, Stephen (1991) Configuring the User, in J. Law (ed.) *A Sociology of Monsters: Essays on Power, Technology and Domination.* London: Routledge, 57–102.

Woolgar, Stephen (2000) The Social Basis of Interactive Social Science. *Science and Public Policy* 27:3, 165–173.

Wright, Georg Henrik von (1985) *Filosofisia tutkielmia.* Juva: Kirjayhtymä.

Zelizer, Vivian (1990) The Social Meaning of Money: 'Special Monies'. *American Journal of Sociology* 95:2, 342–377.

Zelizer, Vivian (1997) *The Social Meaning of Money: Pin Money, Pay Checks, Poor Relief, and Other Currencies.* Princeton: Princeton University Press.

Zelizer, Vivian (1998) The Proliferation of Social Currencies, in M. Callon (ed.) *The Laws of the Markets.* Oxford: Blackwell, 58–68.

Zelizer, Vivian (2005) Missing Monies: Comment on Nigel Dodd, 'Reinventing Monies in Europe. *Economy and Society* 34:3, 584–588.

Zukin, Sharon & Smith Maguire, Jennifer (2004) Consumers and Consumption, *Annual Review of Sociology* 30, 173–197.

# Index

action(s), 6, 8, 13, 14–18, 47, 121–2
activity, need and, 47–50
actor-network theory (ANT), 188
addiction, 69
Adorno, Theodor W., 4, 55, 173, 174
aesthetics of commodities, 6, 53–4
agency theory, 7, 120–1
Alexander, Jeffrey, 209n4
Allardt, Erik, 153
anthropology, 37, 43, 105, 123
anticipatory socialization, 52, 53
anti-fashion movements, 150
appropriation, of commodities,
    191–204
Archer, Mary, 212n9
Aristotle, 59, 60
authenticity, 144, 146
authority, 53

Barbon, Nicholas, 59
basic needs, 46–8
Baudelaire, Charles, 71
Baudrillard, Jean, 5
behaviour
    action and, 121–2
    forms of, 122–6
Belk, Russell, 94
Bell, Daniel, 26
benefit maximization, 15
Benjamin, Walter, 3, 5, 117–18
Bennett, Merrill K., 77–8
Berlin, Isaiah, 21
blaxploitation, 176
Blumer, Herbert, 3
bodily dispositions, 166–7
bodily practices, 116
body, attitude toward, 107–9, 209n4
body language, 116, 126
boredom, 71–2
boundary conditions, 102
bounded rationality, 29
Bourdieu, Pierre, 5, 125, 130–2, 135,
    138, 171, 176, 209n4, 210n6

brand loyalty, 46, 127–8
brands, 168–71, 173
Braudel, Fernand, 209n5
breakfast, 106, 129
bribery, 97–8
Bush, George W., 27

calculation, 18, 30, 32
Callon, Michel, 30, 196, 203, 207n13
calories, 107
Campbell, Colin, 6, 63–9, 121
capitalism, 2, 14, 17, 113, 205n1
capital markets, 26
Cartalism, 86
Castells, Manuel, 28
Castiglione, Baldassare, 134
Catholic Church, 62
certificates of deposit, 83
charity, 95
Chicago School, 15
Christianity, 93, 107
church, 90
circulation of goods, 6
circumstances, 122–6
cities, 24–5
civic religions, 118
civil society, 28, 83, 114
classes, *see* social classes
classification, consumption as means
    of, 172–6
class structure, 5, 25
class styles, 142–3
clothing, 80, 135, 147, 168, 171–2,
    177–8, 180–2
Coase, Ronald, 31
code, 168, 169
cognitive appropriation, 195, 196–7
Colbert, Jean-Baptiste, 206n11
collectibles/collecting, 6, 38, 41, 94–6
collective choice, 20
collective disposition, 145
collective memory, 51, 52, 114–15,
    117

229

| DATE DUE | RETURNED |
|---|---|
|  |  |
|  |  |
|  |  |
|  |  |
|  |  |
|  |  |
|  |  |
|  |  |
|  |  |
|  |  |
|  |  |
|  |  |
|  |  |
|  |  |